The Charlton Standard Catalogue of Canadian Coins

New and revised edition

The Charlton Press

TORONTO

TRADEMARK NOTICE

PRICING NOTICE

The values quoted in this catalogue are based on the latest auction and retail prices. They are neither buying nor selling offers but give the most accurate appraisal of market values at the time of publication. In the case of some rare coins that seldom change hands, prices are subject to wide fluctuations between sales, so the publisher has listed the prices for the latest recorded sales.

The Charlton Press,
299 Queen Street West,
Toronto, Ontario.
M5V 1Z9

ISSN 0706-0424
ISBN 0-88968-015-9

PANEL OF CONTRIBUTORS

TABLE OF CONTENTS

INTRODUCTION

The Charlton Standard Catalogue of Canadian Coins is an illustrated, descriptive price catalogue for the principal types of commercial and commemorative coins used in Canada over the years, including pre-Confederation regions. As a standard catalogue, it provides an accurate overview and introduction to Canadian numismatics and current market values. Every major variety of all issues of Canadian coins is listed, illustrated and priced. Several minor varieties which have a wide appeal to collectors, such as Arnprior dollars, are also included. Historical introductions provide important background information for each series, and relevant technical information is provided wherever available.

The new reader should find in this catalogue all the basic information needed to identify and evaluate individual coins as he or she embarks upon an old and widely enjoyed hobby. The more familiar reader will be pleased to find the text of the present edition completely revised. Dr. James A. Haxby has enlarged the scope of the catalogue, with additional historical data, new high-quality photographs, and more technical data and statistics than has ever before been compiled for a Canadian coin catalogue. New to this edition is a summary of the principal foreign coins used during the French and British regimes, as well as local, pre-decimal issues. The decimal series is complete for the provinces of British North America and Canada from its inception to the present, and also includes patterns, essais, and test tokens.

Since this is a standard catalogue, no attempt has been made to list every minor variety, nor to remark upon all the nuances of interest to the specialist. More specialized treatments are available elsewhere and they should be consulted for issues not covered in this text.

Welcome, then, to the 31st Edition of the Charlton Standard Catalogue of Canadian Coins and the exciting field of Canadian numismatics. This new edition is just the latest chapter in the coordinated efforts and contributions of numismatic scholars, collectors, dealers and students. It marks another important step and maturing sense of direction for one of our most popular and profitable pastimes.

THE COLLECTING OF CANADIAN DECIMAL COINS PAST AND PRESENT

Today, the majority of those collecting Canadian numismatic material specialize in the decimal coin series. The collecting popularity of decimal coins is a relatively recent phenomenon, however. When Canada's first coin club was formed in Montreal in 1862, there was little interest in either decimal coins or paper money. Eighty years later this was still the case. Most collectors specialized in Canadian tokens, the private coppers that served for so long as a medium of exchange in the absence of official coins. Decimal coins were mostly collected by type. One or two examples of each design were sufficient, and there was little concern regarding the relative scarcity of the various dates and varieties.

The current preoccupation with collecting decimal coins by date and variety arose in the 1940's, under the influence of U.S. dealer Wayte Raymond. Shortly after World War II and on into the 1950's, Canadian pioneers J. Douglas Ferguson, Fred Bowman, Sheldon Carroll and Leslie Hill attempted to establish the relative rarities of the decimal coins issued up to that time.

In 1950 collectors in the Ottawa area joined with scattered groups and individuals to form the Canadian Numismatic Association. Its official publication, and annual conventions beginning in 1954, served to bridge the miles and facilitate the exchange of information and ideas.

Two years after the CNA was formed, the Charlton Standard Catalogue made its appearance. Early editions were modest paperback pamphlets with line drawings, but they were a serious attempt to list and price Canadian coins, tokens, paper money and some medals. The first hard-cover edition of 128 pages appeared in 1960. By 1971 it had grown to 200 pages, and by 1978 so much additional numismatic information was available that it was decided the needs of collectors could best be met by splitting the catalogue into separate, specialized works.

The 27th (1979) Edition became the Standard Catalogue of Canadian Coins, now issued twice yearly. This was followed by the Standard Catalogue of Canadian Paper Money in early 1980. Two new volumes on tokens and medals will be released in 1981.

BUILDING A COLLECTION

Decimal coin collections can be formed in a variety of ways. Coins may come from pocket change, family hoards, the bank, the Mint or from other collectors. In general, older coins no longer circulate and the excitement of searching through change for missing dates has been diminished by the withdrawal of most silver coins from circulation.

Today's collectors of Canadian coins are fortunate in having the Royal Canadian Mint, which produces a series of high-quality special coins for collectors. These attractively-packaged coins are available from coin dealers or direct from the Mint. Persons wishing to purchase direct from the Mint can obtain information from:

The Royal Canadian Mint,
355 River Road,
Ottawa, Ontario K1N 8V5

Collecting is a matter of individual taste. Some people collect by design type, others concentrate on one or two denominations or monarchs, while some brave souls try to collect the entire decimal series. Regardless of which path you choose, there is a variety of coin boards, envelopes and other supplies available to help house and organize your collection. For reasons of security many collectors keep their best coins in a bank vault.

Another decision that must be made when building a collection is the minimum state of preservation one will accept when buying coins. As a general rule, it is advisable to buy the best condition coins one can afford.

COMMEMORATIVES

A group of decimal coins that has attracted considerable international interest is the commemorative series. These coins have special designs to mark an event or the anniversary of an event.

The first commemoratives, beginning with the 1935 silver dollar, were issued for general circulation. However, in 1967 a new trend of producing commemoratives as collectors pieces only began, with no corresponding issue for general circulation. The two groups are listed separately below.

Commemorative Coins Struck for Collectors and for General Circulation

$1 1935 — George V Silver Jubilee
$1 1949 — Newfoundland
5¢ 1951 — Discovery & Naming of Nickel
$1 1958 — B.C. as a Crown Colony
$1 1964 — Confederation Conferences
1¢-$1 1967 — Confederation
$1 1970 (nickel) — Manitoba
$1 1971 (nickel) — British Columbia
25¢ & $1 1973 (nickel) — R.C.M.P.
$1 1974 (nickel) — Winnipeg

Commemorative Coins Struck for Collectors Only

$20 1967 — Confederation
$1 1971 (silver) — British Columbia
$1 1973 (silver) — R.C.M.P.
$5 & $10 1973-76 — Olympics

$1 1974 (silver) — Winnipeg
$1 1975 (silver) — Calgary
$1 1976 (silver) — Library of Parliament
$1 (silver) & $100 1977 — Elizabeth II Silver Jubilee
$1 1978 (silver) — Commonwealth Games
$100 1978 — Canadian Unity
$1 1979 — the Griffin
$100 1979 — Year of the Child
$1 1980 — Arctic Territories
$100 1980 — Arctic Territories

AGE - RARITY - DEMAND - CONDITION - VALUE

The value of a coin on the numismatic market is dictated by a complex mixture of factors. One feature which those unfamiliar with coins often mistakenly believe to be of great importance is age. That age is a minor contributor to value is illustrated by the fact that the 1969 Large Date variety ten cents is worth far more than the 1870 ten-cent piece, a coin nearly 100 years older!

Basically, a coin's value is determined by a combination of supply and demand. The 1870 fifty-cent piece does not command as high a premium as the 1921 coin of the same denomination because there are many more 1870's than 1921's available. On the other hand, the variety of the 1872H fifty cents with an "A" punched over the "V" in "VICTORIA" on the obverse (see page 142) sells for about the same as the variety with a normal "V" even though the coins from the blundered die are much rarer. The modest price difference reflects the slight difference in demand.

Finally, the state of preservation of a coin markedly influences its value. It is not unusual for an uncirculated (brand new) George V silver coin, for example, to sell for fifty times what a coin of the same date and denomination would bring in well-worn condition.

GRADING CANADIAN COINS

In the years since they first appeared in the 1952 Charlton Catalogue, grading standards for Canadian coins have been considerably enlarged and refined. These standards used a set of terms, such as Very Good or Extremely Fine, to describe the different grades or states of preservation.

The recent step taken by the ANA, in which a numerical grading system for United States coins was adopted, has caused a re-examination of the Canadian standards. After much deliberation, including a collector survey, it has been decided to use a similar numerical grading system for Canadian coins listed in this catalogue.

Much of the following general text has been taken verbatim from "Official Grading Standards for United States Coins." We wish to express our appreciation to the American Numismatic Association for allowing us to do so.

WHY IS GRADING IMPORTANT?

Why are there differences of opinion in the field of grading coins? There are numerous reasons, but the most common are as follows:

Grading coins can never be completely scientific in all areas. One may weigh a coin and also obtain its specific gravity by mechanical devices, and the results will be factual if accurate equipment was used carefully. There are no scientific means available to measure the surface condition - the amount of wear - of a coin.

In grading coins, consideration such as striking, surface of the planchet, the presence of heavy toning (which may obscure certain surface characteristics), the design, and other factors each lend an influence. A panel of a dozen of the foremost numismatic hobby leaders justifiably could have some slight differences of opinion on the precise grade of some coins.

However, it is not slight differences which concern us here; it is serious or major differences. The term "overgrading" refers to describing a coin as a grade higher than it actually is. For example, if a coin in AU (About Uncirculated) is called Uncirculated, it is overgraded. If a coin in Very Fine condition is called Extremely Fine, it is overgraded.

What induces overgrading? Here are some of the factors:

Buyers Seeking Bargains. The desire to get a bargain is part of human nature. If a given Uncirculated coin actively traded at $100 is offered at $70, it will attract a lot of bargain seekers. These same buyers would reject an offering such as: "I am offering $100 bills for $70 each."

In coins, as in any other walk of life, you get what you pay for. If a coin which has a standard value of $100 is offered for $70 there may be nothing wrong, but chances are that the piece is overgraded.

False Assumptions. Buyers often assume falsely that any advertisement which appears in a numismatic publication has been approved by that publication. Actually, publishers cannot be expected to examine coins and approve of all listings offered. A person who has no numismatic knowledge or expertise whatsoever can have letterheads and business cards printed and, assuming he had good financial and character references (but not necessarily numismatic expertise), run large and flashy advertisements. Months or years later it is often too late for the deceived buyer to get his money back. The solution to this is to learn how to grade coins and think for yourself. Examine the credentials of the seller. Is he truly an expert in his field? To what professional organization does the dealer belong? It is usually foolish to rush and spend your hard earned money with a coin seller who has no professional credentials and whose only attraction is that he is offering "bargains." Think for yourself!

The Profit Motive. Sellers seeking an unfair markup may overgrade. For purposes of illustration, let us assume that a given variety of coin is worth the following prices in these grades: AU $75, and Uncirculated $150. A legitimate dealer in the course of business would buy, for example, an AU coin at $50 or $60 and sell it retail for $75, thus making a profit of $15 to $25. However, there are sellers who are not satisfied with the normal way of doing business. They take shortcuts. They pay $50 or $60 for the same AU coin which is worth $75 retail, but rather than calling it AU they call it "Uncirculated" and sell it for $150. So, instead of making $15 or $25 they make $90 to $100!

Inexperience. Inexperience or error on the part of the seller may lead to incorrect grading - both overgrading and undergrading.

UNCIRCULATED COINS

The term "Uncirculated," interchangeable with "Mint State," refers to a coin which has never seen circulation. Such a piece has no wear of any kind. A coin as bright as the time it was minted or with very little light natural toning can be described as "Brilliant Uncirculated." A coin which has natural toning can be described as "Toned Uncirculated." Except in the instance of copper coins, the presence or absence of light toning does not affect an Uncirculated coin's grade. Indeed, among silver coins, attractive natural toning often results in the coin bringing a premium.

The quality of lustre or "mint bloom" on an Uncirculated coin is an essential element in correctly grading the piece, and has a bearing on its value. Lustre may in time become dull, frosty, spotted or discoloured. Unattractive lustre will normally lower the grade.

With the exception of certain Special Mint Sets made in recent years for collectors, Uncirculated or normal production strike coins were produced on high speed presses, stored in bags together with other coins, run through counting machines, and in other ways handled without regard to numismatic posterity. As a result, it is the rule and not the exception for an Uncirculated coin to have bag marks and evidence of coin-to-coin contact, although the coin might not have actual commercial circulation. The number of such marks will depend upon the coin's actual size. Differences in criteria in this regard are given in the individual sections under grading descriptions for different denominations and types.

Uncirculated coins can be divided into three major categories:

MS-70 (Perfect Uncirculated). MS-70 or Perfect Uncirculated is the finest quality available. Such a coin under 4x magnification will show no bag marks, lines, or other evidence of handling or contact with other coins.

A brilliant coin may be described as "MS-70, Brilliant" or "Perfect Brilliant Uncirculated." A lightly toned nickel or silver coin may be described as "MS-70, toned" or "Perfect Toned Uncirculated." Or, in the case of particularly attractive or unusual toning, additional adjectives may be in order such as "Perfect Uncirculated with attractive iridescent toning around the borders."

Copper and bronze coins: To qualify as MS-70 or Perfect Uncirculated, a copper or bronze coin must have its full lustre and natural surface colour, and may not be toned brown, olive, or any other colour. (Coins with toned surfaces which are otherwise perfect should be described as MS-65 as the following text indicates).

MS-65 (Choice Uncirculated). This refers to an above average Uncirculated coin which may be brilliant or toned (and described accordingly) and which has fewer bag marks than usual; scattered occasional bag marks on the surface or perhaps one or two very light rim marks.

MS-60 (Uncirculated). MS-60 or Uncirculated (typical Uncirculated without any adjectives) refers to a coin which has a moderate number of bag marks on its surface. Also present may be a few minor edge nicks and marks, although not of a serious nature. Unusally deep bag marks, nicks and the like must be described separately. A coin may be either brilliant or toned.

Striking and Minting Peculiarities on Uncirculated Coins

Certain early coins have mint-caused planchet or adjustment marks, a series of parallel striations. If these are visible to the naked eye they should be described adjectivally in addition to the numerical or regular descriptive grade. For example: "MS-60 with adjustment marks," or "MS-65 with adjustment marks," or "Perfect Uncirculated with very light adjustment marks," or something similar.

If an Uncirculated coin exhibits weakness due to striking or die wear, or unusual (for the variety) die wear, this must be adjectivally mentioned in addition to the grade. Examples are: "MS-60, lightly struck," or "Choice Uncirculated, lightly struck," and "MS-70, lightly struck."

CIRCULATED COINS

Once a coin enters circulation it begins to show signs of wear. As time goes on the coin becomes more and more worn until, after a period of many decades, only a few features may be left.

Dr. William H. Sheldon devised a numerical scale to indicate degrees of wear. According to this scale, a coin in condition 1 of "Basal State" is barely recognizable. At the opposite end, a coin touched by even the slightest trace of wear (below MS-60) cannot be called Uncirculated.

While numbers from 1 through 59 are continuous, it has been found practical to designate specific intermediate numbers to define grades. Hence, this text uses the following descriptions and their numerical equivalents:

Choice About Uncirculated-55. Abbreviation: AU-55. Only a small trace of wear is visible on the highest points of the coin. As is the case with the other grades here, specific information is listed in the following text under the various types, for wear often occurs in different spots on different designs.

About Uncirculated-50. Abbreviation: AU-50. With traces of wear on nearly all of the highest areas. At least half of the original mint lustre is present.

Choice Extremely Fine-45. With light overall wear on the coin's highest points. All design details are very sharp. Mint lustre is usually seen only in protected areas of the coin's surface.

Extremely Fine-40. Abbreviation: EF-40. With only slight wear but more extensive than the preceeding, still with excellent overall sharpness. Traces of mint lustre may still show.

Choice Very Fine-30. Abbreviation: VF-30. With light even wear on the surface; design details on the highest points lightly worn, but with all lettering and major features sharp.

Very Fine-20. Abbreviation: VF-20. As preceeding but with moderate wear on highest parts.

Fine-12. Abbreviation: F-12. Moderate to considerable even wear. Entire design is bold. All lettering visible, but with some weaknesses.

Very Good-8. Abbreviation: VG-8. Well worn. Most fine details such as hair strands, leaf details, and so on are worn nearly smooth.

Good-4. Abbreviation: G-4. Heavily worn. Major designs visible, but with faintness in areas. Other major features visible in outline form without centre detail.

About Good-3. Abbreviation: AG-3. Very heavily worn with portions of the lettering, date, and legends being worn smooth. The date is barely readable.

Note: The exact descriptions of circulated grades vary widely from issue to issue, so the preceeding commentary is only of a very general nature. It is essential to refer to the specific text when grading any coin.

SPLIT AND INTERMEDIATE GRADES

It is often the case that because of the peculiarities of striking or a coin's design, one side of the coin will grade differently from the other. When this is the case, a diagonal mark is used to separate the two. For example, a coin with an AU-50 obverse and a Choice Extremely Fine-45 reverse can be described as: AU/EF or, alternatively, 50/45.

The A.N.A. standard numerical scale is divided into the following steps: 3, 4, 8, 12, 20, 30, 45, 50, 60, 65, and 70. Most advanced collectors and dealers find that the graduations from AG-3 through Choice AU-55 are sufficient to describe nearly every coin showing wear. The use of intermediate grade levels such as EF-42, EF-43, and so on is not encouraged. Grading is not that precise, and using such finely split intermediate grades is imparting a degree of accuracy which probably will not be able to be verified by other numismatists. As such, it is discouraged.

A split or intermediate grade, such as that between VF-30 and EF-40, should be called Choice VF-35 rather than VF-EF or About EF.

An exception to intermediate grades can be found among Mint State coins, coins grading from MS-60 through MS-70. Among Mint State coins there are fewer variables. Wear is not a factor; the considerations are the amount of bag marks and surface blemishes. While it is good numismatic practice to adhere to the numerical classifications of 60, 65, and 70, it is permissible to use intermediate grades.

In all instances, the adjectival description must be of the next lower grade. For example, a standard grade for a coin is MS-60 or Uncirculated Typical. The next major category is MS-65 or Uncirculated Choice. A coin which is felt to grade, for example, MS-64, must be described as "MS-64 Uncirculated Typical." It may not be described as Choice Uncirculated, for the minimum definition of Choice Uncirculated is MS-65. Likewise, an MS-69 coin must be described as "MS-69 Uncirculated Choice." It is not permissible to use Uncirculated Perfect for any coin which is any degree less than MS-70.

The A.N.A. grading system considers it to be good numismatic practice to adhere to the standard 60, 65, and 70 numerical designations. Experienced numismatists can generally agree on whether a given coin is MS-60 or MS-65. However, not even the most advanced numismatists can necessarily agree on whether a coin is MS-62 or MS-63; the distinction is simply too minute to permit accuracy. In all instances, it is recommended that intermediate grades be avoided, and if there is any doubt, the lowest standard grade should be used. The use of plus or minus signs is also not acceptable practice.

While the above general definitions of grades are quite useful for many series, each particular series is best graded by referring to grading details specifically dealing with it. A new grading text is nearing completion. In the meantime it is suggested that the reader use the following brief descriptions of the obverses of the various Canadian series. At the end of these the reader will find details of both obverse and reverse in the grading of the fifty-cent series.

Victoria Laureated Head

G-4 - Braid worn through near ear.

VG-8 - No detail in braid around ear.

F-12 - Segments of braid begin to merge into one another.

VF-20 - Braid is clear but not sharp.

EF-40 - Braid is slightly worn but generally sharp and clear.

AU-50 - Slight traces of wear on high points. Degree of mint lustre still present.

MS-60 - No traces of wear. High degree of lustre.

Victoria Crowned Head

G-4 - Hair over ear worn through.

VG-8 - No details in the hair over ear.

F-12 - Strands of hair over ear begin to run together.

VF-20 - Hair and jewels no longer sharp but clear.

EF-40 - Hair over ear is sharp and clear. Jewels in diadem must show sharply and clearly.

AU-50 - Slight traces of wear on high points. Degree of mint lustre still present.

MS-60 - No traces of wear. High degree of lustre.

Edward VII All Denominations

G-4 - Band of crown worn through.

VG-8 - Band of crown worn through at the highest point.

F-12 - Jewels in the band of crown will be blurred.

VF-20 - Band of the crown is still clear but no longer sharp.

EF-40 - Band of crown slightly worn but generally sharp and clear, including jewels.

AU-50 - Slight traces of wear on high points. Degree of mint lustre still present.

MS-60 - No traces of wear. High degree of lustre.

George V All Denominations

G-4 - Band of crown worn through.

VG-8 - Band of crown worn through at the highest point.

F-12 - Jewels in the band of crown will be blurred.

VF-20 - Band of the crown is still clear but no longer sharp.

EF-40 - Band of crown slightly worn but generally sharp and clear, including jewels.

AU-50 - Slight traces of wear on high points. Degree of mint lustre still present.

MS-60 - No traces of wear. High degree of lustre.

George VI All Denominations

VG-8 - No details in hair above ear.

F-12 - Only slight detail in hair above the ear.

VF-20 - Where not worn, the hair is clear but not sharp.

EF-40 - Slight wear in hair over ear.

AU-50 - Slight traces of wear on high points. Degree of mint lustre still present.

MS-60 - No traces of wear. High degree of lustre.

Elizabeth II Young Head

F-12 - Leaves worn almost through. Shoulder fold indistinct.

VF-20 - Leaves are considerably worn; fold must be clear.

EF-40 - Laurel leaves on the band are somewhat worn.

AU-50 - Traces of wear on hair. Degree of mint lustre still present.

MS-60 - No traces of wear. High degree of lustre.

UNCIRCULATED, MS-60 OBVERSE — There should be absolutely no wear of any kind on the hair and diadem. There may be a nick, a few bag marks or some discolouration but a high degree of lustre or frost should remain.
REVERSE — All detail in the wreath, crown and bow are sharp and maple boughs clearly defined.

ABOUT UNCIRCULATED, AU-50 OBVERSE — Very slight traces of wear on diadem and in hairlines but details still sharp. Half of mint lustre remaining.
REVERSE — Slight trace of wear on high points - knot in wreath, crown and lower leaves.

EXTREMELY FINE, EF-40 OBVERSE — Trace of wear on eyebrow, four jewels in rim of diadem, strands of hair over the ear, knot at back and hairlines on top of head.
REVERSE — Trace of wear around the outer edges of lower leaves, knot in wreath and crown.

VERY FINE, VF-20 OBVERSE — Slight wear on eyebrow, cheek, nose, ear lobe and all of the jewels. Ribbon end on neck begins to merge. Hair over the ear and knot slightly worn.
REVERSE — All leaves show wear on outer edges. Knot in wreath and centre part of crown worn.

FINE, F-12 OBVERSE — Considerable wear on all facial features, also hair and jewels. Ribbon end fused with cheek. Strands of hair over the ear begin to merge together. Ear lobe barely showing.

REVERSE — All leaves considerably worn over entire area, also crown. Pearls in crown and beads of border begin to merge.

VERY GOOD, VG-8 OBVERSE — Ear lobe fused with cheek. Hairlines separating face from hair obliterated. Practically no details in hair over ear and knot at back. Jewels mostly worn away.

REVERSE — Very little detail in the leaves and crown remain. Border beads are blurred. Value and date are worn.

GOOD, G-4 OBVERSE — Details of jewels, diadem and hair are worn off. Little but outline of portrait remains. Legend is weak.

REVERSE — Leaves and crown badly worn, with little but outlines remaining. Value and date are weak. Border beads are blurred.

UNCIRCULATED, MS-60 OBVERSE — Robe, shoulder bow, crown, ear and side whiskers all show sharp detail. All jewels in the crown including 8 pearls clear and distinct. A high degree of lustre or frost should remain.
REVERSE — All detail in the wreath, crown and bow are sharp and maple boughs clearly defined.

ABOUT UNCIRCULATED, AU-50 OBVERSE — Very slight wear on shoulder bow, ear and crown. Half of mint lustre remaining.
REVERSE — Slight trace of wear on high points - knot in wreath, crown and lower leaves.

EXTREMELY FINE, EF-40 OBVERSE — Eyebrow worn. Slight wear on ear, moustache and side whiskers. Band of crown slightly worn but all jewels, including 8 pearls showing.
REVERSE — Trace of wear around the outer edges of lower leaves and centre arch of crown.

VERY FINE, VF-20 OBVERSE — Eyebrow, moustache and side whiskers considerably worn, also robe, shoulder bow and ornamental chain. Band of crown worn, but 4 to 6 pearls remain.
REVERSE — Wear on outer edges of leaves consists of about 1/3 their area. Central arch of crown shows slight wear.

FINE, F-12 OBVERSE — Robe, shoulder bow, jewels on chain and band of crown are worn considerably. At least half of band remains. Top of ear merges with hair.
REVERSE — Wear on leaves increased to about ½ their area. Pearls in the arches of crown begin to merge.

VERY GOOD, VG-8 OBVERSE — Band of crown is worn through in the centre. Only weak outline of robe, shoulder bow and chain remain. Outlines of ear is indistinct and moustache and beard are blurred.
REVERSE — Very little detail remains in the leaves. Pearls in crown are blurred and the centre is often worn through.

GOOD, G-4 OBVERSE — Band of the crown and ear are worn away, also details of robe, chain, beard and moustache. Legend is weak.
REVERSE — Leaves and crown badly worn with little but outlines remaining. Lettering and numerals are weak. Border beads blurred.

UNCIRCULATED, MS-60 OBVERSE — Robe, shoulder bow, crown and moustache all clearly defined. Ornamental chain detail sharp and clear. A high degree of lustre remains.
REVERSE — No trace of wear showing on wreath, crown or bow. All detail on maple boughs sharp and clear.

ABOUT UNCIRCULATED, AU-50 OBVERSE — Very slight wear on moustache, crown, ear and hairlines. Half of mint lustre remaining.
REVERSE — Slight trace of wear on high points - knot in wreath, crown and lower leaves.

EXTREMELY FINE, EF-40 OBVERSE — Eyebrow worn. Band of crown slightly worn near centre but all 8 pearls showing. Trace of wear on tip of moustache and side whiskers. All 6 pearls down centre of crown are clearly defned.
REVERSE — Trace of wear around outer edges of most leaves and centre arch of crown.

VERY FINE, VF-20 OBVERSE — Eyebrow, moustache, beard and side whiskers are considerably worn, also robe, shoulder bow and ornamental chain. Band of crown is worn but 4 to 6 pearls remain, also at least 2 pearls at top of crown.
REVERSE — Wear on outer edges of leaves consists of about 1/3 their area. Slight wear on centre arch of crown.

FINE, F-12 OBVERSE — Jewels in the band of crown blurred, but 4 pearls and ½ to ¾ of band remains. Eyebrow indistinct. Beard and moustache worn together. Details of robe, shoulder bow and chain begin to blur. Top of ear merges with hair.
REVERSE — Wear on leaves about ½ their area. Pearls in centre arch of crown begin to merge.

VERY GOOD, VG-8 OBVERSE — Band of crown is worn through in centre with only front and rear portions remaining. Eyebrow worn off. Little detail remains in robe, bow and chain.
REVERSE — Very little detail remains in the leaves. Considerable wear on the centre arch of crown.

GOOD, G-4 OBVERSE — Band of crown worn away, also most of ear and other details. Legend is weak.
REVERSE — Leaves and crown badly worn with little but outlines remaining. Lettering and numerals are weak.

UNCIRCULATED, MS-60 OBVERSE — Hairlines, ear, eyebrow all sharp and distinct. Could be a nick or some bag marks but a high degree of lustre still remains.
REVERSE — No wear on lion or unicorn. All details in shield and crown sharp and clear.

ABOUT UNCIRCULATED, AU-50 OBVERSE — Only a slight trace of wear showing on cheek, ear and hairlines. Half of mint lustre remaining.
REVERSE — Very slight wear showing on shield. All details still sharp.

Many of the fifty cent pieces, particularly the 1947, 1947ML and 1948 were weakly struck in the area at the top left corner of shield and base of crown. The weakness should not be mistaken for wear on strictly uncirculated coins.

EXTREMELY FINE, EF-40 OBVERSE — Slight wear at eyebrow, ear lobe and hair above ear. Sideburn in front of ear clearly showing.
REVERSE — Slight wear on thighs and forelegs of lion and unicorn. Trace of wear on details of crown and shield.

VERY FINE, VF-20 OBVERSE — Eyebrow indistinct. Hairlines above the ear and side of head are blurred. Exposed portions of ear and cheek-bone show wear. Sideburn barely showing.
REVERSE — Some overall wear on bodies of lion and unicorn. Slight wear at bottom of crown and top of shield.

FINE, F-12 OBVERSE — Eyebrow worn off. Only slight detail in hair between the ear and part in hair. Considerable wear on ear, facial features and back of neck.
REVERSE — Considerable wear on lion and unicorn, bottom of crown and upper portion of shield. Border beads begin to merge.

VERY GOOD, VG-8 OBVERSE — No detail in hair above ear. Outer rim of ear is worn flat and merges with hair. Much wear on nose and other facial features.
REVERSE — Lion and unicorn worn. Crown and shield somewhat worn but most of details remain.

Young Head 1953 - 1964

UNCIRCULATED, MS-60 OBVERSE — All 11 leaves of laurel wreath, hairlines and shoulder fold sharply defined. High degree of lustre.
REVERSE — No wear showing on lion or unicorn. All details in shield and crown sharp and clear.

ABOUT UNCIRCULATED, AU-50 OBVERSE — Very slight wear on hairlines, shoulder and laurel wreath. Half of mint lustre remaining.
REVERSE — Trace of wear on lion, unicorn and crown.

EXTREMELY FINE, EF-40 OBVERSE — Slight wear at eyebrow, cheek, shoulder and laurel wreath. All 11 leaves showing.
REVERSE — Slight wear on thighs and forelegs of lion and unicorn, and at base of crown and top of shield.

VERY FINE, VF-20 OBVERSE — Considerable wear at eyebrow, bottom of ear and hair between ear and forehead. Laurel wreath is worn but 8 to 10 leaves showing. Shoulder is worn but shoulder fold visible on that variety.
REVERSE — Slight wear on lion and unicorn and at base of crown and upper panels of shield.

Young Head 1953 - 1964

FINE, F-12 OBVERSE — Much wear over entire portrait with few hairlines visible. Only faint outlines of the bottom of ear, nose and mouth remain. Outlines of 4 to 7 leaves showing.
REVERSE — Lion and unicorn considerably worn. Crown and shield slightly worn but most of details remain.

Mature Head 1965 -

UNCIRCULATED, MS-60 OBVERSE — No evidence of wear at eyebrow, the hair over the ear, temple and forehead. Drapery over the shoulder and band of the diadem sharply defined.
REVERSE — No signs of wear on lion or unicorn. All details in shield and crown are sharp and clear.

ABOUT UNCIRCULATED, AU-50 OBVERSE — Slight trace of wear on cheek, hairlines, tiara and drapery on shoulder. Half of mint lustre remaining.
REVERSE — Very slight wear on lion, unicorn and crown.

EXTREMELY FINE, EF-40 OBVERSE — Slight wear at eyebrow and hair over the ear. Also hair at temple and forehead. Drapery over the shoulder will show slight wear, particularly the line at top of Queen's gown.
REVERSE — Slight wear on crown, front of helmet and the forelegs of the lion and unicorn.

THE MANUFACTURE OF CANADIAN COINS

The steps involved in the production of Canadian coins can be divided into the following: a) production of a large three-dimensional model (for a new design); b) the engraving of the dies and collar; c) production of the blanks (planchets); and d) the coining of them.

A. The Production of the Large Three-Dimensional Model

The design for a new coinage usually begins as a sketch. After the theme for the design is chosen, a suitable sketch is obtained in one of three ways. The most direct way is to generate the sketch "in house." This was done, for example, in the case of the 1977 Queen's Silver Jubilee silver dollar when Royal Canadian Mint engraver Walter Ott made an ink drawing of the throne of the Senate. On other occasions, such as for the 1937 coinage, a select group of outside artists was invited to submit designs. To date, this has been the method most frequently used by the Royal Canadian Mint. The final method is to have an open competition which any Canadian can enter. The designs for the 1951 commemorative five-cent piece and the 1964 silver dollar were the results of open competitions.

Once a suitable sketch is at hand, a three-dimensional plaster model of the design about 8 inches in diameter is made. This is sometimes produced by the original artist, but more often the modelling is done in the Mint. Such models are usually made as a positive (i.e. the design elements are raised as on the final coin). A plastic, negative mould made from this model serves as the starting point for the next series of operations.

B. Die Production

The plastic, negative mould (design elements sunken) is placed in a device called a reducing machine. This machine works on the principal of the pantograph, reproducing on a reduced scale in three dimensions the design of the plastic model in metal. Generally the reduction proceeds in two steps. The first is to reproduce the plastic model as a brass block, making the design about 3 inches in diameter. This brass intermediate model then serves as the pattern for the machine during the reduction to coin scale. In the second reduction the design is engraved into a soft steel block. After the beads are added and other finishing touches applied, the steel block is hardened to become a reduction matrix.

From the reduction matrix one or more punches are made by placing it in a powerful press and impressing its design into soft steel blocks, which are later hardened. A punch has its design elements raised just as on the coins. The next step is to make the dies. Dies are made in the same way as punches, except it is a punch that is used to sink the design into soft steel blocks in the press. A single punch can produce thousands of dies before it must be retired.

The collar (the piece of metal that restrains the sideways expansion of the blank during striking and gives the coin its shape and edge design) is made at the Ottawa Mint. For plain edge coins a hole is simply drilled in the centre of an appropriate piece of steel. If the collar is to be for a reeded edge coin, a smooth-edge hole is first drilled. Then the hole is given a serrated edge by the use of a small, hardened steel wheel.

If the design for the reverse is to be used for more than one year, the final digit or digits of the date are ground from a punch and a new matrix made from the modified punch. The missing digit(s) is then punched into the blank space in the matrix. From this matrix new punches are made.

Since 1945 dies for Canadian coinages have, with rare exceptions, been chromium plated. This extends the die-life and gives the coins a superior finish.

C. Preparation of the Blanks

At the present time Canadian coins are struck in bronze, nickel, silver or gold. The blanks for gold coins are obtained from an outside source. When blanks are produced in the Ottawa Mint, as is the case with bronze and silver, the components of the metal alloys are mixed together in the melting pot and cast into bars. The bars are annealed (softened by heat treatment) and rolled to an exact thickness. The rolled metal is bent into the form of a large coil, which is then sent to the cutting room. In the cutting room the coils are fed into blanking presses, which punch blanks out of them. Following passage over a vibrating screen to remove defective (undersize) blanks, the good blanks are put through a machine which compresses their edges so as to produce raised rims. This facilitates coining by reducing the amount of metal that has to be displaced in the blank during striking. The rimmed blanks are next fed through a special furnace in which they are annealed. Finally, the cooled blanks are cleaned and dried, ready for the coining press.

Nickel is a difficult metal to work with, so both the Ottawa and the Winnipeg Mints obtain this metal in strip or coil form. Winnipeg also obtains its blank bronze in this form.

D. Coining

Blanks are fed into the coining chamber of the press through a feed tube attached to a vibrating hopper of blanks contained above. A metal fork pushes a fresh blank over the hole in the collar and at the same time pushes away the coin just struck. The blank, being slightly smaller than the diameter of the hole in the collar, drops in and comes to rest on the bottom (obverse) die. The top die then descends and makes contact with the blank. This causes the blank to expand, filling the crevices of the dies and the collar to become a coin. Both dies rise, forcing the coin out of the collar so that it can be pushed away by the next blank being positioned. Struck coins are collected, examined, counted and bagged for issue.

TECHNICAL INFORMATION

This catalogue presents the most complete set of technical statistics ever assembled for the Canadian decimal series.

It is important to note that the artistic talent that goes into the production of a new coinage design does not end with the individual who did the original drawing. The designing, modelling and engraving of the master tools for a modern coinage also require great skill and, in some cases, each step may be the work of a different person. As far as possible, these are all listed.

Compositions are given as decimal fractions, adding up to 1.00; they can be converted to percentages by multiplying by 100. Weights are given in grams and can be converted into troy ounces by dividing by 31.1035. Diameters are given in millimetres and can be converted into inches by multiplying by .03937.

Canadian coins have been struck with both major die axis arrangements. In the medal arrangement (designated ↑↑) a coin held vertically between one's fingers with its obverse design right side up finishes with its reverse design right side up when it is rotated on its vertical axis. Dies in the coinage arrangement (↑↓) will result in the reverse being upside down when the coin is turned as previously described.

THE TREATMENT OF VARIETIES

The subject of varieties and other differences is always controversial, and there will inevitably be disagreement, regardless of their treatment in the Standard Catalogue. It must be remembered that as a catalogue for general collectors, this work cannot list all minor differences which the specialist may find fascinating. Recently, the complex question of variety listings was carefully reviewed. It was decided that the best course was to omit some differences listed in previous editions (eg. 1946 "hoof" fifty cents, 1947 "dot" coins, 1956 "dot" ten cents, 1977 nickel dollar varieties), and include them in a separate catalogue specifically devoted to varieties. This new catalogue, The Charlton Standard Catalogue of Canadian Coin Varieties, will be released soon.

MINTS, MINT MARKS AND OTHER LETTERS

Until 1908, all Canadian coins were produced in England. Most were coined at the Royal Mint in London and have no identifying mint mark. From time to time, however, the Royal Mint was so busy with other coinages that Canadian authorities were allowed to have their coins struck by a private mint in Birmingham. This mint, called Heaton's Mint until 1889 and The Mint, Birmingham thereafter, used a small "H" mint mark on all its Canadian issues except for the Prince Edward Island cent of 1871.

January 2, 1908 saw the opening of a mint in Ottawa, authorized under the Imperial Coinage Act, 1870. Until 1931 it was the Ottawa Branch of the Royal Mint. Its issues for the

Dominion of Canada bear no mint mark, but those for elsewhere (British sovereigns and Newfoundland and Jamaica coinages) have a small "C" on the reverse. In 1931 the name of the Ottawa Mint was changed to the Royal Canadian Mint and it came under the full control of the Canadian government as a branch of the Department of Finance. The status of the Mint was altered in March, 1969 by the Government Organization Act, 1969, and it became a Crown Corporation effective April 1, 1969.

Today, Canada has three mints: the Ottawa Mint, the Hull Mint (established in 1965 for striking collectors' coins) and the Winnipeg Mint (opened in 1975). None of these mints employs mint marks.

The only recent occasion when Canadian coins were produced outside the country was in 1968. In that year part of the ten cents issue was coined at the U.S. Mint in Philadelphia. The Philadelphia Mint did not place a mint mark on these coins, but the Canadian and U.S. strikings can be distinguished by the shape of the grooves in the edge (see page 121).

Other identifying letters refer to designers, modellers, or engravers. They include the following:

B	Patrick Brindley	H.P.	T. Humphrey Paget
PC	Paul Cedarberg	DDP	Donald D. Paterson
DES	George W. DeSaulles	PP	Paul Pederson
M.G.	Mrs. Mary Gillick	B.P.	Benedetto Pistrucci
EH or H	Emmanuel Hahn	WWP	William Weseley Pole
K.G or K G	George E. Kruger-Gray	TS or T.S.	Thomas Shingles
B.M.	Sir E. Bertram MacKennal	RT	Raymond Taylor
TM	Terry Manning	ST or ST monogram	Stephan Trenka
P.M.	Percy Metcalfe	D.V.	Dinko Vodanovic
WO or WO monogram	Walter Ott	L.C.W.	Leonard C. Wyon

The location of all mint marks and other initials is indicated in the listings of each series. Since 1977, designers' and modellers' initials no longer appear on Canadian coins.

THE PRICES IN THIS CATALOGUE

The values quoted in this catalogue were determined by averaging the opinions of a group of highly-qualified numismatists who, in turn, based their estimates on the latest auction and retail prices. These prices are neither buying nor selling offers but are our best estimate of retail selling prices at the time of publication. In any case they are merely a guide; coins might sell for more or less in individual transactions.

There are a number of individual foreign coins in this catalogue which occur in several types with differing values. As well, some of the issues listed are for a particular denomination spanning many years; the value of these coins is dependent, to some degree, upon the year of issue. The prices listed here for these types are for the most common coins only. The reader is advised to see a specialized catalogue for specific varieties, dates and prices.

THE ILLUSTRATIONS IN THIS CATALOGUE

The photographs in this catalogue are, for the most part, of coins in the National Currency Collection in Ottawa. We acknowledge with deep appreciation the important role the Bank of Canada has played in this catalogue by allowing portions of their fine collection to be photographed.

FRATERNAL AFFILIATION

Over the years, coin clubs have sprung up in many Canadian communities. In addition both Canada and the United States have national organizations which hold annual conventions. Coin clubs constitute one of the most attractive features of present-day collecting. They offer beginning collectors the opportunity for good fellowship and the encouragement and knowledge of more experienced collectors. The larger groups maintain lending libraries and publish a journal or newsletter on a regular basis.

Memberships and other information can be obtained from:

The Canadian Numismatic Association,
Post Office Box 226,
Barrie, Ontario, Canada. L4M 4T2

The American Numismatic Association,
Post Office Box 2366,
Colorado Springs, Colorado, U.S.A. 80901

FOREIGN COINS IN CANADA

Strictly speaking, Canada (rather, the areas which now form Canada) did not have a coinage struck for its specific use until the mid-19th century. After 1820, some provincial governments issued their own coppers, but this was without Imperial Government sanction until the 1850's. Thus, for some two centuries Canada relied on foreign coins to provide the lifeblood for its commerce.

The importance of foreign coins in our currency history has not been given the emphasis it deserves in Canadian catalogues. Certainly it is difficult to deal with this subject. None of the foreign coins which were once so important here can strictly be called Canadian. This includes the coins of the French regime, some of which have been listed in past catalogues. To simply list some French issues is both misleading and illogical. The Spanish-American dollar, for example, was a more important coin in our overall currency history than any French (or British) coin ever was. A more realistic listing must include coins of France, Great Britain, Spain and Spanish America, Portugal, and the United States.

It has been decided to attempt to list the most important foreign coins that circulated in Canada, regardless of their country of origin. In order to qualify for listing a coin must have been specifically imported and in reasonable quantity. The many coins that filtered into North America in small quantities through trade cannot be listed.

The prices listed below for broad types of coins which may encompass several separate types and a span of many years, are for the most commonly encountered form of the coin only. Readers are advised to see specialized foreign catalogues for specific varieties, dates and prices.

COINS OF FRANCE

During the French regime (ca. 1600-1760), French Imperial coins were intermittently shipped to New France by the King or were imported by local merchants. Occasionally these were supplemented by general colonial coinages intended for circulation in France. But, as New France was just one of the recipients of the colonial issues, they cannot be considered to be specifically for Canada. French coins became less important in Canada after 1760. The silver ecus and ½ ecus, however, remained in commercial use well into the next century.

Between 1680 and the early 1720's, French coins were subject to considerable variations in the rate at which they were to be officially current. We will not attempt to detail these changes or "reformations" for each coin. A single example is sufficient to make the point. One of the few French coins with its original value actually stated on it is the "mousquetaire" or 30-denier piece minted between 1710 and 1713. Its initial rate of 30 deniers was lowered to 27 deniers in 1714 and to 22 deniers the next year. It remained at that level until the wild inflation of John Law (1720-1721), when it soared to 60 deniers and quickly fell back to 45 deniers. In 1724 its rate was returned to 27 deniers and in 1732 it was lowered to 24 deniers. It continued at that level in New France until the Conquest.

By 1726 the French Government realized the folly of frequent changes in the value of coins and generally the currency was stabilized.

MINT MARKS ON FRENCH COINS

Numerous mints produced French coins. Only for issues produced by a small number of mints will the listings by mint be separated. The following mint marks were employed on coins that circulated in quantity in New France and British Canada:

A - Paris	K - Bordeaux	S - Reims	& - Aix
B - Rouen	L - Bayonne	T - Nantes	AA - Metz
C - Caen	M - Toulouse	V - Troyes	BB - Strasbourg
D - Lyon	N - Montpellier	W - Lillie	(- Besancon
E - Tours	O - Riom	X - Amiens	a cow - Pau
G - Poitiers	P - Dijon	Y - Bourges	
H - LaRochelle	O - Perpignan	Z - Grenable	
I - Limoges	R - Orleans	9 - Rennes	

COPPER COINS

DENIER

Along with the copper double and liard, the denier was one of the predominant coins in circulation in New France up to the early 1660's. The denier, although rated at 1 denier in France, circulated as a two-denier piece in New France. The merchants saw a chance for a quick profit and imported these coins in large quantities. This resulted in an oversupply, prompting the Government at Quebec to ban the denier altogether in 1664.

Type and Denomination	VF	EF	Unc.
Louis XIII or XIV Denier*	10.00	25.00	100.00

DOUBLE

In 1664 the Order of the Sovereign Council which demonitized the denier allowed the double to remain in circulation but reduced its value to 1 denier to curb its excessive importation. It had formerly circulated at 4 deniers in New France.

Type and Denomination	VF	EF	Unc.
Louis XIII or XIV Double*	10.00	20.00	60.00

* Several types probably circulated in New France, but they are not listed separately here.

LIARD

Until the Order of Sovereign Council of 1664, the liard passed in New France as a six-denier piece. After 1664 its value was reduced to 2 deniers to discourage its excessive importation.

Type and Denomination	VF	EF	Unc.
Louis XIII or XIV Liard*	20.00	50.00	200.00

½ SOL COINAGE OF 1710-1712

The first coinage of this denomination in copper took place in 1710-1712. When first issued it was rated at 6 deniers.

Date and Denomination	VF	EF	Unc.
1710-1712 ½ Sol**	15.00	75.00	250.00

COPPER COINAGE OF 1719 - 1724

This coinage consisted of a liard, a ½ sol and a double sol. The two middle denominations are believed to have been sent to New France and placed in circulation.

½ SOL 1719-1724

Date and Denomination	VF	EF	Unc.
1719-1724 ½ Sol**	15.00	40.00	150.00

* Several types probably circulated in New France, but they are not listed separately here.
** Dates not listed separately.

COPPER SOL 1719-1724

Date and Denomination	VF	EF	Unc.
1719-1724 Sol**	15.00	40.00	225.00

COLONIAL 9 DENIER COINAGE 1721-1722

   This was a special colonial issue imported by a private trading company, the Company of the Indies. Following difficulties in circulating their new coins, the Company attempted to have them transferred to the Government of New France. This was not successful, so most of the coinage was returned to France in 1726. These coins were also sent to other French colonies.

Date and Denomination	VG	F	VF	EF	Unc.
1721B 9 Deniers	200.00	300.00	400.00	500.00	1,300.00
1721H 9 Deniers	50.00	75.00	100.00	175.00	650.00
1722H 2 over 1	50.00	75.00	100.00	175.00	650.00
1722H Normal Date	50.00	75.00	100.00	175.00	650.00

** Dates not listed separately.

BILLON SOLS MARQUES COINAGES

The most important coinages in circulation during the French regime were a group of billon (low-grade silver) pieces collectively called sols (or sous) marques. They often constituted the smallest denomination coins because copper was generally unpopular with the colonists. There were no less than six coinages of sols marques; the coinages of 1709-1713 and 1738-1764 also had double sol denominations.

COUNTERSTAMPED DOUZAINS (1640)

During the Middle Ages a new French coin called a gros tournois made its appearance. It was about the size of a 25¢ piece and made of good silver. By the first part of the 17th century this coin had become a billon piece called a douzain. The douzain or sol was rated at 12 deniers. In 1640 the French Government called in all douzains and counterstamped them with a small fleur-de-lis in an oval to change their rating to 15 deniers. The term sol marque (marked sol) came from the fact that these coins were counterstamped. It later came to apply to all sols.

Date and Denomination	VF	EF	Unc.
Counterstamped Douzain (1640)	125.00	500.00	1,200.00

COINAGE OF 1641

The next billon coin in the series was a new design dated 1641. It was initially rated at 15 deniers and supplemented the douzains counterstamped the year before. Its relation to these coins is clearly shown by its design (both obverse and reverse) containing a fleur-de-lis in an oval, in imitation of the counterstamp on the earlier issue.

Date and Denomination	VF	EF	Unc.
1641 15 Deniers	150.00	400.00	1,000.00

COINAGE OF 1658

The douzain of 1658 was rated at 12 deniers in France but was given a rating of 20 deniers when it made its first appearance in New France in 1662. A six-denier piece was also struck, but there is no reason to believe that denomination circulated in quantity in the colony.

Date and Denomination	VF	EF	Unc.
1658 Douzain**	200.00	400.00	800.00

COINAGE OF 1692-1698

Beginning in 1692 and continuing through 1698, a new issue of sols marques was made. The designs were new, but instead of being struck on fresh blanks, many were struck over previous issues of sols. It is sometimes possible to detect parts of the undertypes on the overstruck coins. The new issue was rated at 15 deniers when it first came out. Some of these coins dated 1693 and 1697 seem to be counterstamped with a fleur-de-lis in an oval as was done in 1640.

15 Deniers without counterstamp

15 Deniers with fleur-de-lis counterstamp

Date and Denomination	VF	EF	Unc.
1692-1698 15 Deniers, no counterstamp**	15.00	30.00	100.00
1693, 1697 15 Deniers, with fleur-de-lis**	10.00	20.00	70.00

** Dates not listed separately.

6

"MOUSQUETAIRE" ISSUES OF 1709-1713

This issue consisted of a 15-denier piece and a 30-denier piece. The name mousquetaire is believed to have come from the cross on the reverse of the coins, which resembled the crosses on the cloaks of the legendary musketeers.

15 DENIERS

Date and Denomination	VF	EF	Unc.
1710-1713 15 Deniers	30.00	100.00	250.00

30 DENIERS

Date and Denomination	VF	EF	Unc.
1709-1713 30 Deniers	15.00	50.00	175.00

COINAGE OF 1738 - 1764

The final billon coinage used in New France was that of 1738-1764, consisting of a sol and double sol. The double sol has often been mistakenly referred to as "the" sou marque. First, there is no single sol marque; some six coinages are involved. Second, the sol or sou was by 1738 a coin about the size of our present small cent. The larger coin so often called a sou marque is in fact a double sol.

SOL (SOU) 1738-1754

This coin was rated at 12 deniers in both France and New France.

Date and Denomination	VF	EF	Unc.
1738-1754 Sol	15.00	50.00	200.00

DOUBLE SOL (2 SOUS) 1738-1764

Although this type was struck until 1764, it is unlikely that any dated later than 1760 circulated in New France. This coin was rated at 24 deniers.

Large quantities of contemporary counterfeits were made of the double sol, particularly of the dates 1740, 1741, 1742, 1750, 1751, 1755 and 1760. Differences in the rendition of the crown are the easiest way to tell the genuine from the counterfeit.

Original

Typical Counterfeit

Date and Denomination	VF	EF	Unc.
1738-1760 Double Sol, genuine	2.50	15.00	70.00
1740-1760 Double Sol, counterfeit	2.50	15.00	70.00

SILVER COINS

½ ECU

The ½ ecu was not routinely imported into French America; nevertheless, it did circulate in some quantity during the British regime in the first third of the 19th century. It is assumed that these coins came primarily from issues of Louis XIV and XV.

Type and Denomination	VF	EF	Unc.
½ Ecu of Louis XIV and XV*	30.00	250.00	675.00

ECU

The ecu, a large silver coin about the size of the Canadian silver dollar, was imported into French America in significant quantities. The ecu continued in use after the fall of New France, when it was called the French crown. Most types of ecu minted between 1640 and the 1750's probably circulated in Canada.

Type and Denomination	VF	EF	Unc.
Ecu of Louis XIII, XIV, or XV*	45.00	200.00	800.00

* Numerous types circulated in Canada, but they are not listed separately here.

COLONIAL COINAGE OF 1670

In 1670 a special coinage of silver 5 and 15-sol pieces was produced for circulation in the French colonies in the New World. On the reverse was "GLORIAM REGNI TVI DICENT" meaning "They shall speak of the glory of Thy kingdom" and taken from the 145th Psalm of the Bible. Despite their fame, these coins barely qualify as "Canadian." Period documents suggest that they probably were much more intended for the West Indies than New France. Authorities in the West Indies were anxious to obtain a subsidiary silver coinage for payment of day labourers and artisans, who were being paid in goods. In New France these coins were not particularly wanted because they could not be used for buying goods in France; they were not legal tender there. In any case it is quite clear that these coins had a very limited circulation in French America.

5 SOLS

Date and Denomination	Quantity Minted	VG	F	VF	EF	Unc.
1670A 5 Sols	200,000	400.00	600.00	800.00	1,200.00	2,750.00

15 SOLS

Date and Denomination	Quantity Minted	VG	F	VF	EF	Unc.
1670A 15 Sols	40,000	3,000.00	5,000.00	7,500.00	10,000.00	25,000.00

REDUCED SILVER COINAGES OF 1674 - 1709

In the late 17th and early 18th centuries the French Government was in a rather precarious financial condition. As a money-raising scheme it struck seven coinages with reduced silver content (ca. .800 fine) at the same time as the regular .917 fine silver types were being produced. Most of the reduced fineness types were sent to New France in quantity.

4 SOLS ISSUES OF 1674-1677

By 1679 there were so many of these coins in circulation in New France that they were being used in payment by the bagfull. An ordinance passed in that year lowered their value to 3 sols 6 deniers and placed strict limits on the amount that could be used for any one payment.

Date and Denomination	VF	EF	Unc.
1674-1677 4 Sols **	15.00	35.00	80.00

4 SOLS ISSUES OF 1691-1700

This coin was the successor to the previous reduced silver 4-sol piece and was struck over it.

Date and Denomination	VF	EF	Unc.
1691-1700 4 Sols **	20.00	40.00	110.00

** Dates not listed separately.

5 SOLS OF 1702-1709

The next reduced silver coinage used in New France was a piece of approximately the same weight as the old 4-sol pieces, but which was called a 5-sol piece instead.

Date and Denomination	VF	EF	Unc.
1702-1709 5 Sols**	20.00	40.00	110.00

10 SOLS OF 1702-1708

This 10-sol piece is from the same series as the 5-sols.

Date and Denomination	VF	EF	Unc.
1702-1708 10 Sols**	20.00	50.00	175.00

LIVRE OF 1720

In 1720, during the wild inflation brought about by the schemes of John Law, a special coin was produced in pure silver and issued at the overvalued rating of one livre. The Company of the Indies imported a quantity of these coins into French America in 1722.

Date and Denomination	Quantity Minted	VF	EF	Unc.
1720A Livre	6,918,853	225.00	500.00	700.00

** Dates not listed separately.

12

SMALL SILVER LOUIS 1720

In 1720 a new coin called a small silver louis (petit louis d'argent) was brought into Canada. Its initial rating was 55 sols, but this was soon reduced to 40 sols.

Date and Denomination	VF	EF	Unc.
1720 Small Silver Louis	40.00	150.00	500.00

GOLD COINS

THE GOLD LOUIS

The only French gold coin to see significant circulation in the French North America was the gold louis (louis d'or). Louis d'or were regularly sent over and saw use even after the Conquest. Any of the types struck between the 1640's and the 1750's potentially circulated here in quantity.

Type of 1680   Type of 1723-1725

Type and Denomination	VF	EF	Unc.
Gold Louis of Louis XIV or XV*	2,000.00	3,000.00	4,000.00

* The numerous types are not listed separately.

COINS OF GREAT BRITAIN

For most of the British colonial period (ca. 1760-1870) the British Government was hardly better than the French Government had been at supplying Imperial coins for use in Canada. British coinage was struck infrequently during the last half of the 18th century, and England and her colonies alike suffered for the lack of coin.

A major alteration took place in the British coinage in 1816. The silver coinage was reduced to a subsidiary status (along with the coppers) by lowering the amount of silver it contained to bring the bullion value of the coins below the face value. This left gold as the sole standard coinage and marks the beginning of the British gold standard. The coinage of silver was begun on a large scale and British coins gradually became more available. In 1825-1826 a serious attempt was made to establish Imperial coins as the principal coinage of the colonies and to drive out the Spanish-American coins. This attempt largely failed in British North America. Nevertheless, at various times some British coins did achieve a significant circulation here, particularly in Nova Scotia. That province came the closest to adopting sterling coinage; when it was decided to institute a deciaml currency in 1859, the dollar was rated so as to allow the continued cirulcation of British coins. The 2-shilling piece (florin) became a 50¢ piece, the shilling became a 25¢ piece and so on. The halfpenny and shilling also saw much use in Upper and Lower Canada and later in the united Province of Canada.

COPPER COINS

HALFPENNY

GEORGE II ISSUES OF 1740-1754

These coins, along with the George III halfpenny listed below, formed the most important part of the British North American copper currency until the War of 1812. After that time they were supplemented by the tokens issued by local merchants and others. But, until the first bank tokens, they were the only copper sanctioned by the British Government.

Date and Denomination	VG	F	VF	EF	AU	Unc.
1740-1754 ½d **	4.00	7.50	25.00	50.00	100.00	175.00

** Dates not listed separately.

GEORGE III ISSUES OF 1770-1775

The majority of the coins of this issue that circulated in both Great Britain and America were contemporary counterfeits. Issues of halfpennies during later reigns seem not to have circulated in quantity in British North America.

Genuine Issue

Typical Counterfeit

Date and Denomination	VG	F	VF	EF	AU	Unc.
1770-1775 1d, genuine	2.00	5.00	20.00	50.00	90.00	150.00

PENNY

The penny was not a frequently-used denomination in British North America. In 1832, however, a special shipment was made to Upper Canada. This is known to have consisted of coins dated 1831.

Date and Denomination	VG	F	VF	EF	AU	Unc.
1831 Penny	5.00	10.00	50.00	150.00	250.00	400.00

SILVER COINS

British silver coins became more important in circulation in some parts of British North America after about 1830. The intermediate denominations were the most common.

SIX PENCE

Type and Denomination	VG	F	VF	EF	AU	Unc.
Six Pence of William IV*	2.00	3.50	12.00	30.00	45.00	60.00
Six Pence of Victoria (Young Head)*	1.75	2.75	3.50	7.00	14.00	20.00

SHILLING

Type and Denomination	VG	F	VF	EF	AU	Unc.
Shilling of William IV*	3.00	6.00	15.00	40.00	60.00	80.00
Shilling of Victoria (Young Head)*	3.00	5.00	12.00	35.00	50.00	70.00

* Types are not listed separately.

FLORIN

This denomination probably saw use in Nova Scotia during the 1850's and 1860's.

Date and Denomination	F	VF	EF	Unc.
1851-ca. 1870 Florin*	10.00	25.00	60.00	150.00

* On these coins the date is on the obverse in the form of a Roman numeral.

HALFCROWN

Type and Denomination	F	VF	EF	Unc.
Halfcrown of George IV*	15.00	40.00	100.00	200.00
Halfcrown of William IV*	15.00	40.00	90.00	175.00
Halfcrown of Victoria (Young Head)*	10.00	15.00	20.00	60.00

* Types are not listed separately.

GOLD COINS

GEORGE III ½ GUINEA

The ½ guinea was usually rated at 10 shillings 6 pence in Great Britain.

Type and Denomination	F	VF	EF	Unc.
½ Guinea of George III*	150.00	225.00	275.00	375.00

GEORGE III GUINEA 1761-1813

The guinea or 21-shilling piece, was one of the principal gold coins to circulate in British North America.

Type of 1761-1786

Type and Denomination	F	VF	EF	Unc.
Guinea of George III*	175.00	200.00	275.00	450.00

½ SOVEREIGN

The ½ sovereign was the successor to the ½ guinea and probably saw enough circulation in British North America and the Dominion of Canada to warrant its inclusion in this listing.

Type and Denomination	F	VF	EF	Unc.
½ Sovereign of George III*	85.00	125.00	200.00	300.00
½ Sovereign of George IV*	100.00	150.00	275.00	425.00
½ Sovereign of William IV*	125.00	250.00	500.00	1,200.00
½ Sovereign of Victoria (Young Head)*	85.00	100.00	125.00	175.00

* Types are not listed separately.

SOVEREIGN

The sovereign was perhaps the most widely used gold coin in Canada. It was used extensively by banks and the government for redeeming paper money right up to the 20th century.

Type and Denomination	F	VF	EF	Unc.
Sovereign of George III*	165.00	200.00	400.00	650.00
Sovereign of George IV*	175.00	250.00	400.00	650.00
Sovereign of William IV*	175.00	250.00	400.00	650.00
Sovereign of Victoria (Shield)*	165.00	175.00	185.00	200.00

* Types are not listed separately.

COINS OF PORTUGAL

During the 18th and early 19th centuries, several types of gold coins issued by Portugal found their way into British North America and were used extensively there.

MOIDORE

This coin had a denomination of 4,000 reis in Portugal and bore on its reverse the Cross of Jerusalem. It was struck from the reign of Alfonso VI (1656-1683) to the reign of John V (1706-1750).

Type and Denomination	VF	EF	Unc.
Moidore of Alfonso VI to John V*	350.00	450.00	800.00

6,400 REIS (HALF JOE)

This coin, with a formal denomination of 6,400 reis, was introduced in the 1720's, along with a 12,800 reis coin of similar design. The king of Portugal at the time was John (Joao) V and from his name on the coins, Johannes V, came the nickname "Joe" for the 12,800 reis coin and "½ Joe" for the 6,400 reis coin. Half Joe was also applied to the 6,400 reis coins issued in subsequent reigns. The larger coin was not issued in later reigns and Joe was eventually used for the 6,400 reis denomination.

Type and Denomination	VF	EF	Unc.
"½ Joe" 6,400 Reis of John V to John VI*	500.00	900.00	1,500.00

* Types are not listed separately.

12,800 REIS (JOE)

This was a coin of 12,800 reis issued during the reign of John V (see above).

Type and Denomination	VF	EF	Unc.
"Joe" 12,800 Reis of John V*	1,500.00	2,500.00	3,500.00

* Several types probably circulated in British North America, but are not listed separately here.

COINS OF SPAIN, SPANISH AMERICA
AND FORMER SPANISH COLONIES

This group of coins was more important in the currency history of what is now Canada for a longer period of time than any other foreign coinage. It was the Spanish-American dollar that served as the basis for the United States dollar, upon which in turn was based the decimal dollar of the Province of Canada in 1858.

COINS OF SPAIN

The Spanish metropolitan coinage is relatively unimportant compared to that of her New World colonies, with one exception: the pistareen. This was the nickname for a reduced standard two-real piece minted only in Spain and which enjoyed wide circulation in British North America in the first half of the 19th century.

Type and Denomination	VF	EF	Unc.
Spanish Pistareen 18th Century*	10.00	20.00	50.00

* Numerous types circulated here; they are not listed separately.

COINS OF SPANISH AMERICA

The coinage of Spain's colonies emanated from the following principal mints: Potosi in Bolivia, Santiago in Chile, Sante Fe de Bogota and Popayan in Colombia (Nueva Granada), Guatemala in Guatemala, Mexico City in Mexico and Lima and Cuzco in Peru. Minting of Spanish-American coins began in the early 16th century with the coins being of conventional round appearance. These were replaced about 1580 by the "cob" series: crude-appearing coins hand-struck on irregular blanks hewn from bars of refined bullion.

The cob series was finally superceded by round coins in 1732. The first round gold issues bore the portrait of the reigning Spanish monarch from the first; however, the silver did not carry portraits until 1772. In the intervening 40 years the obverses featured the "two world" or "pillar" design, consisting of two crowned hemispheres between the crowned pillars of Hercules.

The Spanish-American series came to an end in the 1820's as Spain's colonies successfully revolted and became independent. Nevertheless, the Spanish-American coins had been minted in such great quantities that they continued to exert an important influence for decades. Probably the most important coinages for Canada are those struck under the rulers Charles III (1760-1788), Charles IV (1788-1808) and Ferdinand VII (1808-1821).

1 REAL

Type and Denomination	VF	EF	Unc.
Real of Charles III to Ferdinand VII*	10.00	20.00	50.00

2 REALES

Type and Denomination	VF	EF	Unc.
2 Reales of Charles III to Ferdinand VII*	10.00	20.00	50.00

* The various types are not listed separately here.

4 REALES

Type and Denomination	VF	EF	Unc.
4 Reales of Charles III or Ferdinand VII*	30.00	60.00	100.00

8 REALES

This is by far the most important foreign coin to circulate in Canada. It was known and appreciated all over the civilized world and was the principal end product of the vast amounts of silver mined in the New World. The eight-real piece had the nickname dollar (even though it was not a decimal coin) due to its similarity in size to the European thalers and dalders. It is the famous "piece-of-eight" of pirate lore. The first eight-real pieces were produced in 1556 at the Mexico City mint.

Type and Denomination	VF	EF	Unc.
8 Reales (Dollar) of Philip IV to Ferdinand VII*	80.00	100.00	200.00

* The various types are not listed separately here.

2 ESCUDOS

This gold coin was popularly known as the Spanish pistole and, next to the doubloon (see below), was the most widely used Spanish-American gold coin in Canada.

Type and Denomination	VF	EF	Unc.
2 Escudos of Charles III to Ferdinand VII*	200.00	250.00	325.00

4 ESCUDOS

Type and Denomination	VF	EF	Unc.
4 Escudos of Charles III to Ferdinand VII*	175.00	300.00	425.00

8 ESCUDOS (DOUBLOON)

The most important gold coin in Canada was the eight-escudo piece or doubloon. It circulated widely, but was especially popular in the Atlantic provinces. After the Spanish colonies gained their independence, these coins were called "Royal" doubloons (as opposed to "Patriot" doubloons discussed below).

Type and Denomination	VF	EF	Unc.
8 Escudos (Doubloon) of Charles III to Ferdinand VII*	1,750.00	2,750.00	6,000.00

* The various types are not listed separately here.

COINS OF FORMER SPANISH COLONIES

By 1826 Spain had lost all her colonies in the New World. This ushered in new coinages on the existing standards by each of the former colonies. They were accepted and circulated alongside the coins of the Spanish-American series. Probably only two denominations are necessary in this listing - the silver dollar and the gold doubloon.

8 REALES (DOLLAR)

The most important dollars of former Spanish colonies to circulate in Canada are undoubtedly those of Mexico.

Type and Denomination	VF	EF	Unc.
Mexican 8 Reales (Dollar) of the 1820's to 1840's*	75.00	100.00	200.00

8 ESCUDOS (DOUBLOON)

In the case of the doubloon it is more difficult to single out any one former colony's coinage as being the most important for Canada. Therefore a general listing is given. Contemporary sources refer to such doubloons as "Patriot" doubloons to distinguish them from the "Royal" doubloons of the Spanish-American series. It is known that "Patriot" doubloons were specifically imported into such provinces as Nova Scotia.

Typical "Patriot" Doubloon from Chile

Type and Denomination	VF	EF	Unc.
"Patriot" 8 Escudos (Doubloon) of ca. 1817 to the 1830's**	(See Specialized Catalogues)		

* The various types are not listed separately here.

** Dates not listed separately.

COINS OF THE UNITED STATES

It is to the United States coinage that we owe our present decimal currency system. By the 1850's trade links between British North America and the U.S. were so strong and its coinage so commonplace here that the proponents of a currency akin to that of the U.S. instead of Great Britain won out.

The U.S. coinage on a decimal basis began in the 1790's and it has circulated here to varying degrees ever since. A great influx of U.S. silver coins took place during the 1850's and 1860's, after the proportion of silver contained in the five, ten, twenty-five and fifty-cent pieces was reduced. Previous to that time, U.S. large cents came across the border in quantity and large numbers of half dollars were imported to help pay for work on such projects as the Rideau Canal. The larger denominations of U.S. gold coins were important in Canada almost up to the beginning of this century because they were widely imported by banks and the government for use in backing and redeeming paper money.

1 CENT

Type and Denomination	VG	F	VF	EF	Unc.
Coronet Large Cent 1816-1857**	5.00	7.00	10.00	25.00	180.00

½ DIME

Type and Denomination	VG	F	VF	EF	Unc.
Seated Liberty ½ Dime 1837-1873**	6.00	9.00	14.00	30.00	225.00

** Dates not listed separately.

DIME

Type and Denomination	VG	F	VF	EF	Unc.
Seated Liberty Dime 1837-1891**	7.50	12.50	17.50	25.00	225.00

QUARTER DOLLAR

Type and Denomination	VG	F	VF	EF	Unc.
Seated Liberty Quarter 1838-1891**	9.00	11.00	20.00	40.00	350.00

HALF DOLLAR

Type and Denomination	VG	F	VF	EF	Unc.
Capped Bust and Seated Liberty Half Dollar 1807-1891**	13.00	20.00	30.00	55.00	400.00

** Dates not listed separately.

½ EAGLE (5 DOLLARS)

Type and Denomination	VF	EF	Unc.
Coronet and Bare Head ½ Eagle 1834-1908**	150.00	175.00	275.00

EAGLE (10 DOLLARS)

Type and Denomination	VF	EF	Unc.
Capped Bust, Heraldic Eagle and Coronet Eagle 1797-1907**	300.00	350.00	450.00

DOUBLE EAGLE (20 DOLLARS)

Type and Denomination	VF	EF	Unc.
Coronet Double Eagle 1849-1907**	650.00	700.00	900.00

** Dates not listed separately.

LOCAL PRE-DECIMAL COINAGES

Although it is sometimes stated that the first coins produced for local use in Canada were the 1858-1859 decimal coins for the Province of Canada, this is not the case. A small but important group of local coinages was produced prior to the adoption of decimal currency. These coinages were at first specially modified Spanish-American silver coins, but coppers were added to this group in the 1850's.

NEW FRANCE (FRENCH REGIME)

COUNTERSTAMPED SPANISH-AMERICAN COINS

During the last part of the 17th century, the quantity of Spanish-American silver coins in circulation in New France increased. This increase was due primarily to the illegal trade in furs which the colonists were carrying on with the Dutch and English. At that time such coins circulated at a value that depended upon their weight; the more worn the coin was, the lower it was valued compared to unworn pieces. Since many Spanish-American coins in New France had varying amounts of wear, their use in commerce was difficult. Colonial authorities were not anxious to see these coins used in preference to French coins, but the latter were so scarce that they relented. In the early 1680's treasury officials weighed a quantity of these coins and counterstamped each with a fleur-de-lis. Underweight coins also received a Roman numeral counterstamp (from I to IV) to indicate the amount by which the weight was deficient. The coins could then be compared to a table to determine the exact value at which they were current.

Unfortunately for collectors, no surviving examples of this interesting local issue are known.

NEW BRUNSWICK

COINAGE OF 1854

Unlike most other pre-Confederation British American colonies, New Brunswick did not have a serious deficiency of copper currency until the late 1830's and early 1840's. In 1843 the provincial government obtained copper pence and halfpence from Boulton and Watt, a private mint in England. These pieces are technically tokens because they were obtained without the permission of the British government.

In 1853 a further issue of copper was required. The adoption of a decimal currency was being seriously considered but was still up in the air. Therefore, it was decided to order more coppers in the £.d.s. system. It was at this time that the British government learned of the "spurious" token issue of 1843. The master tools for the 1843 coppers were sent to the Royal Mint in London where the reverses were modified by substituting "CURRENCY" for "TOKEN." Totally new obverses were prepared.

The actual striking of the 1854 coinage took place at Heaton's Mint in Birmingham, but the coins lack the familiar "H" mint mark.

VICTORIA HALFPENNY 1854

Engraver: Obverse - Leonard C. Wyon, using Williams Wyon's portrait for the British shilling
Reverse - Soho Mint Staff (except for Leonard Wyon's modification of the legend)
Composition: 1.00 copper
Weight: 7.78 grams
Diameter: 28.3 mm
Edge: Plain
Die Axes: ↑↑

Date and Denomination	Quantity Minted	VG	F	VF	EF	Unc.
1854 ½d	480,000	4.00	7.50	15.00	35.00	100.00

VICTORIA PENNY 1854

Engraver: as the halfpenny above
Composition: 1.00 copper
Weight: 15.55 grams

Diameter: 34.3 mm
Edge: Plain
Die Axes: ↑↑

Date and Denomination	Quantity Minted	VG	F	VF	EF	Unc.
1854 1d	480,000	5.00	10.00	20.00	50.00	125.00

NOVA SCOTIA

"MAYFLOWER" COINAGE OF 1856

From 1823 to 1843 the government of Nova Scotia imported a series of unauthorized pence and halfpence which collectors have come to call the "thistle" series. These tokens are in the same category as the 1843 New Brunswick coppers and like them are treated in a separate catalogue.

In the 1850's, when the British government was more willing to allow local coinages in the colonies, the Nova Scotia government officially applied for and received a true coinage, its first. These pence and halfpence feature a sprig of mayflower, now the provincial flower, on their reverses and are considered by many to be among the most beautiful coins ever made for North America. They were produced at Heaton's Mint in Birmingham (without the "H" mint mark), but the master tools were made by the Royal Mint.

VICTORIA HALFPENNY 1856

This denomination is represented by two obverse varieties, one with and the other without the designer's initials (L.C.W.) below the Queen's bust. It appears that the variety with L.C.W. was struck only as a proof. Proofs of the No L.C.W. variety were also struck; it is most interesting that a rare variety of the No L.C.W. proof was struck from a blundered die where an "A" punch was used to repair a defective "V" in "PROVINCE" in one of the reverse dies, resulting in "PROVINCE."

A scarce vareity of the circulation strikes of the No L.C.W. halfpenny was coined in brass instead of the normal bronze. It can be recognized by its light yellow colour.

Designer & Modeller:
Leonard C. Wyon (L.C.W. under the bust on some varieties)
Composition: .95 copper, .04 tin, .01 zinc (except for the brass variety)
Weight: 7.78 grams
Diameter: 27.9 mm
Edge: Plain
Die Axes: ↑↑

Date and Denomination	VG	F	VF	EF	Unc.
1856 ½d, L.C.W.			PROOF ONLY		750.00
1856 ½d, No L.C.W., "PROVINCE"			PROOF ONLY		750.00
1856 ½d, No L.C.W., Normal Legend				PROOF	750.00
1856 ½d, No L.C.W., bronze	4.00	7.50	15.00	35.00	100.00
1856 ½d, No L.C.W., brass	4.00	7.50	15.00	35.00	100.00

VICTORIA PENNY 1856

Both the L.C.W. and the No L.C.W. varieties of the penny were coined for circulation.

Designer & Modeller:
     as the halfpenny above
Composition: .95 copper, .04 tin, .01 zinc
Weight: 15.55 grams
Diameter: 33.3 mm
Edge: Plain
Die Axes: ↑↑

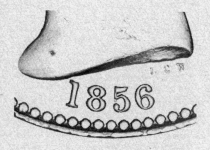

L.C.W. Under Bust   No L.C.W.

Date and Denomination	VG	F	VF	EF	Unc.
1856 1d, L.C.W.	5.00	10.00	20.00	35.00	100.00
1856 1d, No L.C.W.	5.00	10.00	20.00	35.00	100.00

PRINCE EDWARD ISLAND

"HOLEY" DOLLAR AND PLUG COINAGE 1813

The principal coin used on Prince Edward Island in the early 19th century was the Spanish-American dollar. When a new governor arrived there in 1813 to take up his post however, he found that all coins were very scarce creating something of a commercial crisis. The scarcity was due to the tendency of local businessmen to hoard coins for the purpose of sending them abroad to pay for purchases of goods.

The governor decided that a remedy to the problem was the creation of a local coinage from mutilated Spanish-American coins, similar to that taking place in the West Indies and Australia. He ordered that a quantity of Spanish-American dollars be perforated to form two kinds of coins. The piece punched out of the centre (the plug) was to be a shilling and the large ring that remained ("holey" dollar) was to be a five-shilling piece.

Each plug and holey dollar was given an official counterstamp. The nature of this counterstamp seems not to have been specified. Circumstantial evidence suggests it consisted of ten triangles arranged in a circle, like a symbol for the sun. On the holey dollar the triangles are well separated from each other and the symbol touches the King's forehead. However, on the plug the triangles are larger and run together at the corners.

The reasoning behind the creation of the plug and holey dollar coinage was that the coins would remain on the island, being overvalued (as they were by some 20%) compared to the unmutilated coins. Anyone using the mutilated coins for payments abroad would thus sustain a loss of 20% because the coins would only be accepted at the inflated rate on the island. This proved to be correct, but the merchants saw a chance to make a quick profit by creating their own holey dollars. This forced the government to withdraw the official issue in 1814, leaving the merchants' forgeries behind. The merchants' piece are thought to have continued in circulation for about another ten years.

Authenticating a holey dollar or plug is not an easy matter. Pedigree, the appearance of the counterstamp, the appearance and placement of the counterstamp, and the appearance of the hole in the centre of the dollar are all important. Differentiating the original issue from the merchants' imitations is made doubly difficult by the fact that from about 1890 onward forgeries have been made to sell to collectors. Most are made from genuine Spanish-American dollars. The forgeries made for collectors are, of course, worth much less than an original or merchants' imitation. Recently lightweight counterfeits of the holey dollar and plug have also begun to appear.

At the present time it is not possible to positively differentiate the originals from the contemporary merchants' imitations. It is assumed that certain of the holey dollars with counterstamps consisting of small squares or radiating lines instead of triangles are merchants' imitations, but it is also possible that the counterstamp on the merchants' imitations were always more like the originals and that all pieces with squares, lines, etc. are later forgeries for collectors. For this reason, we have listed the merchants' forgeries along with the originals. Pieces of particularly good appearance and with a good pedigree are worth a premium over the prices given below.

GEORGE III ONE SHILLING (1813)

Type and Denomination	Quantity Minted	VG	F	VF
One Shilling, Original or Merchants' Imitation Plug	ca. 1,000	1,500.00	2,000.00	3,000.00

GEORGE III FIVE SHILLINGS (1813)

Type and Denomination	Quantity Minted	VG	F	VF
Five Shillings, Original or Merchants' Imitation Holey Dollar	ca. 1,000	2,000.00	2,500.00	4,000.00

HISTORY OF THE CANADIAN DECIMAL COINAGES

The decimal coins which we take so much for granted today have a history that stretches back into the last century and beyond. During the 1700's, the single most important coin in North America was the Spanish-American dollar, a large silver coin produced in great quantities by mints in Mexico, Peru and other parts of the New World. The Spanish-American dollar was not a decimal coin; its formal denomination was 8 reales. It was nicknamed dollar in deference to its resemblance in size to German thalers and other large European coins of similar name. This Spanish-American coin was so important in the United States that when the U.S. adopted a decimal system of dollars and cents in the 1790's, the silver dollar was made with the same amount of silver as it contained.

In British North America in the first half of the 19th century each colony used a system of accounting which consisted of pounds, shillings and pence. However, the coins actually in circulation were mostly Spanish-American and U.S. As trade with the United States increased in the 1840's and 1850's, the British North American colonies (provinces) were naturally drawn closer toward the adoption of currency systems more like those of the U.S. than Great Britain.

All through the 1850's British North America struggled with the problem of currency standards. The Province of Canada, under Francis Hincks, took the lead in fighting for a decimal system. Acts passed in 1851 and 1853 stipulated that public accounts be kept in dollars and cents, but no coins were issued under their provisions. An 1857 act provided a broader base for a decimal currency system. It directed that both government and private accounts be kept in dollars, cents and mils. A decimal coinage followed in 1858-1859, based upon a dollar equal in value to the U.S. gold dollar.

Other British North American provinces soon followed Canada's lead. New Brunswick and Nova Scotia adopted decimal systems in 1859-1860, Newfoundland followed suit in 1864 and Prince Edward Island went decimal in 1871. Thus, even before Confederation the use of decimal coins was firmly established.

NOVA SCOTIA

In the years immediately preceding the adoption of a decimal currency system in Nova Scotia in 1859 British coins formed an important part of the circulating currency, much more so than in the other British North American provinces. Consequently, the Nova Scotia government chose a decimal dollar equal to 1/5 of a £ sterling (i.e. $5 = £1), allowing British silver coins to conveniently fit into the new system and continue circulating. The British two-shilling piece (florin) became a 50¢ piece, the shilling became a 25¢ cent piece and the 6 pence became a 12½¢ piece. The only coins the province needed to have specially produced were a cent, and to make change for the 6 pence and half crown, a half cent.

HALF CENT

VICTORIA   1861 - 1864

The half cent was coined the same diameter as the British farthing and utilized the same obverse. Pattern pieces incorporated the royal crown and a wreath of roses (cf. NS-1 to NS-3 and NS-5 on page 218). However, a local compaign in favour of the provincial flower, the mayflower, resulted in the adoption of a design using the royal crown surrounded by a wreath of both roses and mayflowers.

Designer & Modeller:
Obverse - Leonard C. Wyon
Reverse - Leonard C. Wyon,
from a model by C. Hill
Composition: .95 copper, .04 tin, .01 zinc
Weight: 2.84 grams
Diameter: 20.65 mm
Edge: Plain
Die Axes: ↑↑

Date	Quantity Minted	G-4	VG-8	F-12	VF-20	EF-40	AU-50	MS-60	MS-65
1861	400,000	4.00	7.00	10.00	12.50	18.00	25.00	50.00	110.00
1864	400,000	4.00	7.00	10.00	12.50	18.00	25.00	50.00	110.00

ONE CENT

VICTORIA

1861 - 1864

The cent was minted the same diameter as the British halfpenny and used the same obverse. The reverse designs are similar to that used for the half cent, including pattern pieces with a wreath of roses (cf. NS-4 and NS-6 on page 218).

The circulation issues of this denomination have two distinct reverses. The first (1861) has much detail in the crown and a large rosebud at the lower right part of the wreath. On the second reverse (1861-1864) the crown has a narrower headband and generally less detail, the rosebud at the lower right is smaller, and the rosebud and certain other parts of the design come closer to the lettering and the raised line just inside the rim denticles.

MINTAGE FIGURES 1861 - 1862

The mintage figures of 800,000 for 1861 and 1,000,000 for 1862 have puzzled collectors for many years since the 1862-dated coins are scarcer. The probable explanation is that some, perhaps most, cents struck in 1862 were from dies dated 1861. Therefore, the mintages for the two years have been combined.

Designer & Modeller:
Obverse - Leonard C. Wyon
Reverse - Leonard C. Wyon,
from a model by C. Hill
Engraver: Leonard C. Wyon
Composition: .95 copper, .04 tin, .01 zinc
Weight: 5.67 grams
Diameter: 25.53 mm
Edge: Plain
Die Axes: ↑↑

Large Rosebud   Small Rosebud

Date		Quantity Minted	G-4	VG-8	F-12	VF-20	EF-40	AU-50	MS-60	MS-65
1861	Large Bud	1,800,000	1.50	2.50	5.00	10.50	15.00	30.00	60.00	175.00
1861	Small Bud	Incl. above	1.25	2.00	3.00	7.00	12.00	24.00	50.00	110.00
1862		Incl. above	12.00	18.00	25.00	50.00	100.00	150.00	250.00	500.00
1864		800,000	1.35	2.25	3.50	8.00	13.00	25.00	50.00	110.00

NEW BRUNSWICK

When New Brunswick adopted a decimal dollar in 1860, it chose the same rating for its dollar and ordered the same denominations as the Province of Canada: cents in bronze and 5, 10 and 20 cent pieces in silver. The effective date for the decimal currency act was November 1, 1860 but, like Nova Scotia, New Brunswick had to wait until early 1862 before the first coins arrived from England. In the meantime, the government introduced other decimal coins as a temporary expedient. Thus, in late 1861 and early 1862 some 500,000 Province of Canada cents and a quantity of United States small denomination silver coins were put into circulation in the province.

HALF CENT

VICTORIA 1861

This denomination was not required by the province since its dollar and hence British coins went at a different rating than in the sister province of Nova Scotia. Nevertheless, the Royal Mint became confused and struck a half cent for New Brunswick. Over 200,000 of these coins came off the presses before the error was discovered. Most of the mintage was retu. ned to the melting pot. The circulation strikes that survived are thought to have become mixed with the Nova Scotia half cents and sent to Halifax.

The obverse is that of the British farthing and the reverse is a royal crown and a rose-mayflower wreath very similar to that used for Nova Scotia.

Designer & Modeller:
　　Obverse - Leonard C. Wyon
　　Reverse - Leonard C. Wyon,
　　from a model by C. Hill
Engraver: Leonard C. Wyon
Composition: .95 copper, .04 tin, .01 zinc
Weight: 2.84 grams
Diameter: 20.65 mm
Edge: Plain
Die Axes: ↑↑

Date	Quantity Minted	G-4	VG-8	F-12	VF-20	EF-40	AU-50	MS-60
1861	222,800*	30.00	50.00	70.00	90.00	125.00	175.00	350.00

*most were melted prior to issue.

ONE CENT

VICTORIA   **1861 - 1864**

The New Brunswick one-cent pieces have the British halfpenny obverse and a reverse similar to that used for the Nova Scotia cent.

For the 1864 issue two styles of 6 were used in the date: a figure with a round centre in its loop and a short top, and a figure with a more oval centre and a longer top.

Designer & Modeller:
   Obverse - Leonard C. Wyon
   Reverse - Leonard C. Wyon,
   from a model by C. Hill
Engraver: Leonard C. Wyon
Composition: .95 copper, .04 tin, .01 zinc
Weight: 5.67 grams
Diameter: 25.53 mm
Edge: Plain
Die Axes: ↑↑

Short 6   Tall 6

Date	Quantity Minted	G-4	VG-8	F-12	VF-20	EF-40	AU-50	MS-60
1861	1,000,000	1.25	2.00	3.00	6.00	12.00	24.00	50.00
1864 Short 6	1,000,000	1.25	2.00	3.00	6.00	12.00	24.00	50.00
1864 Tall 6	Incl. above	1.25	2.00	3.00	6.00	12.00	24.00	50.00

FIVE CENTS

The production of New Brunswick's first silver decimal coinage had to await the completion of the bronze coinage. Consequently, it could not commence until 1862. The five-cent piece designs were basically those of the Province of Canada with an appropriately modified obverse legend.

Two styles of 6 were employed in dating the 1864 issue: a small 6 and a large 6.

Engraver: Obverse - Leonard C. Wyon
Composition: .925 silver, .075 copper
Weight: 1.16 grams
Diameter: 15.49 mm
Edge: Reeded
Die Axes: ↑↓

Small 6   Large 6

Date	Quantity Minted	G-4	VG-8	F-12	VF-20	EF-40	AU-50	MS-60
1862	100,000	25.00	35.00	50.00	100.00	200.00	450.00	900.00
1864 Small 6	100,000	25.00	35.00	50.00	100.00	200.00	450.00	900.00
1864 Large 6	Incl. above	25.00	35.00	50.00	100.00	200.00	450.00	900.00

TEN CENTS

VICTORIA

The designs for the New Brunswick ten-cent piece were adapted from existing Province of Canada designs. The reverse was used without modification and the obverse involved changing the legend only.

The 1862 issue is usually collected as two varieties. One has a normal date and the other has an obviously double-punched 2.

Engraver: Obverse - Leonard C. Wyon
Composition: .925 silver, .075 copper
Weight: 2.32 grams
Diameter: 17.91 mm
Edge: Reeded
Die Axes: ↑↓

Normal Date

Double-punched 2

Date and Mint Mark	Quantity Minted	G-4	VG-8	F-12	VF-20	EF-40	AU-50	MS-60
1862 Normal Date	150,000	20.00	30.00	40.00	90.00	200.00	450.00	900.00
1862 D-P 2	Incl. above	18.00	25.00	35.00	75.00	175.00	400.00	800.00
1864	150,000	20.00	30.00	40.00	90.00	200.00	600.00	1,200.00

TWENTY CENTS

VICTORIA 1862 - 1864

    The New Brunswick twenty-cent piece has an unusual reverse design once rejected for the Province of Canada (cf. PC-4 on page 217). The reverse adopted by the Province of Canada differs in style, although using the same elements, from the reverse chosen by New Brunswick. This stylistic difference, plus the fact a die for the New Brunswick 20¢ of 1862 was used to strike one side of George W. Wyon's obituary medalet, suggests that it was George Wyon and not Leonard Wyon who engraved this reverse. The obverse utilizes the Province of Canada 20¢ portrait with a special legend for New Brunswick.

Designer & Modeller:
                Reverse - possibly Geo. W. Wyon
Engraver: Obverse - Leonard C. Wyon
Composition: .925 silver, .075 copper
Weight: 4.65 grams
Diameter: 23.27 mm
Edge: Reeded
Die Axes: ↑↓

Date	Quantity Minted	G-4	VG-8	F-12	VF-20	EF-40	AU-50	MS-60
1862	150,000	10.00	15.00	25.00	50.00	100.00	300.00	600.00
1864	150,000	11.00	17.00	30.00	60.00	125.00	300.00	600.00

PRINCE EDWARD ISLAND
ONE CENT

Prince Edward Island adopted a decimal currency system in 1871. Its dollar was given the same rating as those of the provinces of Canada and New Brunswick. The only coinage in the new system was bronze cents in 1871. The island entered Confederation two years later. The provincial government experienced considerable difficulty placing its cents in circulation. It took almost ten years to deplete the stock and the last of it was sold at a 10% discount.

The reverse was prepared specifically for the Prince Edward Island government, incorporating the seal of the island and a Latin phrase, PARVA SUB INGENTI, meaning "The small beneath the great." The seal shows a large oak tree, representing England, sheltering three young oak trees, representing the three counties on the island.

Because of pressure to produce domestic coin, the Royal Mint in London made arrangements with Heaton's Mint in Birmingham to strike P.E.I. cents. For some unknown reason Heaton's familiar H mint mark is absent from the coins.

Designer & Modeller:
Obverse - Leonard C. Wyon,
from a portrait model by
Willian Theed
Reverse - Leonard C. Wyon
Composition: .95 copper, .04 tin, .01 zinc
Weight: 5.67 grams
Diameter: 25.40 mm
Edge: Plain
Die Axes: ↑↑

Date	Quantity Minted	G-4	VG-8	F-12	VF-20	EF-40	AU-50	MS-60	MS-65
1871	2,000,000	1.00	1.50	3.00	7.00	15.00	45.00	100.00	275.00

NEWFOUNDLAND

Since Newfoundland remained separate from Canada until 1949, it has a much larger decimal coin series than the other pre-Confederation British colonies. The island adopted decimal currency in 1863, hoping to have coins on the new standard in circulation in 1864. The most important coin in Newfoundland had been the Spanish-American dollar or 8-real piece, so the government set its dollar equal in value to this coin. This made the new decimal cent equal to the British halfpenny and $4.80 equal to £1 sterling.

ONE CENT

VICTORIA   **1865 - 1896**

Beginning in 1864, several designs were considered for the Newfoundland cent. The first tendency was to use the same designs as New Brunswick. Pattern dies are known for an 1864 Newfoundland cent with the royal crown, rose/mayflower design (cf. NF-1 on page 224). This design was rejected in favour of a royal crown and wreath of pitcher plant (the provincial flower) and oak, with unusual broad, bold lettering and date. The obverse incorporated the British halfpenny portrait with the legend VICTORIA QUEEN, also in the same bold type (cf. NF-6 on page 225). However, it was decided that this legend was inappropriate and the cents struck for circulation in 1865 use the British halfpenny obverse legend - VICTORIA D:G:REG:.

An interesting variation in die axes occurs on this denomination. For all dates except 1872 the dies are in the medal arrangement (↑ ↑) but on the 1872's they are coinage arrangement (↑ ↓). The most reasonable explanation for this difference is that the Heaton Mint, which struck the 1872 cents, did not receive specific instructions regarding which die arrangement to use and chose the same arrangement as for the silver. The error was corrected in 1876 when Heaton's next coined cents for Newfoundland.

Designer: Reverse - Horace Morehen
Engraver: Thomas J. Minton
Composition: .95 copper, .04 tin, .01 zinc
Weight: 5.67 grams
Diameter: 25.53 mm
Edge: Plain
Die Axes: ↑↑   (1865, 1873-1896);
↑↓   (1872)

Heaton Mint issues have an "H" mint mark at the bottom of the wreath (1872-1876). London Mint strikings have no letter.

Date and Mint Mark	Quantity Minted	G-4	VG-8	F-12	VF-20	EF-40	AU-50	MS-60	MS-65
1865	240,000	1.25	2.50	3.50	7.00	15.00	50.00	150.00	300.00
1872H	200,000	1.25	2.50	3.50	7.00	15.00	50.00	125.00	250.00
1873	200,025	1.25	2.50	3.50	7.00	15.00	75.00	150.00	325.00
1876H	200,000	1.25	2.50	3.50	7.00	15.00	75.00	150.00	400.00

VARIETIES 1880

Three date varieties exist for 1880. The first has a narrow 0 in the date, while the second and third have a wide 0, in different positions. The positional differences between the second and third varieties are not felt to be important, so they are combined into one variety: wide 0.

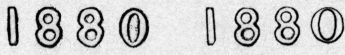

1880 Narrow 0   1880 Wide 0

Date and Mint Mark	Quantity Minted	G-4	VG-8	F-12	VF-20	EF-40	AU-50	MS-60	MS-65
1880 Narrow 0	400,000	50.00	80.00	100.00	125.00	200.00	350.00	700.00	1,400.00
1880 Wide 0	Incl. above	1.50	2.50	5.00	10.00	15.00	60.00	150.00	300.00
1885	40,000	15.00	33.00	30.00	40.00	80.00	150.00	300.00	500.00
1888	50,000	12.50	18.00	25.00	30.00	50.00	100.00	200.00	450.00
1890	200,000	1.00	2.00	3.50	6.00	10.00	30.00	100.00	225.00
1894	200,000	1.00	2.00	3.50	6.00	10.00	30.00	100.00	225.00
1896	200,000	1.00	2.00	3.50	6.00	10.00	30.00	100.00	225.00

ONE CENT

EDWARD VII 1904 - 1909

The reverse design is a modification of the Victorian reverse, substituting the Imperial State crown for the St. Edward's crown. The obverses of most Edward VII denominations were those of the corresponding Dominion of Canada coinage; however, the Newfoundland cent has a distinctive design. The bust is very large and the letter size in the legend correspondingly small.

Designer & Modeller:
      Portrait - G.W. DeSaulles,
      (DES below bust)
Engraver: Reverse - W.H.J. Blakemore,
      modifing existing coinage tools
Composition: .95 copper, .04 tin, .01 zinc
Weight: 5.67 grams
Diameter: 25.53 mm
Edge: Plain
Die Axes: ↑↑

The Mint, Birmingham issue (1904 only) has an "H" mint mark at the bottom of the wreath. Royal Mint strikings have no letter.

Date and Mint Mark	Quantity Minted	G-4	VG-8	F-12	VF-20	EF-40	AU-50	MS-60	MS-65
1904H	100,000	5.00	7.00	10.00	20.00	30.00	90.00	200.00	450.00
1907	200,000	1.25	2.00	3.00	6.00	15.00	45.00	100.00	300.00
1909	200,000	1.25	2.00	3.00	6.00	15.00	45.00	100.00	300.00

ONE CENT

GEORGE V   1913 - 1936

    The reverse for the cents of this reign is that established for the Edward VII series and the obverse is that of the Dominion of Canada cents.

Designer & Modeller:
    Portrait - Sir E.B MacKennal,
    (B.M. on the truncation)
Composition: .95 copper, .04 tin, .01 zinc
    (1913-1920);
    .955 copper, .030 tin,
    .015 zinc (1929-1936)
Diameter: 25.53 mm (1913, 1929-1936);
    25.40 mm (1917-1920)
Edge: Plain
Die Axes: ↑↑

Ottawa Mint issues (1917-1920) have a "C" mint mark at the bottom of the wreath. Royal Mint strikings have no letter.

Date and Mint Mark	Quantity Minted	G-4	VG-8	F-12	VF-20	EF-40	AU-50	MS-60	MS-65
1913	400,000	.75	1.25	1.75	3.00	5.00	15.00	50.00	150.00
1917C	702,350	.75	1.25	1.75	3.00	5.00	15.00	50.00	150.00
1919C	300,000	.75	1.25	1.75	3.00	5.00	15.00	50.00	175.00
1920C	302,184	.75	1.25	1.75	3.00	5.00	15.00	50.00	185.00
1929	300,000	.75	1.25	1.75	3.00	5.00	15.00	50.00	150.00
1936	300,000	.75	1.25	1.75	3.00	5.00	12.50	40.00	125.00

ONE CENT

GEORGE VI
1938 - 1947

In 1937 the Newfoundland government reviewed the question of converting to a small cent, similar to those used in Canada and the United States. The smaller coin was less expensive to produce and Newfoundlanders objected to the reverse design of the large cent, in which their provincial flower was forced into an unnatural configuration.

The reverse design adopted for the new coin was a very life-like rendition of the pitcher plant in bloom. The plant is native to Newfoundland, and is one of the insectivores of the plant kingdom. The large leaves are pitcher-like receptacles, the inner surfaces being covered with downward-sloping bristles. Insects are attracted onto their leaves by a sweet sticky syrup at the bottom and the bristles help prevent their escape. The digestable portions of the insects are then absorbed by the plant.

During World War II, Newfoundland cents were coined at Ottawa rather than in England to avoid the risks of transatlantic shipping. In 1940 and 1942 the C mint mark was omitted in error.

Designer & Modeller:
    Portrait - Percy Metcalfe,
    (P.M. below bust)
    Reverse - Walter J. Newman
Composition: .955 copper, .03 tin,
                  .015 zinc
Weight: 3.24 grams
Diameter: 19.05 mm
Edge: Plain
Die Axes: ↑↑

Royal Canadian Mint issues (1940-1947) have a "C" mint mark to the right of CENT on the reverse (except for the 1940 and 1942 issues, which have none). The Royal Mint issue (1938) has no mint mark.

Date and Mint Mark	Quantity Minted	VG-8	F-12	VF-20	EF-40	AU-50	MS-60	MS-65
1938	500,000	1.00	1.25	2.25	4.50	9.00	20.00	35.00
1940	300,000	3.00	4.00	7.00	14.00	25.00	50.00	100.00
1941C	827,662	.50	.75	1.25	3.00	7.00	15.00	30.00
1942	1,996,889	.50	.75	1.25	3.00	7.00	15.00	30.00
1943C	1,239,732	.50	.75	1.25	3.00	7.00	15.00	30.00
1944C	1,328,776	2.00	3.00	4.00	6.00	18.00	30.00	75.00
1947C	313,772	1.00	1.25	2.25	4.00	20.00	20.00	50.00

FIVE CENTS

VICTORIA

1865 - 1896

Work on the coinage tools for the silver began later than for the cent, so there are no legend wording varieties for this denomination. The first pattern is a bronze striking of the adopted obverse (derived from the New Brunswick obverse by substitution of NEWFOUNDLAND for NEW BRUNSWICK) and the Canada/New Brunswick reverse with a maple wreath and royal crown (cf. NF-2 on page 224). A later pattern, in silver, has an arabesque design similar to the adopted design, except the arches are thinner (cf. NF-8 on page 225).

Designer & Modeller:
 Reverse - Leonard C. Wyon
Engraver: Obverse - Leonard C. Wyon
Composition: .925 silver, .075 copper
Weight: 1.18 grams
Diameter: 15.49 mm
Edge: Reeded
Die Axes: ↑↓

Heaton Mint issues have an "H" mint mark either on the obverse under the bust (1872-1876) or on the reverse under the date (1882). London Mint strikings have no letter.

Date and Mint Mark	Quantity Minted	G-4	VG-8	F-12	VF-20	EF-40	AU-50	MS-60
1865	80,000	20.00	45.00	70.00	125.00	250.00	500.00	1,000.00
1870	40,000	20.00	45.00	70.00	125.00	250.00	500.00	1,000.00
1872H	40,000	20.00	40.00	65.00	100.00	200.00	600.00	1,000.00
1873	44,260	25.00	50.00	75.00	125.00	250.00	600.00	1,000.00
1873H	Incl. above	400.00	800.00	1,200.00	1,600.00	2,500.00	3,500.00	5,000.00
1876H	20,000	35.00	75.00	125.00	200.00	350.00	1,000.00	3,000.00
1880	40,000	25.00	40.00	60.00	110.00	225.00	700.00	1,500.00
1881	40,000	20.00	30.00	40.00	75.00	150.00	550.00	1,000.00
1882H	60,000	15.00	25.00	40.00	75.00	150.00	550.00	1,000.00
1885	16,000	75.00	125.00	200.00	300.00	700.00	1,200.00	2,500.00
1888	40,000	20.00	30.00	45.00	75.00	150.00	500.00	1,000.00
1890	160,000	8.00	15.00	30.00	60.00	100.00	450.00	750.00
1894	160,000	8.00	15.00	30.00	60.00	100.00	450.00	750.00
1896	400,000	6.00	10.00	20.00	40.00	75.00	350.00	600.00

FIVE CENTS

EDWARD VII   **1903 - 1908**

The obverse for this denomination is that of the Dominion of Canada issues. The reverse, a new design by G.W. DeSaulles, is one of the last coinage designs he did before his death.

Designer & Modeller:
   George W. DeSaulles,
   (DES. below bust)
Composition: .925 silver, .075 copper
Weight: 1.18 grams
Diameter: 15.49 mm
Edge: Reeded
Die Axes: ↑↓

The Mint, Birmingham issue of 1904 has an "H" mint mark below the oval at the bottom on the reverse. Royal Mint issues have no letter.

Date and Mint Mark	Quantity Minted	G-4	VG-8	F-12	VF-20	EF-40	AU-50	MS-60
1903	100,000	2.50	4.00	8.00	20.00	70.00	300.00	600.00
1904H	100,000	2.50	4.00	8.00	18.00	65.00	300.00	600.00
1908	400,000	2.00	3.50	6.50	15.00	50.00	200.00	400.00

FIVE CENTS

GEORGE V  1912 - 1929

The obverse is the same as for the Dominion of Canada issue and the reverse is the same as the Newfoundland Edward VII issue.

Designer & Modeller:
    Portrait - Sir E.B. MacKennal,
    (B.M. on the truncation)
Composition: .925 silver, .075 copper
Weight: 1.18 grams (1912);
    1.17 grams (1917-1929)
Diameter: 15.49 mm (1912-1919);
    15.69 mm (1929)
Edge: Reeded
Die Axes: ↑↓

The Ottawa Mint issues (1917-1919) have a "C" mint mark below the oval at the bottom on the reverse. Royal Mint strikings have no letter.

Date and Mint Mark	Quantity Minted	G-4	VG-8	F-12	VF-20	EF-40	AU-50	MS-60
1912	300,000	1.25	2.50	4.00	8.00	30.00	150.00	400.00
1917C	300,319	1.25	2.50	4.00	8.00	30.00	150.00	300.00
1919C	100,844	2.25	3.50	7.00	15.00	40.00	150.00	400.00
1929	300,000	1.25	2.50	3.50	7.00	25.00	125.00	300.00

FIVE CENTS

  While considering the replacement of the large cent, the Newfoundland government also contemplated dropping its "fish scale" silver five-cent piece in favour of a nickel coin similar to Canada's. At that time, because of a strong conservative element it was decided to change only the cent. The reverse design was continued from the previous reign and the obverse used the standard portrait for British colonial coinages.

Designer & Modeller:
  Portrait - Percy Metcalfe,
  (P.M. below bust)
Composition: .925 silver, .075 copper
       (1938 - 1944);
       .800 silver, .200 copper
       (1945-1947)
Weight: 1.17 grams
Diameter: 15.69 mm (1938);
      15.49 mm (1940-1947)
Edge: Reeded
Die Axes: ↑↓

Royal Canadian Mint issues (1940-1947) have a "C" mint mark below the oval at the bottom on the reverse. The Royal Mint issue (1938) has no letter.

Date and Mint Mark	Quantity Minted	VG-8	F-12	VF-20	EF-40	AU-50	MS-60
1938	100,000	1.25	1.50	3.00	7.00	40.00	125.00
1940C	200,000	1.25	1.50	2.50	5.00	20.00	75.00
1941C	612,641	1.25	1.50	2.50	4.00	15.00	60.00
1942C	298,348	2.00	2.50	3.50	6.00	20.00	75.00
1943C	351,666	1.25	1.50	2.50	4.00	15.00	60.00
1944C	286,504	1.25	1.50	2.50	5.00	20.00	75.00
1945C	203,828	1.25	1.50	2.50	4.00	15.00	60.00

1946C - 1947C ISSUES

The 1946C issue is an anomaly. Published official mint reports, as well as unpublished mint accounting records, do not indicate any mintage of this denomination during 1946. It appears that this scarce issue was actually coined during 1947. The mintage figures given for the years 1946 and 1947 must be considered unofficial although they are believed to have come from a mint officer many years ago.

Date and Mint Mark	Quantity Minted	VG-8	F-12	VF-20	EF-40	AU-50	MS-60
1946C	2,041	250.00	300.00	400.00	600.00	1,000.00	2,000.00
1947C	38,400	5.00	8.00	10.00	15.00	40.00	125.00

TEN CENTS

Like the five cents, the ten cents has a bronze pattern with the adopted obverse (derived from the New Brunswick obverse by substituting NEWFOUNDLAND for NEW BRUNSWICK) and the Canada/New Brunswick reverse (cf. NF-3 on page 224). As well there is a silver pattern with very thin arches in the arabesque design on the reverse (cf. NF-9 on page 225).

Designer & Modeller:
Reverse - Leonard C. Wyon
Engraver: Obverse - Leonard C. Wyon
Composition: .925 silver, .075 copper
Weight: 2.36 grams
Diameter: 17.98 mm
Edge: Reeded
Die Axes: ↑↓

Heaton Mint issues have an "H" mint mark either on the obverse under the bust (1872-1876) or on the reverse under the date (1882). London Mint strikings have no letter.

Date	Quantity Minted	G-4	VG-8	F-12	VF-20	EF-40	AU-50	MS-60
1865	80,000	10.00	20.00	35.00	75.00	200.00	900.00	1,500.00
1870	30,000	100.00	150.00	250.00	450.00	1,000.00	2,000.00	4,000.00

1871H NEWFOUNDLAND/CANADA MULE

A rare variety exists because an 1871H Dominion of Canada reverse die was muled, apparently accidentally, with an "H" Newfoundland obverse die. All known examples are in well-worn condition.

1871H Newfoundland/Canada Mule

Date and Mint Mark	Quantity Minted	G-4	VG-8	F-12	VF-20	EF-40	AU-50	MS-60
1871H Mule	40,000				VERY	RARE		
1872H	Incl. above	10.00	20.00	35.00	75.00	200.00	1,000.00	1,800.00
1873	23,614	15.00	30.00	50.00	100.00	300.00	1,250.00	2,500.00
1876H	10,000	20.00	35.00	75.00	175.00	400.00	1,500.00	3,000.00

All examples of the 1880 issue are from dies in which the second 8 of the date is punched over a 7.

1880 Second 8 over 7

Date and Mint Mark	Quantity Minted	G-4	VG-8	F-12	VF-20	EF-40	AU-50	MS-60
1880	10,000	20.00	35.00	75.00	175.00	400.00	1,500.00	3,000.00
1882H	20,000	10.00	18.00	30.00	80.00	200.00	900.00	1,800.00
1885	8,000	40.00	80.00	160.00	325.00	750.00	2,000.00	3,500.00
1888	30,000	15.00	25.00	35.00	70.00	200.00	900.00	1,750.00
1890	100,000	5.00	10.00	18.00	50.00	160.00	600.00	1,000.00
1894	100,000	5.00	10.00	18.00	50.00	160.00	600.00	1,000.00
1896	230,000	4.50	9.00	18.00	45.00	125.00	500.00	900.00

TEN CENTS

The obverse is that used for the Dominion of Canada issues. The reverse is a new design by G.W. DeSaulles.

Designer & Modeller:
    G.W. DeSaulles,
      (DES. below bust)
Composition: .925 silver, .075 copper
Weight: 2.36 grams
Diameter: 17.96 mm
Edge: Reeded
Die Axes: ↑↓

The Mint, Birmingham issue of 1904 has an "H" mint mark below the oval at the bottom on the reverse. The Royal Mint issue (1903) has no letter.

Date and Mint Mark	Quantity Minted	G-4	VG-8	F-12	VF-20	EF-40	AU-50	MS-60
1903	100,000	3.00	5.00	10.00	30.00	100.00	400.00	800.00
1904H	100,000	3.00	5.00	10.00	30.00	100.00	400.00	800.00

TEN CENTS

GEORGE V **1912 - 1919**

The obverse is the same as for the Dominion of Canada issues. The reverse is a continuation of the Newfoundland Edward VII designs.

Designer & Modeller:
 Portrait - Sir E.B. MacKennal,
 (B.M. on the truncation)
Composition: .925 silver, .075 copper
Weight: 2.36 grams (1912-1917)
 2.33 grams (1919)
Diameter: 17.96 mm (1912)
 18.03 mm (1917-1919)
Edge: Reeded
Die Axes: ↑↓

Ottawa Mint issues (1917-1919) have a "C" mint mark below the oval at the bottom on the reverse. The Royal Mint issue (1912) has no letter.

Date and Mint Mark	Quantity Minted	G-4	VG-8	F-12	VF-20	EF-40	AU-50	MS-60
1912	150,000	3.00	4.00	10.00	20.00	50.00	300.00	700.00
1917C	250,805	2.50	3.00	7.00	15.00	40.00	200.00	400.00
1919C	54,342	3.00	4.50	9.00	22.00	60.00	300.00	600.00

TEN CENTS

The obverse for this denomination used Percy Metcalfe's standard portrait of George VI for British colonial coinages and the existing Edward VII/George V reverse. The 1946C issue was probably coined in 1947 (see preceding comments on the 1946C 5¢ on page 58); the mintage figures for 1946 and 1947 must be considered unofficial.

Designer & Modeller:
    Portrait - Percy Metcalfe,
    (P.M. below bust)
Composition: .925 silver, .075 copper
    (1938-1944);
    .800 silver, .200 copper
    (1945-1947)
Weight: 2.33 grams
Diameter: 18.03 mm
Edge: Reeded
Die Axes: ↑↓

Royal Canadian Mint issues (1941-1947) have a "C" mint mark below the oval at the bottom on the reverse. The Royal Mint issue (1938) and the Royal Canadian Mint issue of 1940 have no letter.

Date and Mint Mark	Quantity Minted	VG-8	F-12	VF-20	EF-40	AU-50	MS-60
1938	100,000	2.50	3.00	5.00	12.00	40.00	125.00
1940	100,000	2.50	3.00	4.50	10.00	30.00	100.00
1941C	483,630	2.50	3.00	4.50	8.00	22.00	75.00
1942C	292,736	2.50	3.00	4.50	8.00	22.00	75.00
1943C	104,706	2.50	3.00	4.50	8.00	22.00	75.00
1944C	151,471	2.50	3.00	4.50	8.00	30.00	100.00
1945C	175,833	2.50	3.00	4.50	7.00	20.00	70.00
1946C	38,400	7.00	9.00	12.00	25.00	80.00	150.00
1947C	61,988	3.00	4.50	7.00	10.00	30.00	100.00

TWENTY CENTS

VICTORIA

The first pattern known for the Newfoundland twenty-cent piece is a bronze striking with the adopted obverse (derived from the New Brunswick obverse) and a reverse from a die for the 1864 New Brunswick 20¢ (cf. NF-4 on page 224). Later patterns in silver have an arabesque design similar to that finally adopted. The first (cf. NF-10 on page 226) has very thin arches and corresponds to similar 5¢ and 10¢ patterns. The second stands alone and has arches more like the adopted design and a raised line just inside the denticles (cf. NF-13 on page 226).

This denomination proved popular with Newfoundlanders and was minted on a regular basis throughout the remainder of Victoria's reign. With the passing years, however, it became increasingly unpopular with Canadians (due to its similarity to their 25¢ piece) and was replaced with a 25¢ coin during World War I.

Designer: Reverse - Horace Morehen
Modeller: Reverse - Leonard C. Wyon
Engraver: Obverse - Leonard C. Wyon
Composition: .925 silver, .075 copper
Weight: 4.71 grams
Diameter: 23.19 mm
Edge: Reeded
Die Axes: ↑↓

Heaton Mint issues have an "H" mint mark either on the obverse under the bust (1872-1876) or on the reverse under the date (1882). London Mint strikings have no letter.

Date and Mint Mark	Quantity Minted	G-4	VG-8	F-12	VF-20	EF-40	AU-50	MS-60
1865	100,000	7.00	12.00	25.00	65.00	200.00	800.00	1,500.00
1870	50,000	10.00	20.00	40.00	80.00	200.00	900.00	1,800.00
1872H	90,000	6.00	10.00	20.00	60.00	175.00	800.00	1,500.00
1873	45,799	7.00	12.00	25.00	70.00	200.00	900.00	1,800.00
1876H	50,000	10.00	20.00	35.00	80.00	250.00	1,000.00	2,000.00
1880	30,000	10.00	20.00	35.00	80.00	250.00	1,000.00	2,000.00
1881	60,000	5.00	8.00	15.00	60.00	160.00	700.00	1,400.00
1882H	100,000	5.00	8.00	13.00	55.00	160.00	650.00	1,300.00
1885	40,000	5.00	8.00	13.00	55.00	160.00	650.00	1,300.00
1888	75,000	5.00	8.00	13.00	50.00	150.00	600.00	1,200.00
1890	100,000	5.00	8.00	13.00	30.00	85.00	500.00	1,000.00
1894	100,000	5.00	8.00	13.00	30.00	85.00	500.00	1,000.00

Photo Not
Available

1896 Small 96   1896 Large 96   1899 Small 99   1899 Large 99

Date	Quantity Minted	G-4	VG-8	F-12	VF-20	EF-40	AU-50	MS-60
1896 Small 96	125,000	5.00	8.00	13.00	30.00	85.00	500.00	1,000.00
1896 Large 96	Incl. above	6.00	10.00	20.00	50.00	100.00	600.00	1,200.00
1899 Small 99	125,000	6.00	8.00	18.00	45.00	100.00	500.00	1,000.00
1899 Large 99	Incl. above	5.00	8.00	12.00	30.00	80.00	500.00	1,000.00
1900	125,000	5.00	8.00	10.00	20.00	75.00	450.00	900.00

TWENTY CENTS

Coins of this denomination were required on only one occasion during Edward's short reign, making the 1904 issue a one-year type.

Designer & Modeller:
  Portrait - G.W. DeSaulles,
  (DES below bust)
  Reverse - W.H.J. Blakemore,
  copying DeSaulles design for the
  reverse of 5¢ & 10¢ pieces
Composition: .925 silver, .075 copper
Weight: 4.71 grams
Diameter: 23.19 mm
Edge: Reeded
Die Axes: ↑↓

The issue was coined by The Mint, Birmingham and bears an "H" mint mark below the oval at the bottom on the reverse.

Date and Mint Mark	Quantity Minted	G-4	VG-8	F-12	VF-20	EF-40	AU-50	MS-60
1904H	75,000	9.00	15.00	30.00	100.00	300.00	800.00	1,500.00

TWENTY CENTS

GEORGE V

Like its Edwardian predecessor, the George V 20¢ is a one-year type. The reverse established for the previous reign was reused.

Designer: Portrait - Sir E.B. MacKennal,
(B.M. on truncation)
Composition: .925 silver, .075 copper
Weight: 4.71 grams
Diameter: 23.19 mm
Edge: Reeded
Die Axes: ↑↓

Date	Quantity Minted	VG-8	F-12	VF-20	EF-40	AU-50	MS-60
1912	350,000	5.00	8.00	25.00	65.00	400.00	800.00

TWENTY-FIVE CENTS

GEORGE V

The second time twenty-cent pieces were required during George V's reign was toward the end of World War I. By that time, however, arrangements had been made for the Ottawa Mint to produce Newfoundland's coins. Canada took a dim view of the 20¢ because it circulated in Canada as well, and was confused with the Canadian 25¢. The Canadian government convinced the Newfoundland government to drop the 20¢ and adopt a 25¢, struck on the same standard as the corresponding Canadian coin. Indeed, the obverse of the new coin was identical to that for the Canadian 25¢.

Designer & Modeller:
      Portrait - Sir E.B. MacKennal,
      (B.M. on truncation)
Engraver: Reverse - W.H.J. Blakemore,
      modifying the 20¢ reverse
Composition: .925 silver, .075 copper
Weight: 5.83 grams
Diameter: 23.62 mm
Edge: Reeded
Die Axes: ↑↓

This denomination was coined by the Ottawa Mint and bears a "C" mint mark below the oval at the bottom on the reverse.

Date and Mint Mark	Quantity Minted	VG-8	F-12	VF-20	EF-40	AU-50	MS-60
1917C	464,779	5.00	7.00	10.00	25.00	100.00	200.00
1919C	163,939	5.00	7.00	10.00	25.00	125.00	250.00

FIFTY CENTS

VICTORIA

The fifty-cent piece was the last denomination to be added to the Victorian coinage, coming in 1870. Its laureate portrait is stylistically unlike anything used for the rest of the British North America series. This denomination became popular on the island and assumed even greater importance after the failure of the Commercial and Union Banks of Newfoundland during the financial panic of 1894.

Designer & Modeller:
    Leonard C. Wyon
Composition: .925 silver, .075 copper
Weight: 11.78 grams
Diameter: 29.85 mm
Edge: Reeded
Die Axes: ↑↓

Heaton Mint issues have an "H" mint mark either on the obverse under the bust (1872-1876) or on the reverse under the date (1882). London Mint strikings have no letter.

Date and Mint Mark	Quantity Minted	G-4	VG-8	F-12	VF-20	EF-40	AU-50	MS-60
1870	50,000	10.00	18.00	25.00	60.00	250.00	1,500.00	2,500.00
1872H	48,000	10.00	18.00	25.00	60.00	250.00	1,500.00	2,500.00
1873	37,675	10.00	18.00	25.00	60.00	250.00	1,500.00	2,500.00
1874	80,000	10.00	18.00	25.00	60.00	250.00	1,500.00	2,500.00
1876H	28,000	15.00	30.00	50.00	125.00	500.00	1,800.00	3,500.00

1880

All examples of the 1880 issue are from dies in which the second 8 of the date is punched over a 7.

Date and Mint Mark	Quantity Minted	G-4	VG-8	F-12	VF-20	EF-40	AU-50	MS-60
1880	24,000	15.00	30.00	50.00	110.00	450.00	1,600.00	3,000.00
1881	50,000	10.00	18.00	30.00	60.00	250.00	1,300.00	2,500.00
1882H	100,000	10.00	18.00	30.00	60.00	250.00	1,300.00	2,500.00
1885	40,000	10.00	20.00	40.00	110.00	450.00	1,600.00	3,000.00
1888	20,000	10.00	20.00	50.00	125.00	500.00	1,800.00	3,500.00
1894	40,000	8.00	12.50	20.00	40.00	225.00	1,200.00	2,300.00
1896	60,000	8.00	12.50	17.50	40.00	225.00	1,200.00	2,300.00
1898	76,607	8.00	12.50	17.50	40.00	225.00	1,200.00	2,300.00

Narrow 9's with
thick sides and oval centres

Wide 9's with
thin sides and round centres

Date and Mint Mark	Quantity Minted	G-4	VG-8	F-12	VF-20	EF-40	AU-50	MS-60
1899 Narrow 9's	150,000	8.00	12.50	17.50	40.00	225.00	1,200.00	2,300.00
1899 Wide 9's	Incl. above	8.00	12.50	17.50	40.00	225.00	1,200.00	2,300.00
1900	150,000	8.00	12.50	17.50	35.00	200.00	1,100.00	2,000.00

FIFTY CENTS

The obverse for this denomination is that of the Dominion of Canada issues.

Designer & Modeller:
   Obverse - G.W. DeSaulles,
   (DES below bust)
   Reverse - W.H.J. Blakemore,
   copying DeSaulle's design for
   5¢ and 10¢ pieces
Composition: .925 silver, .075 copper
Weight: 11.78 grams
Diameter: 29.85 mm
Edge: Reeded
Die Axes: ↑↓

The Mint, Birmingham issue (1904)
has an "H" mint mark below the
oval at the bottom on the reverse.
Royal Mint issues have no letter.

Date and Mint Mark	Quantity Minted	G-4	VG-8	F-12	VF-20	EF-40	AU-50	MS-60
1904H	140,000	8.00	12.50	15.00	30.00	110.00	400.00	800.00
1907	100,000	8.00	12.50	15.00	30.00	110.00	400.00	800.00
1908	160,000	—	10.00	12.50	25.00	100.00	325.00	650.00
1909	200,000	—	10.00	12.50	25.00	100.00	325.00	650.00

FIFTY CENTS

GEORGE V 1911 - 1919

The obverse for the Newfoundland fifty-cent piece is the same as that for the 1912-1936 Dominion of Canada coins. That the legend contains DEI GRA: (cf. page 78) indicated that the modification of the Canadian obverses was made during 1911, prior to commencing the production of the Newfoundland issue for that year. The reverse continued the Edwardian design.

In 1917-1919 nearly 1,000,000 50¢ were struck and many were used to replace the discontinued government "cash notes" for making relief payments to the poor. The need for silver for this purpose diminished in 1920, when a new issue of government paper money was made.

Designer: Portrait - Sir E.B. MacKennel, (B.M. on truncation)
Composition: .925 silver, .075 copper
Weight: 11.78 grams (1911);
       11.66 grams (1917-1919)

Diameter: 29.85 mm (1911);
         29.72 mm (1917-1919)
Edge: Reeded
Die Axes: ↑↓

Ottawa Mint issues (1917-1919) have a "C" mint mark below the oval at the bottom on the reverse. The Royal Mint issue has no letter.

Date and Mint Mark	Quantity Minted	G-4	VG-8	F-12	VF-20	EF-40	AU-50	MS-60
1911	200,000	—	10.00	12.50	25.00	100.00	300.00	600.00
1917C	375,560	—	10.00	12.50	25.00	75.00	250.00	500.00
1918C	294,824	—	10.00	12.50	25.00	75.0	250.00	500.00
1919C	306,267	—	10.00	12.50	25.00	75.00	250.00	500.00

TWO DOLLARS

VICTORIA   **1865 - 1888**

In the original planning for the Newfoundland coinage a gold dollar was considered. However, it was decided that such a coin would be so small it could be easily lost by the fishermen, so a two-dollar denomination was chosen instead. The initial bronze pattern combines the adopted obverse (derived from the New Brunswick 10¢ obverse and identical to the Newfoundland 10¢ obverse) with the crown and maple wreath of the Canada/New Brunswick 10¢ reverse (cf. NF-5 on page 224). Later gold patterns (cf. NF-14 and NF-15 on page 227) show a design similar to the adopted design, in which the denomination is expressed, only with block letters similar to those used on the cent. The adopted reverse has more conventional letters and the unusual feature of expressing the denomination three ways: 2 dollars, 200 cents, 100 pence, the last being the equivalent value in sterling (British money). Newfoundland was the only British colony with its own gold issue.

Designer & Modeller:
　　　　Reverse - Leonard C. Wyon
Engraver: Obverse - Leonard C. Wyon
Composition: .917 gold, .083 copper
Weight: 3.33 grams
Diameter: 17.98 mm
Edge: Reeded
Die Axes: ↑↓

The Heaton Mint issue (1882) has an "H" mint mark below the date on the reverse. London Mint strikings have no letter.

Date and Mint Mark	Quantity Minted	F-12	VF-20	EF-40	AU-50	MS-60
1865	10,000	—	400.00	450.00	500.00	950.00
1870	10,000	—	400.00	450.00	500.00	950.00
1872	6,050	—	550.00	700.00	825.00	1,300.00
1880	2,500	—	1,800.00	2,200.00	2,800.00	3,500.00
1881	10,000	—	375.00	425.00	475.00	650.00
1882H	25,000	—	350.00	400.00	450.00	625.00
1885	10,000	—	375.00	425.00	475.00	650.00
1888	25,000	—	350.00	400.00	450.00	625.00

PROVINCE OF CANADA
LARGE CENTS

VICTORIA

After the decision to adopt decimal coins was approved, a number of designs, sizes, and compositions were considered for the cent. The first trials used a reverse design consisting of 19 maple leaves placed side by side, radiating from the centre (cf. PC-1 to PC-3 on page 216). However, a motif of 16 serpentine maple leaves was adopted and trial pieces were struck in a cupro-nickel alloy. Later, it was decided the new cents would be bronze.

The adopted obverse design shows a youthful, idealized bust of the Queen wearing a laurel wreath in her hair. In fact, by the late 1850's the Queen was quite pudgy and appeared decidedly older than the coinage portraits suggested.

The government optimistically ordered ca. 10,000,000 one-cent pieces, which proved to be much more than the province could absorb. At the time both Canada East and Canada West were inundated with the copper tokens issued by banks and individuals. The bank tokens were heavier than the thin cents (which weighed 1/100 lb. avoirdupois) and slowed their public acceptance. The majority of the mintage remained unissued in the original boxes. In late 1861 part of it was sent to the New Brunswick government to provide a temporary supply of decimal coins while the province awaited the arrival of its own issues. But the bulk of the stock went to the Bank of Upper Canada, the government's bank. Until 1866, when it closed its doors, the Bank of Upper Canada experienced considerable difficulty in reducing its stock of cents, even when it offered to sell them at 20% below face value.

A stock of several million Province of Canada cents was inherited by the Dominion of Canada government in 1867 and it proceeded to issue them as Dominion currency.

Designer & Modeller:
  Leonard C. Wyon
Composition: .95 copper, .04 tin, .01 zinc
  (except for the rare brass)
Weight: 4.54 grams
Diameter: 25.4 mm
Edge: Plain
Die Axes: ↑↑

Date	Quantity Minted	G-4	VG-8	F-12	VF-20	EF-40	AU-50	MS-60	MS-65
1858	421,000	20.00	35.00	45.00	60.00	90.00	125.00	200.00	500.00

Since the coining of cents did not begin until the latter part of 1858, production continued throughout most of 1859, with most coins bearing an 1859 date. The first 1859's were undoubtedly overdates, on which a special wide 9 punch was employed to alter the second 8 to a 9, produced from several 1858-dated dies.

The majority of the 1859 dies were not overdates; they were dated with a narrow 9 punch. Many such dies were made and numerous re-punching varieties exist. Only those most widely collected are listed here.

Double-punched Narrow 9 #1: Traces of the original 9 at the left.
Double-punched Narrow 9 #2: Resembles and often designated "narrow 9 over 8." Actually it is a double-punched narrow 9, confused by the presence of die defect causing a small "tail" at the lower left of the 9.

A very rare variety of the plain, narrow 9 exists in brass, which can be identified by its distinctive yellow colour.

Overdate: Plain, Narrow 9
Wide 9 over 8

Date	Quantity Minted	G-4	VG-8	F-12	VF-20	EF-40	AU-50	MS-60	MS-65
1859 W9/8	Incl. above	15.00	25.00	35.00	50.00	75.00	100.00	175.00	350.00
1859 N9, bronze	Incl. above	.85	1.50	3.00	3.50	5.00	15.00	40.00	100.00
1859 N9, brass	Incl. above				VERY	RARE			

Double-punched Narrow 9 #1   Double-punched Narrow 9 #2
Resembles narrow 9 over 8   Traces of original 9 at left

Date	Quantity Minted	G-4	VG-8	F-12	VF-20	EF-40	AU-50	MS-60	MS-65
1859 D-P N9 #1	Incl. above	40.00	75.00	125.00	200.00	300.00	400.00	600.00	1,500.00
1859 D-P N9 #2	Incl. above	25.00	40.00	50.00	60.00	100.00	140.00	200.00	400.00

FIVE CENTS

The five-cent piece chosen by the Province of Canada was a small silver coin, half the weight of the ten-cent piece and similar to the United States half dime. The obverse depicts an idealized, youthful laureated Victoria and the reverse features a maple wreath of 21 leaves surmounted by St. Edward's crown.

The first dies bore small, widely spaced digits in the date. Later strikings carried larger digits punched over the original small figures, making the digits closer together.

Designer & Modeller:
    Leonard C. Wyon
Composition: .925 silver, .075 copper
Weight: 1.16 grams
Diameter: 15.5 mm
Edge: Reeded
Die Axes: ↑↓

  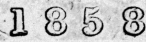

1858 Small Date
Digits widely spaced

1858 Large Date over Small Date
Digits closely spaced

Date	Quantity Minted	G-4	VG-8	F-12	VF-20	EF-40	AU-50	MS-60
1858 SD	1,460,389	6.00	10.00	18.00	25.00	50.00	150.00	300.00
1858 LD/SD	Incl. above	75.00	125.00	175.00	275.00	400.00	800.00	1,500.00

VICTORIA

In design, the Province of Canada ten-cent pieces resemble the five-cent pieces. An interesting variety occured through a dating blunder in which a 5 punch was used to repair a defective first 8. The top of the 5 can be seen rising above the 8.

Designer & Modeller:
    Leonard C. Wyon
Composition: .925 silver, .075 copper
Weight: 2.32 grams
Diameter: 18.0 mm
Edge: Reeded
Die Axes: ↑↓

1858
5 over first 8

Date	Quantity Minted	G-4	VG-8	F-12	VF-20	EF-40	AU-50	MS-60
1858 Normal Date	1,216,402	7.00	12.50	20.00	65.00	130.00	300.00	550.00
1858 5 over first 8	Incl. above	7.00	12.50	20.00	65.00	130.00	300.00	550.00

TWENTY CENTS

VICTORIA

This unusual denomination was chosen as a bridge between the two systems. It apparently deferred to the £, s, d basis of the Halifax currency system while naming the new issue in the $, ¢, mils system. The relationship between the two systems meant twenty cents was equivalent to a shilling in Halifax currency, and it was assumed that consequently the new coin would be found useful. This assumption proved unfounded because there had been no coin representing a shilling in the old system; the British shilling coin was worth just over 20% more than a shilling in Halifax currency. Furthermore, the size and weight of the twenty-cent piece led to confusion with both British shillings and U.S. twenty-five cent pieces. As one would expect, the government had difficulty introducing the twenty-cent piece and by 1860 it was decided to replace it with a twenty-five cent coin as the opportunity arose.

The replacement of the twenty-cent piece with a twenty-five cent coin came after Confederation. The Dominion government actively withdrew the twenty-cent pieces and at various times from 1885 onward sent them back to the Royal Mint in London for melting and recoining as twenty-five cent pieces.

Designer & Modeller:
    Leonard C. Wyon
Composition: .925 silver, .075 copper
Weight: 4.65 grams
Diameter: 23.3 mm
Edge: Reeded
Die Axes: ↑↓

Date	Quantity Minted	G-4	VG-8	F-12	VF-20	EF-40	AU-50	MS-60
1858	730,392	40.00	60.00	80.00	125.00	250.00	800.00	1,500.00

DOMINION OF CANADA
ONE CENT

VICTORIA   1876 - 1901

The large cents produced in 1858-1859 for the Province of Canada were inherited by the Dominion of Canada government at the time of Confederation. It was decided to issue them as Dominion cents. Nearly ten years were required to use up the stock; the first cents struck for the Dominion came out in 1876. An 1876 pattern cent (DC-1 on page 229) with the laureated obverse of 1858-1859 suggests that initially it was intended the Dominion cents be the same design as those of the Province of Canada. However, the obverse of the pieces actually issued bore a crowned bust adapted from that used for the Jamaica halfpenny and Prince Edward Island cent. The government also took the opportunity to increase the weight to 1/80th of an avoirdupois pound, the same as the British halfpenny.

Three varieties of the reverse, from independently engraved master tools, are known to exist: the Provincial Leaves reverse (1876-1882), the Large Leaves reverse (1884-1891), and the Small Leaves reverse (1891-1901). Only in 1891 are two reverses employed for a single year's coinage (see below). Four varieties exist for the obverse; however, their detailed description and listing by year will be included in a separate catalogue (see INTRODUCTION).

Designer & Modeller:
    Obverses - Leonard C. Wyon
    Provincial and Large Leaves
    Reverses - Leonard C. Wyon;
    Small Leaves Reverse -
    G.W. DeSaulles
Composition: .95 copper, .04 tin, .01 zinc
Weight: 5.67 grams
Diameter: 25.4 mm
Edge: Plain
Die Axes: ↑↑

Heaton Mint issues of 1876-1882 and The Mint, Birmingham issue of 1890 have an "H" mint mark on the reverse under the date. London Mint strikings have no letter.

Date and Mint Mark	Quantity Minted	G-4	VG-8	F-12	VF-20	EF-40	AU-50	MS-60	MS-65
1876H	4,000,000	1.00	2.00	2.50	3.75	7.50	15.00	35.00	100.00
1881H	2,000,000	1.25	2.50	3.50	5.00	10.00	18.00	40.00	115.00
1882H	4,000,000	1.00	2.00	2.75	4.00	8.00	15.00	35.00	100.00
1884	2,500,000	1.00	2.25	3.00	5.00	7.00	15.00	35.00	110.00
1886	1,500,000	1.50	2.50	3.50	6.00	10.00	20.00	50.00	135.00
1887	1,500,000	1.65	3.00	4.50	7.00	11.00	25.00	55.00	150.00
1888	4,000,000	1.00	2.00	2.50	3.50	7.00	12.50	30.00	100.00
1890H	1,000,000	3.00	6.00	9.00	12.00	18.00	30.00	75.00	200.00

Three major varieties of the 1891 cent are known. The first two have the Large Leaves reverse. The broad, flat leaves have very little detail and the bottom leaf runs into the rim denticles. The third variety has the Small Leaves reverse, which has slightly smaller leaves with much more detail. The bottom leaf ends well short of the rim denticles. The first variety has a large date; the second and third varieties have a small date.

Large Leaves, Large Date - leaves close to beads and vine; note broad figure "9".

Large Leaves, Small Date - leaves close to beads and vine; note narrow figure "9".

Small Leaves, Small Date - leaves far from beads and vine; note narrow figure "9".

Date	Quantity Minted	G-4	VG-8	F-12	VF-20	EF-40	AU-50	MS-60	MS-65
1891 LL, LD	1,452,500	3.00	6.00	9.00	12.00	18.00	30.00	75.00	200.00
1891 LL, SD	Incl. above	30.00	45.00	55.00	75.00	100.00	160.00	350.00	900.00
1891 SL, SD	Incl. above	25.00	40.00	50.00	65.00	85.00	125.00	300.00	650.00
1892	1,200,000	1.60	3.25	5.50	7.50	12.50	20.00	50.00	150.00
1893	2,000,000	1.50	2.50	3.50	5.00	10.00	17.50	35.00	100.00
1894	1,000,000	4.00	7.00	10.00	12.00	17.00	40.00	75.00	200.00
1895	1,200,000	2.00	3.50	6.00	8.00	13.00	20.00	55.00	150.00
1896	2,000,000	1.10	2.25	3.00	5.00	7.00	15.00	30.00	100.00
1897	1,500,000	1.25	2.50	3.50	5.00	10.00	20.00	40.00	110.00

The Mint, Birmingham issues of 1898 and 1900 have an "H" mint mark on the reverse under the wreath at the bottom. London Mint strikings have no letter.

Date and Mint Mark	Quantity Minted	G-4	VG-8	F-12	VF-20	EF-40	AU-50	MS-60	MS-65
1898H	1,000,000	3.00	5.00	7.00	10.00	15.00	25.00	55.00	160.00
1899	2,400,000	1.00	2.00	3.00	4.00	7.50	12.00	30.00	90.00
1900	1,000,000	4.50	7.50	10.00	13.00	18.00	35.00	85.00	200.00
1900H	2,600,000	1.25	2.50	3.00	4.50	10.00	15.00	35.00	100.00
1901	4,100,000	1.00	2.00	2.50	3.50	7.50	12.00	30.00	75.00

ONE CENT

The reverse of this denomination is a continuation of the Victorian design.

Designer & Modeller:
  Obverse - G.W. DeSaulles
  (DES below bust)
Composition: .95 copper, .04 tin, .01 zinc
Weight: 5.67 grams
Diameter: 25.4 mm
Edge: Plain
Die Axes: ↑↑

The Mint, Birmingham issue of 1907 has an "H" mint mark on the reverse under the wreath at the bottom. London Mint strikings (1902-1907) and Ottawa Mint strikings (1908-1910) have no letter.

Date and Mint Mark	Quantity Minted	G-4	VG-8	F-12	VF-20	EF-40	AU-50	MS-60	MS-65
1902	3,000,000	1.00	2.00	2.50	3.50	7.00	12.00	30.00	75.00
1903	4,000,000	1.50	3.00	4.00	6.00	12.00	16.00	35.00	75.00
1904	2,500,000	1.50	3.00	4.00	6.00	13.00	18.00	35.00	85.00
1905	2,000,000	3.00	6.00	8.00	10.00	15.00	25.00	50.00	125.00
1906	4,100,000	1.00	2.00	2.50	3.50	7.00	12.00	25.00	75.00
1907	2,400,000	1.50	3.00	4.50	7.00	13.00	18.00	35.00	90.00
1907H	800,000	6.00	10.00	15.00	20.00	30.00	60.00	120.00	350.00
1908	2,401,506	2.00	3.50	4.50	7.00	14.00	20.00	35.00	75.00
1909	3,973,339	.80	1.50	1.75	3.00	5.00	8.00	20.00	70.00
1910	5,146,487	.80	1.50	1.75	3.00	4.00	8.00	20.00	60.00

ONE CENT - LARGE

GEORGE V   **1911 - 1920**

"GODLESS" OBVERSE 1911

The obverse introduced in 1911 broke a tradition set by the coins of the previous two reigns in which the Latin phrase DEI GRATIA (or an abbreviation for it) was included in the monarch's titles. Omission of the phrase aroused public criticism during which the coins were labeled "Godless." The coinage tools were modified during the year and cents with "DEI GRA:" in the legend appeared in 1912. The reverse also marked a departure from the previous reigns in the inclusion of "CANADA" in the legend. It had formerly been part of the obverse legend on this denomination.

Designer & Modeller:
　　　Portrait - Sir E.B. MacKennal,
　　　(B.M. on truncation)
　　　Reverse - W.H.J. Blakemore
Composition: .95 copper, .04 tin, .01 zinc
Weight: 5.67 grams
Diameter: 25.4 mm
Edge: Plain
Die Axes: ↑↑

Date	Quantity Minted	G-4	VG-8	F-12	VF-20	EF-40	AU-50	MS-60	MS-65
1911	4,663,486	.90	1.75	2.50	4.00	7.50	12.50	25.00	75.00

MODIFIED OBVERSE LEGEND 1912-1936

1912-1919
Composition: .95 copper, .04 tin, .01 zinc
1919-1920
　　　.955 copper, .030 tin,
　　　.015 zinc
The physical specifications are as for the 1911 issue.

Date	Quantity Minted	G-4	VG-8	F-12	VF-20	EF-40	AU-50	MS-60	MS-65
1912	5,107,642	.65	1.00	1.25	2.25	5.00	7.00	15.00	50.00
1913	5,735,405	.65	1.00	1.25	2.25	5.00	7.00	15.00	50.00
1914	3,405,958	.85	1.50	2.00	3.00	6.00	9.00	20.00	65.00
1915	4,932,134	.70	1.25	1.75	2.75	4.00	6.00	15.00	50.00
1916	11,022,367	.60	1.00	1.25	2.25	5.00	6.00	14.00	40.00
1917	11,899,254	.50	.75	1.15	1.75	3.00	5.00	10.00	35.00
1918	12,970,798	.50	.75	1.15	1.75	3.00	5.00	10.00	35.00
1919	11,279,634	.50	.75	1.15	1.75	3.00	5.00	10.00	35.00
1920	6,762,247	.60	1.00	1.25	2.00	4.00	6.00	12.00	40.00

ONE CENT - SMALL

GEORGE V   **1920 - 1936**

   As a matter of economy the Canadian government introduced in 1920 a small cent similar in size and composition to that of the United States. The large cents were not immediately withdrawn, but were allowed to circulate until the late 1930's. The small coins lacked rim denticles, the first instance of this in the Canadian decimal series. The obverse design was retained while a new reverse design, featuring two maple leaves, was used.

Designer: Portrait - Sir E.B. MacKennal
               (B.M. on truncation)
               Reverse - Fred Lewis
Modeller: Portrait - Sir E.B. MacKennal
               Reverse - W.H.J. Blakemore
Composition: .955 copper, .030 tin,
               .015 zinc
Weight: 3.24 grams
Diameter: 19.05 mm
Edge: Plain
Die Axes: ↑↑

Date	Quantity Minted	G-4	VG-8	F-12	VF-20	EF-40	AU-50	MS-60	MS-65
1920	15,483,923	.20	.40	.75	2.50	3.50	5.50	10.00	30.00
1921	7,601,627	.45	.90	1.50	4.00	7.00	11.00	20.00	40.00
1922	1,243,635	10.00	15.00	20.00	25.00	42.00	70.00	150.00	400.00
1923	1,019,002	15.00	25.00	30.00	35.00	50.00	100.00	225.00	600.00
1924	1,593,195	5.00	7.50	9.00	12.50	22.00	35.00	90.00	200.00
1925	1,000,622	12.00	20.00	25.00	30.00	40.00	75.00	160.00	450.00
1926	2,143,372	1.50	3.00	4.50	6.00	16.00	25.00	50.00	125.00
1927	3,553,928	1.00	1.75	3.00	5.00	12.00	18.00	30.00	60.00
1928	9,144,860	.20	.35	.65	1.25	3.00	5.00	10.00	30.00
1929	12,159,840	.20	.30	.60	1.10	2.75	4.50	9.00	30.00
1930	2,538,613	1.50	2.50	3.50	6.00	15.00	25.00	50.00	100.00
1931	3,842,776	1.25	2.00	3.00	6.00	15.00	22.00	40.00	80.00
1932	21,316,190	.20	.30	.40	.75	2.50	4.00	8.00	30.00
1933	12,079,310	.20	.35	.50	.90	3.50	5.00	10.00	30.00
1934	7,042,358	.25	.45	1.00	1.50	4.00	7.00	12.00	30.00
1935	7,526,400	.25	.45	1.00	1.50	4.00	6.00	10.00	30.00
1936	8,768,769	.20	.40	.90	1.25	3.25	5.00	10.00	25.00

ONE CENT

COINAGE USING GEORGE V DIES 1936

In December, 1936 the reigning British King, Edward VIII, abdicated in favour of his brother, who became George VI. This placed a great strain upon the Royal Mint in London. It was well along in the preparation of the tools for the British Commonwealth coinage obverses, including those for Canada. All this work had to be scrapped and new obverse tools made for George VI.

In 1937, during the delay involved in the preparation of new obverses in London, the Royal Canadian Mint was forced to strike from 1936 dies quantities of all denominations, except the 50¢ piece. The dies for the one, ten and twenty-five cent pieces are said to have been marked with a tiny dot on the reverse. This was to indicate that the coins were struck in a year different than that borne on the dies and with the bust of the preceding monarch.

The 1936 dot cent is an extreme rarity; only one business strike and three specimen strikes, all in mint state, are presently known. Numerous circulated examples of this rarity have come to light over the years; however, none has been satisfactorily authenticated. It seems unlikely that any genuine 1936 dot cents ever circulated, despite the supposedly official mintage of almost 700,000 pieces.

1936 with raised dot below date
struck in 1937

Date and Mint Mark	Quantity Minted	G-4	VG-8	F-12	VF-20	EF-40	AU-50	MS-60	MS-65
1936 Dot	678,823				RARE				

COINAGE IN NAME OF GEORGE VI

In the early part of 1937 the Royal Mint in London decided to speed up the production of the new coinage tools for Canadian coinages by having some of the work done by the Paris Mint. Included in this work was the reverse for the cent. The model was sent to Paris for conversion into master coinage tools.

The reverse of the new cent continued the trend toward modernization of the Canadian coinage designs begun in 1935 with the voyageur silver dollar.

"ET IND: IMP:" IN OBVERSE LEGEND 1937-1947

The initial obverse (1937-1947) bore a legend containing the Latin abbreviation "ET IND: IMP:," indicating the King was the Emperor of India.

Designer & Modeller:
    Portrait - T.H. Paget
    (H.P. below bust)
    Reverse - G.E. Kruger-Gray
    (K G below right-hand maple leaf)
Composition: .955 copper, .030 tin,
                 .015 zinc (1937-1942);
                 .980 copper, .005 tin,
                 .015 zinc (1942-1952)
Weight: 3.24 grams
Diameter: 19.05 mm
Edge: Plain
Die Axes: ↑↑

Date	Quantity Minted	VG-8	F-12	VF-20	EF-40	AU-50	MS-60	MS-65
1937	10,040,231	.40	.60	1.75	3.00	4.00	6.00	7.50
1938	18,365,608	.30	.50	.75	1.00	2.00	4.00	8.00
1939	21,600,319	.30	.40	.65	1.00	2.00	3.00	7.00
1940	85,740,532	.15	.25	.40	.75	1.25	2.00	6.00
1941	56,336,011	.15	.25	.40	.75	2.00	5.00	25.00
1942	76,113,708	.15	.25	.60	1.00	2.00	4.00	20.00
1943	89,111,969	.15	.25	.50	.90	1.25	2.00	5.00
1944	44,131,216	.20	.30	.60	.75	2.00	7.50	25.00
1945	77,269,591	.15	.20	.35	.60	.80	1.00	3.50
1946	56,662,071	.15	.20	.35	.60	.80	1.00	3.50
1947	31,093,901	.30	.40	.60	1.00	1.50	2.50	4.50

MAPLE LEAF ISSUE 1947

The granting of independence to India resulted in a dilemma for the Royal Canadian Mint in the early part of 1948. New obverse coinage tools with "ET IND: IMP:" omitted would not arrive for several months, yet there was a pressing need for all denominations of coins. The Mint satisfied this demand by striking coins dated 1947 and bearing an obverse with outmoded titles. To differentiate this issue from the regular strikings of 1947, a tiny maple leaf was placed after the date.

1947 Maple Leaf Issue
struck in 1948

Date	Quantity Minted	VG-8	F-12	VF-20	EF-40	AU-50	MS-60	MS-65
1947 Maple Leaf	43,855,448	.15	.20	.35	.60	.90	1.50	3.25

MODIFIED OBVERSE LEGEND 1948-1952

Following the arrival of the master tools with the new obverse legend lacking "ET IND: IMP:" in 1948, the 1947 Maple Leaf coinage was suspended. For the remainder of the year coins were produced with the new obverse and the true date 1948. This obverse was employed for the rest of the reign.

The physical and chemical specifications are as for the 1937-1947 issues.

Date	Quantity Minted	VG-8	F-12	VF-20	EF-40	AU-50	MS-60	MS-65
1948	25,767,779	.25	.35	.60	.90	1.50	3.00	6.00
1949	33,128,933	.10	.20	.30	.40	.60	.90	3.00
1950	60,444,992	.10	.20	.30	.40	.60	.90	2.50
1951	80,430,379	.05	.15	.25	.50	.60	.90	2.25
1952	67,631,736	.05	.15	.25	.50	.60	.90	2.25

ONE CENT

The portrait model for the new Queen Elizabeth coinages was prepared in England by a sculptress, Mrs. Mary Gillick. The relief of this model was too high, with the result that the centre portion containing two lines on the shoulder (representing a fold in the Queen's gown) did not strike up well on the coins. This first obverse variety has been commonly termed the "no shoulder strap" variety by many collectors, due to the resemblance of the lines to a strap. Later in 1953, Royal Canadian Mint authorities decided to correct the defects in the obverse design. Thomas Shingles, the Mint's Chief Engraver, lowered the relief of the model, and strengthened the shoulder and hair detail. This modified obverse (often called the "shoulder strap" variety) was introduced before the end of the year and became the standard obverse. By mistake the "no shoulder fold" obverse was used to produce some of the 1954 cents for the proof-like sets and a small quantity of 1955 cents for circulation.

Many collectors have difficulty differentiating the two varieties on slightly worn cents. The best way is to note that the I's on the "no shoulder fold" variety are flared at the ends and that an imaginary line drawn up through the centre of the I in DEI goes between two rim denticles. On the "shoulder fold" variety the I's are nearly straight sided and a line drawn up through the I of DEI runs into a rim denticle.

The reverse was a continuation of the George VI reverse.

Designer & Modeller:
    Portrait - Mrs. Mary Gillick
    (M.G. on truncation)
Engraver: No Shoulder Fold Obverse -
    Thomas Shingles, using the
    Gillick portrait model;
    Shoulder Fold Obverse -
    Thomas Shingles, modifying
    existing NSF coinage tools
Composition: .980 copper, .005 tin,
    .015 zinc
Weight: 3.24 grams
Diameter: 19.05 mm
Edge: Plain
Die Axes: ↑↑

No Shoulder Fold Obverse
note flared ends of I's and I in DEI
points between two rim denticles.

Shoulder Fold Obverse
note straight-sided I's and I in DEI
points at a rim denticle.

Date	Quantity Minted	F-12	VF-20	EF-40	AU-50	MS-60	MS-65
1953 NSF	67,806,016	.15	.25	.50	.75	1.00	2.00
1953 SF	Incl. above	1.75	2.50	5.00	10.00	15.00	50.00
1954 NSF		—	—	—	—	100.00	150.00
1954 SF	22,181,760	.30	.50	.75	1.50	2.50	5.00
1955 NSF	56,403,193	10.00	30.00	50.00	80.00	200.00	500.00
1955 SF	Incl. above	.15	.25	.35	.50	.75	1.25
1956	78,685,535	.15	.25	.35	.50	.75	1.25
1957	100,601,792	.15	.25	.35	.50	.75	1.25
1958	59,385,679	.15	.25	.35	.50	.75	1.25
1959	83,615,343	.10	.20	.30	.40	.50	1.00
1960	75,772,775	.10	.20	.30	.40	.50	.80
1961	139,598,404	.10	.20	.30	.40	.50	.80
1962	227,244,069	.10	.15	.25	.35	.45	.70
1963	279,076,334	.10	.15	.20	.25	.35	.50
1964	484,655,322	.10	.15	.20	.25	.30	.40

CROWNED PORTRAIT & MAPLE TWIG REVERSE 1965-1966

In 1964 the British government decided to introduce a more mature portrait of Queen Elizabeth for domestic and Commonwealth coinages. The new portrait model, by Arnold Machin, features the Queen wearing a tiara instead of a laurel wreath. A copy of the model was forwarded to Canada and was incorporated into the obverses for 1965.

Designer & Modeller:
    Portrait - Arnold Machin

The physical and chemical specifications are as for the 1953-1964 issues.

VARIETIES 1965

During 1965, difficulties were encountered in striking the cents, resulting in the introduction of a second variety obverse. The first variety has small beads at the rim and a flat field; the second has large rim beads and a field that slopes up at the rim. Another way to distinguish the two obverses is by the location of the A in REGINA relative to the rim beads: on the small beads obverse it points between two beads, whereas on the large beads obverse it points at a bead. In addition, two reverses differing in the style of 5 in the date were used in 1965. The obverses and reverses were employed in all possible combinations, creating four varieties for the year.

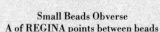

Small Beads Obverse
A of REGINA points between beads

Large Beads Obverse
A of REGINA points at bead

Pointed 5
Top right of 5 comes to point

Blunt 5
Top right of 5 is nearly square

Date	Quantity Minted	MS-60	MS-65
1965 Variety 1 (small beads, pointed 5)	304,441,082	.60	.80
1965 Variety 2 (small beads, blunt 5)	Incl. above	.15	.25
1965 Variety 3 (large beads, blunt 5)	Incl. above	.25	.40
1965 Variety 4 (large beads, pointed 5)	Incl. above	10.00	15.00
1966	183,644,388	.15	.25

COMMEMORATIVE FOR CENTENNIAL OF CONFEDERATION 1967

Alex Colville's design of a rock dove was selected for the 1967 cent reverse, struck in commemoration of Canada's centennial of Confederation. The event was marked by a special design for each denomination coined for circulation, plus a special $20 gold piece for collectors only. The obverse of the cent is the same as that for the 1966 issue.

Designer: Reverse - Alex Colville
Modeller: Reverse - Myron Cook

The physical and chemical specifications are as for the 1953-1966 issues.

Date	Quantity Minted	MS-60	MS-65
1967 Confederation Commemorative	345,140,645	.20	.30

MAPLE TWIG REVERSE RESUMED; LARGE PORTRAIT 1968-1978

Date	Quantity Minted	MS-60	MS-65
1968	329,695,772	.15	.25
1969	335,240,929	.15	.25
1970	311,145,010	.15	.25
1971	298,228,936	.15	.25
1972	451,304,591	.10	.20
1973	457,059,852	.10	.20
1974	692,058,489	.10	.15
1975	642,318,000	.10	.15
1976	701,122,890	.10	.15
1977	453,050,666	.10	.15
1978	911,170,647	.10	.15

MODIFIED OBVERSE; OLD WEIGHT STANDARD CONTINUED   1979

As part of a general standardization of the coinage, the portrait of the Queen was made smaller beginning with the 1979 coinage. The purpose was to make the size of the portrait proportional to the diameter of the coin, regardless of the denomination.

The physical and chemical specifications are as for the 1953-1978 issues.

Date	Quantity Minted	MS-60	MS-65
1979	753,942,953	.10	.15

REDUCED WEIGHT   1980

In 1978 the Mint struck pattern pieces, dated 1979, with a considerably reduced weight and a diameter of 16 mm. The Mint was prompted by the rising price of copper which resulted in the one-cent piece being coined at a loss. Unfortunately, the diameter of the pattern was the same as that for the tokens used by the Toronto Transit Commission and this was enough to result in the cancellation of plans for the new 16 mm cent. The Mint struck cents of the old size and design during 1979. However, in 1980 it introduced a coin of the same design as before, but with a decreased diameter and thickness (hence a decreased weight).

Weight: 2.80 grams
Diameter: 19.00 mm
Thickness: 1.38 mm

Date	Quantity Minted	MS-60	MS-65
1980		.10	.15

FIVE CENTS

VICTORIA

1870 - 1901

The first five-cent pieces for the Dominion of Canada were introduced in 1870. The initial designs were identical to those used for the Province of Canada in 1858. During the reign of Queen Victoria, five obverse varieties, differing primarily in the facial features, were employed. Their detailed description and listing by year will be included in a separate catalogue (see INTRODUCTION). Three varieties of the reverse are known: the Wide Rim reverse (1870), the Narrow Rim, 21 Leaves reverse (1870-1881, 1890-1901) and the Narrow Rim, 22 Leaves reverse (1882-1889).

Designer, Modeller & Engraver:
    Leonard C. Wyon
Composition: .925 silver, .075 copper
Weight: 1.16 grams
Diameter: 15.50 mm
Edge: Reeded
Die Axes: ↑↓

Heaton Mint issues of 1872-1883 and the Mint, Birmingham issue of 1880 have an "H" mint mark on the reverse under the wreath. London Mint strikings have no letter.

VARIETIES 1870

Before the coinage of 1870 was complete, new master tools for the five-cent piece were introduced, with the result that two varieties were created for the year. The first has wide rims (including unusually long rim denticles) on the obverse and reverse and the second has more conventional narrow rims.

1870 Wide Rims   1870 Narrow Rims

Date and Mint Mark	Quantity Minted	G-4	VG-8	F-12	VF-20	EF-40	AU-50	MS-60
1870 Wide Rims	2,800,000	5.00	9.00	15.00	25.00	50.00	150.00	325.00
1870 Narrow Rims	Incl. above	6.00	10.00	16.00	30.00	60.00	200.00	350.00
1871	1,400,000	5.00	9.00	15.00	25.00	50.00	150.00	325.00
1872H	2,000,000	5.00	8.00	12.00	20.00	50.00	150.00	300.00

VARIETIES 1874H & 1875H

In 1874 and 1875 two sizes of digits were used for dating the dies. In addition, the two date sizes for 1874 also differ in the style of 4: the small date contains a plain 4 and the large date contains a crosslet 4.

Through a clerical error part of the mintage of 1874H-dated coins was assigned to the next year's production figures. Therefore the mintage figures for the two years, 800,000 and 1,000,000, respectively, have been combined.

1874H Small Date
(Plain 4)

1874H Large Date
(Crosslet 4)

1875H Small Date

1875H Large Date

Date and Mint Mark	Quantity Minted	G-4	VG-8	F-12	VF-20	EF-40	AU-50	MS-60
1874H SD, Plain 4	1,800,000	8.00	15.00	20.00	40.00	100.00	250.00	500.00
1874H LD, Crosslet 4	Incl. above	5.00	10.00	15.00	30.00	60.00	200.00	400.00
1875H SD	Incl. above	45.00	90.00	125.00	200.00	350.00	750.00	1,500.00
1875H LD	Incl. above	50.00	100.00	150.00	250.00	500.00	1,000.00	2,000.00
1880H	3,000,000	2.00	4.00	6.00	10.00	30.00	150.00	300.00
1881H	1,500,000	3.00	5.00	7.50	15.00	30.00	150.00	300.00
1882H	1,000,000	3.50	6.00	9.00	18.00	40.00	200.00	350.00
1883H	600,000	5.50	10.00	20.00	30.00	60.00	250.00	450.00
1884	200,000	40.00	70.00	110.00	200.00	400.00	800.00	1,500.00

VARIETIES 1885 & 1886

During the year 1885, two markedly different styles of 5 were used in the date. One is the small 5 seen on the 1875H issue; the other is the larger 5 used in the denomination "5 CENTS." In 1886 there is either a small 6 or a large 6 used. The uppermost part of the inner portion of the small 6 comes to a point, whereas that area on the large 6 is almost square.

1885 Small 5

1885 Large 5

1886 Small 6

1886 Large 6

Date and Mint Mark	Quantity Minted	G-4	VG-8	F-12	VF-20	EF-40	AU-50	MS-60
1885 Small 5	1,000,000	3.50	7.00	10.00	17.50	40.00	175.00	350.00
1885 Large 5	Incl. above	3.50	7.00	10.00	17.50	40.00	175.00	350.00
1886 Small 6	1,700,000	2.50	4.00	6.00	11.00	21.00	175.00	300.00
1886 Large 6	Incl. above	2.50	4.00	6.00	12.00	22.00	175.00	300.00
1887	500,000	8.00	15.00	20.00	30.00	60.00	300.00	500.00
1888	1,000,000	2.50	5.00	7.00	14.00	30.00	125.00	250.00
1889	1,200,000	12.00	20.00	30.00	45.00	100.00	375.00	600.00
1890H	1,000,000	3.00	5.00	8.00	15.00	30.00	175.00	300.00
1891	1,800,000	3.00	5.00	8.00	15.00	30.00	125.00	250.00
1892	860,000	4.00	6.00	10.00	17.00	32.00	250.00	500.00
1893	1,700,000	3.00	5.00	8.00	12.00	20.00	125.00	250.00
1894	500,000	7.50	15.00	20.00	30.00	50.00	200.00	350.00
1896	1,500,000	2.50	4.50	7.00	11.00	20.00	100.00	200.00
1897	1,319,283	2.50	4.50	7.00	11.00	20.00	100.00	200.00
1898	580,717	6.00	12.00	18.00	30.00	50.00	125.00	250.00
1899	3,000,000	2.00	3.00	5.00	7.50	15.00	100.00	200.00

VARIETIES 1900

Two sizes of date are seen on the 1900 issue. The large date has been referred to most often as the Round 0's variety and the small date as the Oval 0's variety, but there is a greater difference in the 9's. The large date has a Wide 9 as on the 1898 issue and the small date has a Narrow 9 as on the 1899 and 1901 issues.

1900 Large Date
(Wide 0's and 9)

1900 Small Date
(Narrow 0's and 9)

Date	Quantity Minted	G-4	VG-8	F-12	VF-20	EF-40	AU-50	MS-60
1900 LD, Wide 0's	1,800,000	10.00	20.00	30.00	40.00	75.00	300.00	500.00
1900 SD, Narrow 0's	Incl. above	2.00	3.00	5.00	7.50	15.00	175.00	300.00
1901	2,000,000	2.00	3.00	4.00	6.00	12.00	100.00	200.00

FIVE CENTS

EDWARD VII **1902 - 1910**

In 1902, the coronation year for Edward VII, the Royal Mint was extremely busy producing new coinage tools and striking the new coins and medals. One compromise this necessitated involved the reverse of the Canadian five-cent piece. It had been intended to transfer both the word "CANADA" from the obverse to the reverse legend and to replace the old St. Edward's crown, showing depressed arches at the top, with the Imperial State crown, showing raised arches at the top. Instead, the Mint had to settle for making the legend change only. The following year the crown was changed. The 1903H issue had a reverse with 21 leaves, but a modified design with 22 leaves was instituted for the London issue.

Designer & Modeller:
  Obverse - G.W. DeSaulles
  (DES under bust)
Engraver: Reverse - G.W. DeSaulles
Composition: .925 silver, .075 copper
Weight: 1.16 grams
Diameter: 15.50 mm
Edge: Reeded
Die Axes: ↑↓

The Mint, Birmingham issue has an "H" mint mark on the reverse under the wreath. The London Mint issue has no letter.

MINT MARK VARIETIES 1902

Two sizes of H appear on the 1902 Heaton issue of this denomination. One is a small, narrow H not seen on any other Canadian coins and the other is a large, wide H similar to that on the 1903H.

   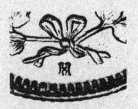

1902 Large H   1902 Small H

Date and Mint Mark	Quantity Minted	G-4	VG-8	F-12	VF-20	EF-40	AU-50	MS-60
1902	2,120,000	1.25	2.50	4.00	6.00	10.00	40.00	90.00
1902H Large H	2,200,000	1.50	3.00	5.00	8.00	14.00	45.00	100.00
1902H Small H	Incl. above	5.00	10.00	15.00	20.00	50.00	150.00	300.00

IMPERIAL CROWN; 21 LEAVES IN REVERSE WREATH 1903
(The Mint, Birmingham Issue Only)

The 1903 issue for The Mint, Birmingham was essentially the same as the 1902 coinage with the St. Edward's crown replaced by the Imperial State crown. This design was employed for only the one year and at the Birmingham Mint only.

Designer & Engraver:
       probably G.W. De Saulles

The physical and chemical specifications are as for the 1902 issue.

Date and Mint Mark	Quantity Minted	G-4	VG-8	F-12	VF-20	EF-40	AU-50	MS-60
1903H	2,640,000	1.50	3.00	4.50	8.00	15.00	70.00	150.00

IMPERIAL CROWN; 22 LEAVES IN REVERSE WREATH 1903
(London Mint - 1910)

In a move unprecedented in Canadian coinage the Royal Mint produced a coin (the five-cent piece) that bore a somewhat different design than that used by its sub-contractor, The Mint, Birmingham, in 1903. The 1903 London issue features a new wreath with 22 instead of 21 leaves.

Designer & Modeller:
       Obverse - G.W. De Saulles
       Reverse - W.H.J. Blakemore
Composition: .925 silver, .075 copper
Weight: 1.16 grams (1903-1910);
       1.17 grams (1910)
Diameter: 15.50 mm
Edge: Reeded
Die Axes: ↑↓ (1903-1907);
       ↑↑ (1908-1910)

Date	Quantity Minted	G-4	VG-8	F-12	VF-20	EF-40	AU-50	MS-60
1903	1,000,000	2.50	4.00	7.00	14.00	20.00	125.00	250.00
1904	2,400,000	2.00	3.50	5.50	8.00	15.00	70.00	150.00
1905	2,600,000	2.00	3.50	5.50	8.00	15.00	70.00	150.00
1906	3,100,000	1.50	3.00	3.50	6.00	10.00	60.00	125.00
1907	5,200,000	1.50	3.00	3.50	6.00	10.00	60.00	125.00
1908	1,220,524	3.50	6.00	10.00	15.00	25.00	100.00	200.00

VARIETIES 1909 & 1910

In 1909 the existing reverse was modified to create a variety in which the maple leaves have sharp points along their edges, causing them to resemble holly leaves. Both the "Maple Leaves" and the "Holly Leaves" reverses saw use in 1909 and 1910.

Maple Leaves Reverse	Holly Leaves Reverse
(1903-1910)	(1909-1910)

Date		Quantity Minted	G-4	VG-8	F-12	VF-20	EF-40	AU-50	MS-60
1909	Maple leaves	1,983,725	—	3.00	4.00	8.00	14.00	70.00	150.00
1909	Holly Leaves	Incl. above	—	3.00	4.00	8.00	14.00	70.00	150.00
1910	Maple Leaves	5,580,325	—	2.00	3.50	5.50	10.00	60.00	125.00
1910	Holly Leaves	Incl. above	—	2.00	3.50	5.50	10.00	60.00	125.00

FIVE CENTS — SILVER

GEORGE V

"GODLESS" OBVERSE 1911

The new obverse introduced in 1911 was criticized by the public because the Latin phrase DEI GRATIA (or an abbreviation for it), indicating that the King ruled by the grace of God, was omitted. The coinage tools were modified during the year and a new obverse with "DEI GRA:" included in the legend appeared on the 1912 issue. The maple leaves design reverse was that of the previous reign.

Designer & Modeller:
    Portrait - Sir E.B. MacKennal
    (B.M. on truncation)
Composition: .925 silver, .075 copper
Weight: 1.17 grams
Diameter: 15.50 mm
Edge: Reeded
Die Axes: ↑↑

Date	Quantity Minted	G-4	VG-8	F-12	VF-20	EF-40	AU-50	MS-60
1911	3,692,350	1.50	3.00	5.00	8.00	18.00	70.00	200.00

MODIFIED OBVERSE LEGEND 1912-1921

Composition: .925 silver, .075 copper
    (1912-1919);
    .800 silver, .200 copper
    (1920-1921)

The physical specifications are as for the 1911 issue.

Date	Quantity Minted	G-4	VG-8	F-12	VF-20	EF-40	AU-50	MS-60
1912	5,863,170	1.25	2.50	3.50	6.00	8.00	30.00	100.00
1913	5,588,048	1.25	2.50	3.50	6.00	8.00	30.00	100.00
1914	4,202,179	1.50	2.50	3.50	6.00	8.00	35.00	110.00
1915	1,172,258	4.00	7.00	12.00	20.00	40.00	125.00	350.00
1916	2,481,675	1.50	2.50	3.50	6.00	12.00	50.00	125.00
1917	5,521,373	1.25	2.50	3.50	5.00	7.00	15.00	85.00
1918	6,052,298	1.25	2.50	3.50	5.00	7.00	15.00	85.00
1919	7,835,400	1.25	2.50	3.50	5.00	7.00	15.00	85.00
1920	10,649,851*	1.25	2.50	3.50	5.00	7.00	15.00	85.00

* Some 1920 5¢ are believed to have remained unissued and returned to the melting pot in 1922.

FIVE CENTS 1921

During 1920-1921 plans moved forward for the replacement of the small silver five-cents piece with a larger coin of pure nickel, the same size as the U.S. nickel. The enabling legislation was passed in May 1921 and thereafter no more five-cent pieces were coined in silver. The Mint melted some 3,022,665 coins of this denomination. The presumed composition of this melt is almost all of the 1921 mintage and a portion of the 1920 mintage, thus explaining the rarity of the 1921 date today. Only about 400 1921's are believed to have survived. A few are specimen coins, issued to collectors in sets and the rest are thought to be circulation strikes sold to visitors to the Mint in the early months of 1921.

Date	Quantity Minted	G-4	VG-8	F-12	VF-20	EF-40	AU-50	MS-60
1921	2,582,495*	1,600.00	2,000.00	3,500.00	4,500.00	6,500.00	9,000.00	15,000.00

* Almost all 1921 5¢ are believed to have remained unissued and returned to the melting pot in 1922.

FIVE CENTS - NICKEL

GEORGE V   1922 - 1936

The new Canadian nickel five-cent piece was introduced in 1922 after two years of planning. The silver coin it replaced was allowed to circulate also until the 1930's, when a more active withdrawal program was instituted.

Designer & Modeller:
Portrait - Sir E.B. MacKennal
(B.M. on truncation)
Reverse - W.H.J. Blakemore
Composition: 1.00 nickel
Weight: 4.54 grams
Diameter: 21.21 mm
Edge: Plain
Die Axes:↑↑

Date	Quantity Minted	G-4	VG-8	F-12	VF-20	EF-40	AU-50	MS-60
1922	4,794,119	.30	.50	.75	2.50	7.00	25.00	85.00
1923	2,502,279	.40	.75	1.25	4.00	10.00	40.00	100.00
1924	3,105,839	.30	.50	1.25	3.50	9.00	35.00	100.00
1925	201,921	25.00	40.00	50.00	80.00	200.00	400.00	900.00

VARIETIES 1926

It was the usual practice in the George V five-cent series to complete the date at the matrix stage, eliminating the necessity to date every reverse die and thereby assuring that there would be no difference in the positioning of the date digits on a given year's coinage. A notable exception was 1926, when the reverse punch (bearing a 6 which nearly touched the maple leaf) was retired before the conclusion of the coinage. The second variety had the 6 slightly farther from the maple leaf.

1926 Near 6   1926 Far 6
the 6 almost touches the maple leaf   the 6 is farther from the maple leaf

Date	Quantity Minted	G-4	VG-8	F-12	VF-20	EF-40	AU-50	MS-60
1926 Near 6	938,162	2.25	3.50	6.00	17.00	60.00	125.00	250.00
1926 Far 6	Incl. above	75.00	125.00	150.00	225.00	350.00	700.00	1,500.00
1927	5,285,627	.30	.50	1.00	3.50	8.00	30.00	100.00
1928	4,577,712	.30	.50	1.00	3.50	8.00	30.00	100.00
1929	5,611,911	.30	.50	1.00	3.50	8.00	30.00	100.00
1930	3,704,673	.30	.50	1.00	3.50	8.00	30.00	110.00
1931	5,100,000	.30	.50	1.00	3.50	8.00	30.00	110.00
1932	3,198,566	.30	.50	1.00	3.50	9.00	30.00	110.00
1933	2,597,867	.40	.75	1.25	3.50	9.00	35.00	150.00
1934	3,827,304	.30	.50	1.00	3.00	8.00	30.00	125.00
1935	3,900,000	.30	.50	1.00	3.00	8.00	30.00	125.00
1936	4,400,000	.30	.50	1.00	3.00	8.00	30.00	100.00

FIVE CENTS

GEORGE VI   1937 - 1942

In 1937 Canada introduced new coinage designs for the lower denominations, in keeping with a trend towards modernization begun in 1935 with the silver dollar. The reverse of the five-cent piece bore a beaver on a rock-studded mound of earth rising out of the water. At the left is a log on which the beaver has been chewing. The master tools for this reverse were produced at the Paris Mint because the Royal Mint in London was pressed for time.

Designer & Modeller:
Portrait - T.H. Paget
(H.P. below bust)
Reverse - G.E. Kruger-Gray
(K.G above water at left)
Composition: 1.00 nickel
Weight: 4.54 grams
Diameter: 21.21 mm
Edge: Plain
Die Axes: ↑↑

Date and Mint Mark	Quantity Minted	VG-8	F-12	VF-20	EF-40	AU-50	MS-60
1937 Dot*	4,593,263	.25	.75	2.50	4.00	12.50	25.00
1938	3,898,974	.35	1.25	3.50	12.50	45.00	125.00
1939	5,661,123	.25	.75	2.50	7.50	30.00	75.00
1940	13,920,197	.20	.50	1.50	4.00	15.00	35.00
1941	8,681,785	.20	.50	1.50	5.00	17.50	40.00
1942 Nickel	6,847,544	.20	.50	1.50	5.00	16.00	35.00

* All 1937 5¢ have the dot after the date.

BEAVER DESIGN; TOMBAC COINAGE 1942

Nickel is an important component of stainless steel and other alloys needed for producing war materials, so World War II put a great strain upon Canada's nickel producers. By 1942 it was decided that nickel would have to be suspended as a coinage material for the duration of the war and experiments were initiated to find a substitute metal for the five-cent piece. This led to the adoption of a 12-sided coin made of tombac, a kind of brass. The idea had come from the British 3-penny piece first issued in 1937. The tombac 5¢ was given its shape so that when tarnished it would still not be confused with one-cent pieces.

Designer: Royal Canadian Mint staff,
modifying existing designs
Engraver: Thomas Shingles, modifying
Royal Mint coinage tools
Composition: .88 copper, .12 zinc
Weight: 4.54 grams
Diameter: ca. 21.3 mm (opposite corners)
& ca. 20.0 mm (opposite sides)
Edge: Plain
Die Axes: ↑↑

Date	Quantity Minted	VG-8	F-12	VF-20	EF-40	AU-50	MS-60
1942 Tombac	3,396,234	.75	1.00	1.25	1.60	2.75	5.00

TORCH & V DESIGN; TOMBAC COINAGE 1943

In 1943 a new reverse design came into use for this denomination. Its purpose was to help promote the war effort. The idea for the design came from Churchill's famous "V" sign and the V denomination mark on the U.S. five-cent pieces of 1883-1912. A novel feature was the use of an International Code message meaning, "We Win When We Work Willingly." It was placed along the rim on the reverse instead of denticles. The original master matrix was engraved entirely by hand by Royal Canadian Mint Chief Engraver Thomas Shingles. The obverse was the same as that for 1942, except rim denticles were added.

Designer: Obverse - Thomas Shingles, modifying existing design; Reverse - Thomas Shingles (T.S. at lower right of V and torch)

Engraver: Obverse - Thomas Shingles modifying Royal Mint coinage tools; Reverse - Thomas Shingles

Composition: .88 copper, .12 zinc

Weight: 4.54 grams

Diameter: ca. 21.3 mm (opposite corners) & ca. 20.9 mm (opposite sides)

Edge: Plain

Die Axes: ↑↑

Date	Quantity Minted	VG-8	F-12	VF-20	EF-40	AU-50	MS-60
1943	24,760,256	.35	.50	.75	1.00	2.50	5.00

TORCH & V DESIGN; STEEL COINAGE 1944-1945

War demands for copper and zinc forced a suspension in the use of tombac for the five-cent piece and the institution of plated steel. The steel was plated with nickel and then returned to the plating tank for a very thin plating of chromium. The chromium was hard and helped retard wear. Unfortunately it was necessary to plate the strips prior to the blanks being punched out. This resulted in the edges of the blanks (and hence the coins) being unplated and vulnerable to rusting.

Some collectors have noted steel five-cent pieces which have a dull gray colour instead of the normal bluish-white colour. This is due to some of the strips being plated with nickel only and not nickel and chromium. Such coins do not ordinarily command a significant premium.

Composition: Steel with .0127 mm plating of nickel and .0003 mm plating of chromium

All other statistics are as for the 1943 coinage.

Date	Quantity Minted	VG-8	F-12	VF-20	EF-40	AU-50	MS-60
1944	11,532,784	.20	.30	.50	.85	1.75	3.50
1945	18,893,216	.20	.30	.50	.75	1.75	3.50

BEAVER DESIGN RESUMED; "ET IND: IMP:" IN OBVERSE LEGEND 1946-1947

After the end of World War II, the Mint returned to the issue of nickel five-cent pieces of the beaver design. However, it was decided to retain the 12-sided shape, because it had become popular. The obverse was a continuation of that of 1943-1945.

Designer: Reverse - Thomas Shingles, modifying existing design
Engraver: Reverse - Thomas Shingles, modifying existing coinage tools
Composition: 1.00 nickel
Weight: 4.54 grams
Diameter: ca. 21.3 mm (opposite corners) & ca. 20.9 mm (opposite sides)
Edge: Plain
Die Axes: ↑↑

Date	Quantity Minted	VG-8	F-12	VF-20	EF-40	AU-50	MS-60
1946	6,952,684	.25	.40	.85	3.50	7.00	15.00
1947	7,603,724	.25	.35	.75	2.50	6.00	14.00

MAPLE LEAF ISSUE 1947

The granting of independence to India provided a dilemma for the Royal Canadian Mint in the early part of 1948. The new obverse coinage tools (with "ET IND: IMP:" omitted) would not arrive for several months, yet there was a great need for all denominations of coins. Therefore, the Mint struck coins dated 1947 and bearing the obverse with the outmoded titles. To differentiate this issue from the regular strikings of 1947, a tiny maple leaf was placed after the date.

1947 Maple Leaf Issue, struck in 1948

The physical and chemical specifications are as for the 1946-1947 issues.

Date	Quantity Minted	VG-8	F-12	VF-20	EF-40	AU-50	MS-60
1947 Maple Leaf	9,595,124	.20	.30	.75	2.00	5.00	12.00

MODIFIED OBVERSE LEGEND; BEAVER REVERSE 1948-1950

Following the arrival of the master tools with the new obverse legend lacking "ET IND: IMP:" in 1948, the 1947 Maple Leaf coinage was suspended from production. For the remainder of the year coins were produced with the new obverse and the true date, 1948.

The physical and chemical specifications are as for the 1946-1947 issues.

Date	Quantity Minted	VG-8	F-12	VF-20	EF-40	AU-50	MS-60
1948	1,810,789	.75	1.00	2.00	5.00	12.50	30.00
1949	13,037,090	.20	.25	.50	1.00	3.00	7.00
1950	11,970,520	.20	.25	.50	1.00	3.00	7.00

COMMEMORATIVE FOR ISOLATION & NAMING OF NICKEL 1951

In 1950 plans were made to strike a coin to commemorate the isolation and naming of the element nickel by the Swedish chemist A.F. Cronstedt in 1751. The two Canadian commemorative coins issued up to that time had been silver dollars, but the five-cent piece was selected for use in 1951 because it was the only denomination struck in nickel. The design was chosen from entries submitted to the Mint in an open competition, the first of its type in Canada for a coinage that was actually issued. The winning design depicts a nickel refinery, with low buildings flanking a smoke stack in the centre. The obverse is the same as that for the 1948-1950 issues.

Some members of the public became confused and believed that the dates 1751-1951 should have read 1851-1951. This caused hoarding of these coins in the mistaken belief that they would become extremely valuable.

Designer & Modeller:
    Reverse - Stephen Trenka
    (ST monogram below the building
    at the right)
Composition: 1.00 nickel
Weight: 4.54 grams
Diameter: ca. 21.3 mm (opposite corners)
    & ca. 20.9 mm (opposite sides)
Edge: Plain
Die Axes: ↑↑

Date	Quantity Minted	VG-8	F-12	VF-20	EF-40	AU-50	MS-60
1951 Nickel Commemorative	9,028,507	.20	.25	.45	.65	1.50	2.75

BEAVER DESIGN RESUMED; STEEL COINAGE 1951-1952

The Korean War placed strong demands for nickel, forcing suspended production of the commemorative nickel five-cent piece before the end of 1951. In its place steel coins of the beaver design were struck. It was found during trials that the beaver design was not as easy to strike in steel as in nickel, so new, lower relief coinage tools were prepared for both obverse and reverse. By mistake, a High Relief obverse die was used to strike a small proportion of the 1951 steel coinage, resulting in two varieties for the year. Aside from the difference in relief the High and Low Relief obverses differ in the position of the last A of GRATIA relative to the rim denticles. On the High Relief variety the A points to a rim denticle; on the Low Relief variety it points between denticles. The entire 1952 issue was coined with the Low Relief obverse.

Modeller: Thomas Shingles, modifying existing models
Composition: Steel with .0127 mm plating of nickel and .0003 mm plating of chromium
Weight: 4.54 grams
Diameter: ca. 21.3 mm (opposite corners) & ca. 20.9 mm (opposite sides)
Edge: Plain
Die Axes: ↑↑

A in GRATIA points to a rim denticle

1951 High Relief Obverse

A in GRATIA points between rim denticles

1951 Low Relief Obverse

Date	Quantity Minted	VG-8	F-12	VF-20	EF-40	AU-50	MS-60
1951 High Relief Obverse	4,313,310	20.00	30.00	60.00	125.00	250.00	400.00
1951 Low Relief Obverse	Incl. above	.25	.50	1.00	2.00	4.00	8.00
1952	10,891,148	.25	.40	1.00	2.00	3.00	5.00

FIVE CENTS

ELIZABETH II

1953 to date

STEEL FIVE CENTS (12-SIDED) 1953-1954

Two obverse varieties, termed the No Shoulder Fold and Shoulder Fold obverses, saw use during 1953 (see page 83 for full explanation). On the five-cent piece these varieties are best distinguished on worn coins by observing the styles of the letters in the obverse legends: they are more flared (particularly the I's) on the No Shoulder Fold variety. The reverses combined with the two obverses also show slight differences.

Designer & Modeller:
    Portrait - Mrs. Mary Gillick,
    (M.G. on truncation)
Engraver: No Shoulder Fold Obverse -
    Thomas Shingles, using the
    Gillick portrait model;
    Shoulder Fold Obverse -
    Thomas Shingles, modifying
    existing NSF coinage tools
Composition: Steel with .0127 mm plating
    of nickel and .003 mm
    plating of chromium
Weight: 4.54 grams
Diameter: ca. 21.3 mm (opposite corners)
    & ca. 20.9 mm (opposite sides)
Edge: Plain
Die Axes: ↑↑

No Shoulder Fold Obverse
note flared ends of I's

Shoulder Fold Obverse
note straight-sided I's

Date and Mint Mark	Quantity Minted	VG-8	F-12	VF-20	EF-40	AU-50	MS-60
1953 NSF Obverse	16,635,552	.20	.25	.50	1.00	2.50	5.00
1953 SF Obverse	Incl. above	.20	.25	.75	1.50	3.75	7.00
1954	6,998,662	.25	.50	1.00	1.75	5.00	9.00

NICKEL 12-SIDED COINAGE 1955-1962

The Mint returned to nickel for the five-cent piece in 1955. The reverse for the George VI coinage of 1946-1950 was continued.

Composition: 1.00 nickel

The other specifications are as for the 1953-1954 issues.

Date	Quantity Minted	F-12	VF-20	EF-40	AU-50	MS-60
1955	5,355,028	.25	.50	1.00	3.00	5.50
1956	9,399,854	.20	.25	.50	1.25	2.25
1957	7,387,703	.20	.25	.50	1.25	2.00
1958	7,607,521	.20	.25	.50	1.00	2.00
1959	11,552,523	—	.20	.25	.65	1.00
1960	37,157,433	—	—	.20	.40	.50
1961	47,889,051	—	—	—	—	.35
1962	46,307,305	—	—	—	—	.35

LAUREATED BUST; ROUND COINAGE 1963-1964

For strictly economic reasons the production of round five-cent pieces was resumed in 1963 for the first time since 1942. It was cheaper to make round coins because the collars for the coining presses lasted longer.

Engraver: Thomas Shingles, using existing coining tools
Composition: 1.00 nickel
Weight: 4.54 grams
Diameter: 21.21 mm
Edge: Plain
Die Axes: ↑↑

Date	Quantity Minted	AU-50	MS-60
1963	43,970,320	.20	.30
1964	78,075,068	.20	.25

CROWNED PORTRAIT; MAPLE TWIG REVERSE 1965-1966

A new obverse with the Queen showing more mature facial features and wearing a tiara was introduced on all denominations in 1965.

Designer & Modeller:
  Portrait - Arnold Machin

The physical and chemical specifications are as for the 1963-1964 issues.

Date	Quantity Minted	AU-50	MS-60
1965	84,876,019	.20	.25
1966	27,678,469	.20	.25

COMMEMORATIVE FOR CENTENNIAL OF CONFEDERATION 1967

A reverse design showing a hopping rabbit was selected for the 1967 five-cent piece. It was by Alex Colville, who also designed the reverses of the other Confederation commemoratives issued for circulation. The obverse was a continuation of the 1965-1966 design.

Designer: Reverse - Alex Colville
Modeller: Reverse - Myron Cook

The physical and chemical specifications are as for the 1963-1966 issues.

Date	Quantity Minted	AU-50	MS-60
1967 Confederation Commemorative	36,876,574	.20	.25

BEAVER REVERSE RESUMED; LARGE PORTRAIT 1968-1978

The physical and chemical specifications are the same as the 1963-1967 issues.

Date	Quantity Minted	AU-50	MS-60
1968	99,253,330	—	.20
1969	27,830,229	—	.20
1970	5,726,010	.60	.75
1971	27,312,609	—	.25
1972	62,417,387	—	.20
1973	53,507,435	—	.20
1974	94,704,645	—	.20
1975	138,882,000	—	.20
1976	55,140,213	—	.20
1977	89,120,791	—	.20
1978	137,079,273	—	.20

MODIFIED OBVERSE 1979 - 1980

Beginning on the 1979 coinage and as part of a general standardization of the coinage, the portrait of the Queen was made smaller. The purpose was to make the size of the portrait proportional to the diameter of the coin, regardless of the denomination.

The physical and chemical specifications are as the 1963-1978 issues.

Date	Quantity Minted	MS-60
1979	186,295,825	.20
1980		.20

TEN CENTS

VICTORIA 1870 - 1901

The initial designs for the Victoria ten-cent pieces issued by the Dominion government were identical to the 1858 Province of Canada issue. During the reign, six obverse varieties were used. They differed primarily in the features of the Queen's face. A detailed description and listing by year will be included in a separate catalogue (see INTRODUCTION). Two major varieties of the reverse exist; only in 1891 were both used for the same year's coinage (see below).

Designer, Modeller & Engraver:
Leonard C. Wyon
Composition: .925 silver, .075 copper
Weight: 2.32 grams
Diameter: 18.03 mm
Edge: Reeded
Die Axes: ↑↓

Heaton Mint issues of 1871-1883 and the Mint, Birmingham issue of 1890 have an "H" mint mark on the reverse under the wreath. London Mint strikings have no letter.

VARIETIES 1870

Two styles of 0 appear in the date of the 1870 issue. The Narrow 0 with sides of equal thickness is more common than the Wide 0, on which the right-hand side is thicker.

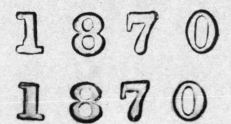

1870 Narrow 0
Sides of equal thickness

1870 Wide 0
Right side is thicker

Date and Mint Mark	Quantity Minted	G-4	VG-8	F-12	VF-20	EF-40	AU-50	MS-60
1870 Narrow 0	1,600,000	6.00	12.00	20.00	60.00	120.00	300.00	600.00
1870 Wide 0	Incl. above	6.50	13.00	25.00	65.00	130.00	325.00	650.00
1871	800,000	8.00	15.00	30.00	65.00	135.00	400.00	700.00
1871H	1,870,000	12.00	20.00	30.00	65.00	150.00	400.00	700.00
1872H	1,000,000	40.00	80.00	135.00	250.00	500.00	1,000.00	1,750.00

MINTAGE FIGURES 1874H & 1875H

Through a clerical error part of the mintage of 1874H-dated coins was assigned to the next year's production figures. Therefore, the mintage figures for the two years, 600,000 and 1,000,000, respectively, have been combined.

Date and Mint Mark	Quantity Minted	G-4	VG-8	F-12	VF-20	EF-40	AU-50	MS-60
1874H	1,600,000	5.00	9.00	18.00	50.00	100.00	300.00	550.00
1875H	Incl. above	100.00	175.00	300.00	500.00	1,500.00	2,500.00	4,000.00
1880H	1,500,000	4.00	8.00	15.00	30.00	75.00	300.00	550.00
1881H	950,000	5.50	10.00	20.00	40.00	100.00	325.00	650.00
1882H	1,000,000	4.00	8.00	15.00	30.00	75.00	300.00	550.00
1883H	300,000	12.50	25.00	50.00	100.00	250.00	600.00	1,100.00
1884	150,000	60.00	125.00	250.00	500.00	1,500.00	2,000.00	4,000.00
1885	400,000	7.00	13.00	30.00	70.00	200.00	500.00	950.00

VARIETIES 1886

For the 1886 coinage three distinctly different styles of 6 were used: a small 6, a large 6 with a point on its tail, and a large 6 with a large knob on its tail.

Photo Not Available

1886 Small 6   1886 Large, Pointed 6   1886 Large, Knobbed 6

Date and Mint Mark	Quantity Minted	G-4	VG-8	F-12	VF-20	EF-40	AU-50	MS-60
1886 Small 6	800,000	7.00	13.00	30.00	70.00	150.00	400.00	700.00
1886 Lg., Pt. 6	Incl. above	6.50	12.50	30.00	70.00	150.00	400.00	700.00
1886 Lg., Knb. 6	Incl. above	6.50	12.50	30.00	70.00	150.00	400.00	700.00
1887	350,000	10.00	20.00	35.00	110.00	300.00	1,000.00	1,700.00
1888	500,000	4.00	6.00	10.00	30.00	70.00	300.00	550.00
1889	600,000	250.00	450.00	800.00	1,500.00	2,500.00	5,000.00	10,000.00
1890H	450,000	6.00	12.00	25.00	60.00	125.00	350.00	700.00

The two major reverse varieties seen on this denomination differ in the number of leaves in the wreath. The first (1870-1881 & 1891) has 21 leaves and the second (1882-1901) has 22 leaves. The 21-leaf reverse in 1891 occurs with small digits in the date, whereas the 22-leaf reverse in 1891 has a large date.

One 1891 large date die was carried over into 1892 and the 1 was overdated with a 2. Aside from the overpunching, the 1892 over 1 differs from the non-overdate 1892's in the style of the 9; the overdate has the large 9 of the 22 leaves, 1891 and the non-overdates have the small 9 of the 21 leaves, 1891 variety.

Dating varieties continued into 1893. In that year one or two dies were dated with a large 9 and round-top 3, while the rest were dated with a medium 9 and a flat-top 3.

1891 21 Leaves, Small Date   1891 22 Leaves, Large Date

1892 2 over 1, Large 9   1892 Normal Date, Small 9

1893 Flat-top 3, Medium 9   1893 Round-top 3, Large 9
                                    The 3 on this variety is often weakly struck.

Date	Quantity Minted	G-4	VG-8	F-12	VF-20	EF-40	AU-50	MS-60
1891 21 Lvs.	800,000	7.00	13.00	25.00	60.00	125.00	275.00	600.00
1891 22 Lvs.	Incl. above	7.00	13.00	25.00	60.00	125.00	300.00	650.00
1892 2 over 1	520,000	4.50	9.00	20.00	50.00	100.00	250.00	500.00
1892 Normal	Incl. above	4.50	9.00	20.00	50.00	100.00	250.00	500.00
1893 F-Top 3	500,000	7.00	14.00	30.00	70.00	125.00	300.00	600.00
1893 R-top 3	Incl. above	300.00	500.00	1,000.00	2,000.00	5,000.00	10,000.00	15,000.00
1894	500,000	4.50	9.00	15.00	30.00	75.00	250.00	500.00
1896	650,000	3.50	7.00	14.00	30.00	75.00	225.00	450.00
1898	720,000	3.50	7.00	14.00	30.00	75.00	250.00	500.00

VARIETIES 1899

During the production of the 1899 ten-cent pieces, two styles of 9 were used for dating the dies: a small, narrow 9 and a large, wide 9. The upper centre of the wide 9 is almost round, compared with the tall, square centre of the narrow 9.

1899 Small 9's   1899 Large 9's

Date	Quantity Minted	G-4	VG-8	F-12	VF-20	EF-40	AU-50	MS-60
1899 Small 9's	1,200,000	3.00	6.00	10.00	25.00	70.00	200.00	400.00
1899 Large 9's	Incl. above	5.00	10.00	20.00	50.00	125.00	350.00	700.00
1900	1,100,000	2.50	4.50	9.00	25.00	65.00	175.00	375.00
1901	1,200,000	2.50	4.50	9.00	25.00	65.00	175.00	375.00

TEN CENTS

EDWARD VII

1902 - 1910

The reverse first employed for the ten-cent pieces of this reign was adapted from the 22-leaf Victorian reverse. The Imperial State crown replaced the St. Edward's crown at the top and the word "CANADA" was transferred from the obverse legend.

Designer & Modeller:
Obverse - G.W. DeSaulles
(DES. under the bust);
Broad Leaves Reverse (1909-10) -
W.H.J. Blakemore
Engraver: Victorian Leaves Reverse
(1902-09) - G.W. DeSaulles
Composition: .925 silver, .075 copper
Weight: 2.32 grams (1902-10);
2.33 grams (1910)
Diameter: 18.03 mm
Edge: Reeded
Die Axes: ↑↑ (1902-07);
↑↓ (1908-10)

The Mint, Birmingham issues (1902-1903) have an "H" mint mark on the reverse under the wreath. London Mint issues have no letter.

Date and Mint Mark	Quantity Minted	G-4	VG-8	F-12	VF-20	EF-40	AU-50	MS-60
1902	720,000	2.50	5.00	10.00	20.00	60.00	200.00	400.00
1902H	1,100,000	2.50	4.50	9.00	18.00	50.00	135.00	275.00
1903	500,000	4.00	8.00	18.00	50.00	125.00	300.00	600.00
1903H	1,320,000	2.50	4.50	9.00	18.00	50.00	175.00	350.00
1904	1,000,000	4.00	8.00	20.00	50.00	110.00	225.00	450.00
1905	1,000,000	3.00	6.00	15.00	40.00	90.00	250.00	500.00
1906	1,700,000	2.50	5.00	10.00	25.00	60.00	200.00	400.00
1907	2,620,000	2.25	4.50	9.00	20.00	40.00	175.00	350.00
1908	776,666	3.00	6.00	11.00	22.00	55.00	175.00	350.00

VARIETIES 1909

In 1909 an entirely new model was prepared for this denomination. The variety thus created has been called the Broad Leaves variety because of its broad leaves with strong, detailed venation.

1909 Victorian Leaves

1909 Broad Leaves

Date	Quantity Minted	G-4	VG-8	F-12	VF-20	EF-40	AU-50	MS-60
1909 Victorian Leaves	1,697,200	3.00	5.00	10.00	25.00	60.00	225.00	450.00
1909 Broad Leaves	Incl. above	3.50	6.00	12.00	30.00	70.00	275.00	550.00
1910	4,468,331	2.25	3.00	6.00	12.00	40.00	160.00	325.00

TEN CENTS

GEORGE V

"GODLESS" OBVERSE 1911

The obverse combined with the 1911 reverse aroused criticism because it lacked reference to the King's ruling "by the grace of God." The coinage tools were modified during 1911 and a new legend containing the Latin abbreviation "DEI GRA:" appeared on the 1912 and subsequent issues. The first reverse was a continuation of the Broad Leaves design introduced in 1909. It was replaced during 1913 (see below).

Designer & Modeller:
Portrait - Sir E.B. MacKennal (B.M. on truncation); Small Leaves Reverse - W.H.J. Blakemore
Composition: .925 silver, .075 copper
Weight: 2.33 grams
Diameter: 18.03 mm
Edge: Reeded
Die Axes: ↑↑

Date	Quantity Minted	G-4	VG-8	F-12	VF-20	EF-40	AU-50	MS-60
1911	2,737,584	6.00	12.00	18.00	35.00	125.00	225.00	450.00

MODIFIED OBVERSE LEGEND 1912-1936

1912-1919
Composition: .925 silver, .075 copper;
1920-1936
.800 silver, .200 copper

The physical specifications are as for the 1911 issue.

Date	Quantity Minted	G-4	VG-8	F-12	VF-20	EF-40	AU-50	MS-60
1912	3,235,557	—	2.50	4.50	8.00	20.00	100.00	250.00

The reverse that replaced the Broad Leaves design during 1913 has smaller leaves with less venation. It is from a completely new model.

1913 Broad Leaves

1913 Small Leaves

Date	Quantity Minted	G-4	VG-8	F-12	VF-20	EF-40	AU-50	MS-60
1913 Broad Leaves	3,613,937	50.00	125.00	175.00	450.00	900.00	2,000.00	3,500.00
1913 Small Leaves	Incl. above	—	2.50	3.50	6.00	18.00	100.00	250.00
1914	2,549,811	—	2.50	4.00	8.00	22.00	100.00	300.00
1915	688,057	4.00	7.00	14.00	50.00	200.00	500.00	1,200.00
1916	4,218,114	—	2.50	3.50	7.00	16.00	100.00	300.00
1917	5,011,988	—	2.50	4.00	6.00	14.00	60.00	150.00
1918	5,133,602	—	2.25	4.00	6.00	14.00	60.00	150.00
1919	7,877,722	—	2.25	4.00	6.00	14.00	60.00	150.00
1920	6,305,345	—	2.25	4.00	6.00	14.00	60.00	150.00
1921	2,469,562	—	2.50	4.00	7.00	17.00	75.00	225.00
1928	2,458,602	—	2.50	4.00	7.00	13.00	65.00	175.00
1929	3,253,888	—	2.50	4.00	7.00	13.00	75.00	225.00
1930	1,831,043	—	2.50	4.25	7.00	15.00	75.00	225.00
1931	2,067,421	—	2.50	5.00	7.00	15.00	75.00	200.00
1932	1,154,317	—	2.50	5.00	9.00	18.00	85.00	250.00
1933	672,368	2.00	3.50	7.00	13.00	40.00	125.00	300.00
1934	409,067	2.25	4.00	7.00	14.00	40.00	200.00	500.00
1935	384,056	2.50	5.00	8.00	20.00	50.00	300.00	750.00
1936	2,460,871	—	2.50	3.50	6.00	13.00	50.00	200.00

TEN CENTS

COINAGE USING GEORGE V DIES   1936

Early in 1937, while the Royal Canadian Mint was awaiting the arrival of the master tools for the new coinage for George VI, an emergency coinage of ten-cent pieces dated 1936 and from George V dies is said to have taken place. To mark the special nature of the coinage the dies bore a small raised dot on the reverse under the wreath.

Although the mintage of the 1936 dot variety is claimed to be nearly 200,000, only four examples seem to survive today. All are specimen strikes, adding to the suspicion that circulation strikes were either never produced or were all melted. No genuine circulation strike has been confirmed.

The physical and chemical specifications are as for the 1911-1936 issues.

1936 With Raised Dot Below Date, struck in 1937

Date	Quantity Minted	SPECIMEN
1936 Dot	191,237	only four known to exist

COINAGE IN NAME OF GEORGE VI   1937-1952

The new reverse design introduced in 1937 was destined to become one of the most loved and most controversial of Canada's coinage designs. It features a "fishing schooner under sail," as the official proclamation states. Proud Nova Scotians, believing the ship represents the famous fishing and racing schooner "Bluenose" have continually pressed for official acknowledgment. Available information indicates that the designer, Emmanuel Hahn, used that ship as his primary model, but that strictly speaking the design must be considered a composite. The original master tools for the reverse were prepared at the Paris Mint. To improve the wearing qualities of the date, larger size digits were introduced in 1938.

"ET IND: IMP:" IN OBVERSE LEGEND   1937-1947

The initial obverse bore a legend containing the Latin abbreviation "ET IND: IMP:" to indicate that the King was the Emperor of India.

Designer & Modeller:
  Portrait - T.H. Paget
  (H.P. below bust);
  Reverse - Emmanuel Hahn
  (H above waves at left)
Composition: .800 silver, .200 copper
Weight: 2.33 grams
Diameter: 18.03 mm
Edge: Reeded
Die Axes: ↑↑

Date	Quantity Minted	VG-8	F-12	VF-20	EF-40	AU-50	MS-60
1937	2,500,095	4.00	6.00	8.00	14.00	20.00	40.00
1938	4,197,323	3.00	4.00	7.00	12.00	50.00	175.00
1939	5,501,748	3.00	4.00	6.00	12.00	30.00	150.00
1940	16,526,470	2.50	3.00	5.00	12.50	25.00	50.00
1941	8,716,386	2.50	3.50	6.50	13.00	60.00	150.00
1942	10,214,011	2.50	3.00	5.00	10.00	35.00	80.00
1943	21,143,229	2.50	3.00	5.00	8.00	17.50	40.00
1944	9,383,582	2.50	3.00	6.00	8.00	25.00	75.00
1945	10,979,570	2.50	3.00	5.00	7.00	15.00	35.00
1946	6,300,066	2.50	3.00	5.00	9.00	30.00	70.00
1947	4,431,926	2.50	3.00	6.00	10.00	40.00	100.00

MAPLE LEAF ISSUE 1947

The granting of independence to India posed a problem for the Royal Canadian Mint in the early part of 1948. The new obverse coinage tools (with the Latin phrase "ET IND: IMP:" omitted to indicate that the King was no longer the Emperor of India) would not arrive for several months, yet there was a need for all denominations of coins. The Mint satisfied the demand by striking coins dated 1947 bearing the obverse with the outmoded titles. To differentiate this issue from the regular strikings of 1947, a tiny maple leaf was placed after the date.

1947 Maple Leaf Issue,
struck in 1948

Date	Quantity Minted	VG-8	F-12	VF-20	EF-40	AU-50	MS-60
1947 Maple Leaf	9,638,793	2.50	3.00	5.00	7.00	12.00	30.00

MODIFIED OBVERSE LEGEND 1948-1952

Following the arrival of the master tools with the obverse legend omitting "ET IND: IMP:" production of the 1947 Maple Leaf coinage was suspended. For the remainder of the year coins were produced with the new obverse and the true date, 1948. This obverse was employed for the rest of the reign.

Photo Not
Available

The physical and chemical specifications are as for the 1937-1947 issues.

Date	Quantity Minted	VG-8	F-12	VF-20	EF-40	AU-50	MS-60
1948	422,741	7.00	9.00	15.00	40.00	60.00	150.00
1949	11,336,172	2.50	3.00	3.50	5.00	7.00	18.00
1950	17,823,075	2.50	3.00	3.50	4.50	6.00	15.00
1951	15,079,265	2.50	3.00	3.50	4.50	6.00	15.00
1952	10,474,455	2.50	3.00	3.50	4.50	6.00	15.00

TEN CENTS

LAUREATED PORTRAIT 1953-1964

Two obverse varieties, termed the No Shoulder Fold and the Shoulder Fold obverses, saw use during 1953 (see page 83 for full explanation). On heavily circulated ten-cent pieces these varieties are most easily distinguished by observing the lettering styles in the legend. The No Shoulder Fold obverse has thicker letters with more flared ends (note the I's). The use of the George VI reverse was continued.

Designer & Modeller:
    Portrait - Mrs. Mary Gillick.
    (M.G. on truncation)
Engraver: No Shoulder Fold Obverse -
    Thomas Shingles, using the
    Gillick portrait model;
    Shoulder Fold Obverse -
    Thomas Shingles, modifying
    existing NSF coinage tools
composition: .800 silver, .200 copper
Weight: 2.33 grams
Diameter: 18.03 mm
Edge: Reeded
Die Axes: ↑↑

No Shoulder Fold Obverse 1953,
note the flared ends of the letters

Shoulder Fold Obverse 1953-1954,
the ends of letters are not as flared

Date		Quantity Minted	VG-8	F-12	VF-20	EF-40	AU-50	MS-60
1953	No Shoulder Fold	17,706,395	2.50	3.00	3.50	4.00	5.00	10.00
1953	Shoulder Fold	Incl. above	2.50	3.00	4.00	5.00	6.00	15.00
1954		4,493,150	2.50	3.00	4.00	5.00	8.00	20.00
1955		12,237,294	—	2.00	3.00	4.00	5.00	7.50
1956		16,732,844	—	2.00	2.75	3.50	4.00	6.00
1957		16,110,229	—	—	2.00	2.25	2.50	4.00
1958		10,621,236	—	—	2.00	2.25	2.50	4.00
1959		19,691,433	—	—	—	—	—	3.00
1960		45,446,835	—	—	—	—	—	3.00
1961		26,850,859	—	—	—	—	—	2.50
1962		41,864,335	—	—	—	—	—	2.50
1963		41,916,208	—	—	—	—	—	2.50
1964		49,518,549	—	—	—	—	—	2.50

CROWNED PORTRAIT; SCHOONER REVERSE 1965-1966

A new obverse with the Queen showing more mature facial features and wearing a tiara was introduced on all denominations in 1965.

Designer & Modeller:
  Portrait - Arnold Machin

The physical and chemical specifications are as the 1953-1964 issues.

Date	Quantity Minted	MS-60
1965	56,965,392	2.50
1966	34,330,199	2.50

COMMEMORATIVE FOR CENTENNIAL OF CONFEDERATION 1967

A reverse design showing a mackerel was chosen as part of the group of commemorative designs for the centennial of Confederation. During the year, the rising price of silver forced a reduction in the silver content to .500 from .800. The two varieties are not distinguishable by eye. The obverse is the same as on the 1965-1966 issues.

Designer: Reverse - Alex Colville
Modeller: Reverse - Myron Cook
Composition: .800 silver, .200 copper, or
.500 silver, .500 copper

The other physical specifications are as for the 1965-1966 issues.

Date	Quantity Minted	MS-60
1967 .800 silver	32,309,135	2.50
1967 .500 silver	30,689,080	2.50

LARGE FISHING SCHOONER REVERSE RESUMED   1968-1969

During 1968 the use of silver in circulation coins was discontinued. Nickel was used in its place. The nickel coins are darker and are attracted to a magnet. In addition about half of the 1968 nickel ten-cent pieces were coined at the Philadelphia Mint in the United States because of the pressure of other work at the Royal Canadian Mint. The Philadelphia and Ottawa issues differ only in the number and shape of the grooves in the edge of the coins; the grooves have square bottoms on the Philadelphia coins and V-shaped bottoms on the Ottawa strikings. The 1969 Large Schooner variety is rare. A small quantity was struck early in the year before it was decided to replace it. The Large Schooner variety also has a large date (see the Small Schooner variety below). The obverse is as on the 1965-1967 issues.

Composition: .500 silver, .500 copper
(1968);
1.00 nickel (1968-69)

The physical specifications are as for the 1965-1967 issues.

1969 Large Schooner, Large Date

Philadelphia Mint
edge grooves have flat bottoms

Royal Canadian Mint
edge grooves have V-shaped bottoms

Date and Mint Mark	Quantity Minted	MS-60
1968 .500 silver	70,460,000	2.00
1968 Nickel, Philadelphia Mint	85,170,000	.35
1968 Nickel, Ottawa Mint	87,412,930	.35
1969 Large Schooner	Incl. below	RARE

SMALL SCHOONER REVERSE: LARGE PORTRAIT 1969-1978

The new reverse introduced early in the 1969 issue was from a completely redone model in which the ship was smaller and the date noticeably smaller. The change was made after it was discovered the original design had deteriorated so much that it was no longer usable.

Designer & Modeller:
    Reverse - Myron Cook, copying
    previous design

The physical and chemical specifications are as for the 1968-1969 Large Schooner nickel issues.

1969 Small Schooner, Small Date

Date	Quantity Minted	MS-60
1969 Small Schooner	55,833,929	.90
1970	5,249,296	.35
1971	41,016,968	.35
1972	60,169,387	.35
1973	167,715,435	.35
1974	201,566,565	.35
1975	207,680,000	.35
1976	95,018,533	.35
1977	128,452,206	.30
1978	170,366,431	.30

MODIFIED OBVERSE 1979-1980

With the 1979 issue a general standardization of the coinage was started. The portrait of the Queen was reduced to make it proportional to the diameter of the coin, regardless of the denomination.

Photo Not
Available

The physical and chemical specifications are as for the 1968-1978 issues.

Date	Quantity Minted	MS-60
1979	236,910,479	.30
1980		.30

TWENTY-FIVE CENTS

VICTORIA

1870 - 1901

The Province of Canada did not issue this denomination so new coinage tools were required for the Dominion of Canada issue. During Victoria's reign, five obverse and two reverse device varieties were employed. Their detailed description and listing by year will be included in a separate catalogue (see INTRODUCTION). The basic design for the reverse is the same as all other silver denominations: crossed boughs of Sweet Maple, tied at the bottom by a ribbon and surmounted by St. Edward's crown.

Designer, Modeller & Engraver:
        Leonard C. Wyon
Composition: .925 silver, .075 copper
Weight: 5.81 grams
Diameter: 23.62 mm
Edge: Reeded
Die Axes: ↑↓

Heaton Mint issues of 1871-1883 and the Mint, Birmingham issue of 1890 have an "H" mint mark on the reverse under the wreath. London Mint strikings have no letter.

Date and Mint Mark	Quantity Minted	G-4	VG-8	F-12	VF-20	EF-40	AU-50	MS-60
1870	900,000	7.00	12.00	22.00	60.00	150.00	500.00	1,000.00
1871	400,000	8.00	15.00	30.00	65.00	275.00	750.00	1,500.00
1871H	748,000	7.50	15.00	25.00	65.00	250.00	750.00	1,500.00
1872H	2,240,000	5.00	8.00	16.00	30.00	100.00	500.00	1,000.00

MINTAGE FIGURES 1874H & 1875H

Through a clerical error part of the mintage of 1874H-dated coins was assigned to the next year's production figures. Therefore the mintage figures for the two years, 1,600,000 and 1,000,000, respectively, have been combined.

Date and Mint Mark	Quantity Minted	G-4	VG-8	F-12	VF-20	EF-40	AU-50	MS-60
1874H	2,600,000	—	8.00	16.00	30.00	100.00	500.00	1,000.00
1875H	Incl. above	125.00	200.00	500.00	1,200.00	2,500.00	4,500.00	9,000.00

VARIETIES 1880H

Two styles of 0 were utilized for dating the dies for the 1880 issue of this denomination. Both the Narrow 0 and the Wide 0 occur alone, but in addition there is a scarce variety with the Narrow 0 punched over the Wide 0. Since the Narrow over Wide 0 variety looks like the plain, Wide 0 when it is worn, it is not listed separately and is considered part of the Wide 0 group.

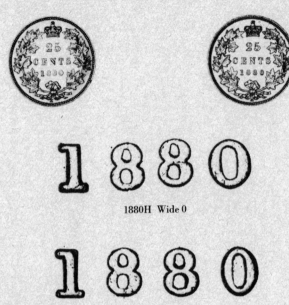

1880H Wide 0

1880H Narrow 0

Date and Mint Mark	Quantity Minted	G-4	VG-8	F-12	VF-20	EF-40	AU-50	MS-60
1880H Wide 0	400,000	50.00	80.00	150.00	400.00	800.00	2,000.00	4,000.00
1880H Narrow 0	Incl. above	12.00	20.00	35.00	100.00	350.00	1,000.00	2,000.00
1881H	820,000	7.00	12.00	25.00	80.00	300.00	800.00	1,600.00
1882H	600,000	8.00	15.00	30.00	90.00	350.00	850.00	1,700.00
1883H	960,000	6.00	10.00	20.00	50.00	200.00	750.00	1,500.00
1885	192,000	45.00	75.00	125.00	300.00	900.00	1,500.00	3,000.00

VARIETIES 1886

A very interesting and long unrecognized overdate occurs on the 1886 twenty-five cents. The overdate 1886/3 seems unlikely in view of the fact that the 1885 date came in between and the 1883 coins were all produced at The Mint, Birmingham with the H mint mark; however, in an article to be published soon it is proved conclusively that the overdate here illustrated is indeed 6/3.

Date and Mint Mark	Quantity Minted	G-4	VG-8	F-12	VF-20	EF-40	AU-50	MS-60
1886 6 over 3	540,000	7.00	12.00	25.00	100.00	300.00	1,200.00	2,000.00
1886 Normal Date	Incl. above	7.00	12.00	25.00	100.00	300.00	1,200.00	2,000.00
1887	100,000	45.00	75.00	150.00	300.00	900.00	2,000.00	4,000.00
1888	400,000	7.00	12.50	25.00	75.00	200.00	600.00	1,200.00
1889	66,324	50.00	75.00	150.00	350.00	1,000.00	2,250.00	4,500.00
1890H	200,000	9.00	18.00	35.00	100.00	300.00	1,000.00	2,000.00
1891	120,000	45.00	75.00	100.00	300.00	600.00	1,250.00	2,500.00
1892	510,000	6.00	12.00	22.00	60.00	150.00	700.00	1,400.00
1893	100,000	25.00	40.00	80.00	250.00	500.00	1,250.00	2,500.00
1894	220,000	7.00	12.00	24.00	65.00	175.00	750.00	1,500.00
1899	415,580	5.00	7.50	11.00	25.00	100.00	450.00	1,000.00
1900	1,320,000	—	6.00	10.00	22.00	60.00	375.00	750.00
1901	640,000	—	7.00	11.00	25.00	75.00	425.00	850.00

TWENTY-FIVE CENTS

EDWARD VII   1902 - 1910

SMALL CROWN REVERSE   1902-1905

The initial reverse for the Edward VII coins of this denomination has an almost unaltered wreath from the Victorian issues coupled with a small Imperial State crown and a new legend containing "CANADA" (it was formerly on the obverse).

Designer & Modeller:
    Obverse - G.W. DeSaulles
    (DES. under the bust)
Engraver: Small Crown Reverse -
    G.W. DeSaulles
Composition: .925 silver, .075 copper
Weight: 5.81 grams
Diameter: 23.62 mm
Edge: Reeded
Die Axes: ↑↓

The Mint, Birmingham issue of 1902 has an "H" mint mark on the reverse under the wreath. London Mint issues have no letter.

Date and Mint Mark	Quantity Minted	G-4	VG-8	F-12	VF-20	EF-40	AU-50	MS-60
1902	464,000	5.00	8.00	14.00	35.00	85.00	400.00	900.00
1902H	800,000	—	6.00	11.00	30.00	75.00	350.00	750.00
1903	846,150	5.00	8.00	18.00	50.00	125.00	450.00	1,000.00
1904	400,000	7.00	14.00	30.00	80.00	200.00	750.00	1,500.00
1905	800,000	5.00	9.00	18.00	50.00	125.00	600.00	1,250.00

LARGE CROWN REVERSE 1906-1910

The reverse for the 1906 coinage was modified to improve die life and impart a better overall appearance to the coins. The wreath was extensively retouched and a larger crown was placed at the top.

Engraver: Reverse - W.H.J. Blakemore
Weight: 5.81 grams (1906-10);
        5.83 grams (1910)
Die Axes: ↑↓ (1906-07);
        ↑↑ (1908-10)

The other specifications are as the 1902-05 issues.

Date	Quantity Minted	G-4	VG-8	F-12	VF-20	EF-40	AU-50	MS-60
1906	1,237,843	5.00	9.00	18.00	40.00	100.00	375.00	800.00
1907	2,088,000	5.00	9.00	18.00	40.00	100.00	300.00	750.00
1908	495,016	6.00	10.00	20.00	50.00	125.00	375.00	800.00
1909	1,335,929	5.00	7.50	12.00	35.00	125.00	350.00	850.00
1910	3,577,569	5.00	7.00	11.00	25.00	75.00	250.00	700.00

TWENTY-FIVE CENTS

GEORGE V

1911 - 1936

"GODLESS" OBVERSE 1911

    The obverse issued on the 1911 coins provoked public outcry because it lacked reference to the King's ruling "by the grace of God." The coinage tools were modified during the year and a new legend including the Latin abbreviation "DEI GRA:" appeared on the 1912 and subsequent issues. The reverse was a continuation of the Large Crown variety of Edward VII.

Designer & Modeller:
    Portrait - Sir E.B. MacKennal
    (B.M. on truncation)
Composition: .925 silver, .075 copper
Weight: 5.83 grams
Diameter: 230.62 mm
Edge: Reeded
Die Axes: ↑↑

Date	Quantity Minted	G-4	VG-8	F-12	VF-20	EF-40	AU-50	MS-60
1911	1,721,341	9.00	15.00	35.00	85.00	200.00	500.00	1,000.00

MODIFIED OBVERSE LEGEND 1912-1936

1912-1919
Composition: .925 silver, .075 copper;
1920-1936
.800 silver, .200 copper

The physical specifications are as for the 1911 issue.

Date	Quantity Minted	G-4	VG-8	F-12	VF-20	EF-40	AU-50	MS-60
1912	2,544,199	—	5.00	7.00	18.00	60.00	200.00	600.00
1913	2,213,595	—	5.00	7.00	18.00	55.00	175.00	500.00
1914	1,215,397	—	6.00	8.00	20.00	65.00	300.00	800.00
1915	242,382	7.50	15.00	30.00	150.00	500.00	1,250.00	2,500.00
1916	1,462,566	—	5.00	8.00	20.00	50.00	165.00	600.00
1917	3,365,644	—	—	5.00	15.00	50.00	150.00	400.00
1918	4,175,649	—	—	5.00	15.00	50.00	150.00	400.00
1919	5,852,262*	—	—	5.00	15.00	50.00	150.00	400.00
1920	1,975,278	—	—	6.00	20.00	60.00	150.00	500.00
1921	597,337	6.00	10.00	25.00	75.00	250.00	1,000.00	2,000.00
1927	468,096	12.50	25.00	55.00	125.00	350.00	1,100.00	2,200.00
1928	2,114,178	—	—	6.50	15.00	60.00	200.00	600.00
1929	2,690,562	—	—	6.50	15.00	60.00	200.00	600.00
1930	968,748	—	5.00	7.00	20.00	75.00	250.00	700.00
1931	537,815	—	6.00	9.00	25.00	80.00	300.00	800.00
1932	537,994	—	6.50	10.00	30.00	100.00	325.00	850.00
1933	421,282	—	6.50	10.00	30.00	100.00	325.00	850.00
1934	384,350	—	6.50	10.00	30.00	100.00	350.00	900.00
1935	537,772	—	6.00	9.00	25.00	85.00	300.00	800.00
1936	972,094	—	4.50	6.00	15.00	60.00	125.00	400.00

*51,494 25¢ pieces, .925 fine and presumably all dated 1919, were melted in 1920.

TWENTY-FIVE CENTS

GEORGE VI   **1937 - 1952**

COINAGE USING GEORGE V DIES 1936

Early in 1937, while the Royal Canadian Mint was awaiting the arrival of the master tools for the new coinage for George VI, an emergency issue of twenty-five cent pieces occured to satisfy urgent demands for this denomination. To mark the special nature of the coinage the dies bore a small raised dot on the reverse under the wreath. That such an emergency issue even took place was generally not known until 1940, when collectors began noticing that some of the twenty-five cent pieces dated 1936 had a dot under the wreath. It was learned that supposedly one and ten-cent pieces were issued also. But no circulated examples of the two latter denominations have been proved genuine.

The physical and chemical specifications are as for the 1911-1936 issues.

1936 With Raised Dot Below Date
struck in 1937

Date	Quantity Minted	G-4	VG-8	F-12	VF-20	EF-40	AU-50	MS-60
1936 Dot	153,322	17.50	35.00	75.00	350.00	700.00	1,000.00	2,000.00

COINAGE IN NAME OF GEORGE VI 1937-1952

The design chosen for the reverse of the new George VI coinage in 1937 was Emmanuel Hahn's caribou head. This design was part of the government's program of modernizing the coinage. The original master tools were prepared at the Paris Mint due to a heavy work load at the Royal Mint in London at that time.

"ET IND: IMP:" IN OBVERSE LEGEND 1937-1947

The initial obverse bore a legend containing an abbreviation for the Latin phrase, ET INDAE IMPERATOR, meaning "and Emperor of India," referring to the fact that the British monarch had held that position since Queen Victoria was made Empress of India in 1876.

Designer & Modeller:
Portrait - T.H. Paget
(H.P. below bust);
Reverse - Emmanuel Hahn
(H in front of caribou's neck at bottom)
Composition: .800 silver, .200 copper
Weight: 5.83 grams
Diameter: 23.62 mm
Edge: Reeded
Die Axes: ↑↑

Date	Quantity Minted	F-12	VF-20	EF-40	AU-50	MS-60
1937	2,690,176	5.50	7.00	12.00	25.00	40.00
1938	3,149,245	5.50	8.00	15.00	90.00	175.00
1939	3,532,495	5.50	10.00	15.00	90.00	175.00
1940	9,583,650	5.00	6.00	10.00	25.00	60.00
1941	6,654,672	5.00	6.00	10.00	25.00	60.00
1942	6,935,871	5.00	6.00	10.00	25.00	60.00
1943	13,559,575	5.00	6.00	8.00	25.00	50.00
1944	7,216,237	5.00	6.00	10.00	50.00	100.00
1945	5,296,495	5.00	6.00	8.00	30.00	50.00
1946	2,210,810	5.00	8.00	20.00	60.00	125.00
1947	1,524,554	5.00	8.00	20.00	90.00	175.00

MAPLE LEAF ISSUE 1947

In early 1948 the Royal Canadian Mint was faced with a problem resulting from India's recent independence. The new obverse coinage tools, with the Latin abbreviation "ET IND: IMP:" omitted to indicate that the King's titles had changed, would not arrive for several months, yet there was a great need for all denominations of coins. The Mint satisfied the demand by striking coins dated 1947 and bearing outmoded titles on the obverse. To distinguish this issue from the regular strikings of 1947, a tiny maple leaf was placed after the date.

1947 Maple Leaf Issue
struck in 1948

Date	Quantity Minted	F-12	VF-20	EF-40	AU-50	MS-60
1947 Maple Leaf	4,393,938	5.00	6.00	7.00	20.00	40.00

MODIFIED OBVERSE LEGEND 1948-1952

Following the arrival of the master tools with the new obverse legend lacking "ET IND: IMP:" in 1948, production of the 1947 Maple Leaf coinage was suspended. For the remainder of the year coins were produced with the new obverse and the true date, 1948.

The physical and chemical specifications
are as for the 1937-1947 issues.

Date	Quantity Minted	F-12	VF-20	EF-40	AU-50	MS-60
1948	2,564,424	5.00	8.00	20.00	50.00	135.00
1949	7,988,830	5.00	6.00	8.00	12.00	25.00
1950	9,673,335	5.00	6.00	7.00	10.00	20.00

VARIETIES 1951-1952

In an attempt to improve the appearance of the obverse of this denomination a fresh reduction was made to produce an obverse with a slightly larger, lower relief portrait. Both varieties were used in 1951 and 1952. Aside from the difference in relief and the size of the portrait, the two varieties can be distinguished since the High Relief variety has a plain lettering style in the legend and the first A in GRATIA points to a rim denticle. On the Low Relief variety the letters are more flared and the first A in GRATIA points between rim denticles.

High Relief Obverse

Low Relief Obverse

Date	Quantity Minted	F-12	VF-20	EF-40	AU-50	MS-60
1951 High Relief Obverse	Incl. below	3.00	4.00	5.00	8.00	18.00
1951 Low Relief Obverse	8,290,719	3.00	4.00	5.00	8.00	18.00
1952 High Relief Obverse	Incl. below	3.00	4.00	5.00	8.00	18.00
1952 Low Relief Obverse	8,859,642	3.00	4.00	5.00	8.00	18.00

TWENTY-FIVE CENTS

ELIZABETH II   **1953 to date**

LAUREATED PORTRAIT 1953-1964

Two obverse varieties, called the No Shoulder Fold and Shoulder Fold obverses, saw use during 1953 (see page 83 for full explanation). On the twenty-five cents these obverses are combined with reverses that are readily distinguishable. The No Shoulder Fold obverse comes with a Large Date reverse (carried over from George VI) and the Shoulder Fold obverse was used with a Small Date reverse.

Designer & Modeller:
    Portrait - Mrs. Mary Gillick
    (M.G. on truncation);
    Small Date Reverse - Thomas
    Shingles, modifying existing
    models
Engraver: No Shoulder Fold Obverse -
    Thomas Shingles, using the
    Gillick portrait model;
    Shoulder Fold Obverse -
    Thomas Shingles, modifying
    existing NSF coinage tools
Composition: .800 silver, .200 copper
Diameter: 23.62 mm (1953 Lg. Date);
    23.88 mm (1953 Sm. Date - '64)
Edge: Reeded
Die Axes: ↑↑

1953 No Shoulder Fold Obverse, Large Date Reverse

1953 Shoulder Fold Obverse, Small Date Reverse

Date	Quantity Minted	F-12	VF-20	EF-40	AU-50	MS-60
1953 Large Date, NSF	10,456,769	5.00	6.00	7.00	9.00	15.00
1953 Small Date, SF	Incl. above	5.00	6.00	7.00	9.00	16.00
1954	2,318,891	5.00	8.00	20.00	40.00	70.00
1955	9,552,505	5.00	6.00	7.00	9.00	14.00
1956	11,269,353	—	—	—	5.00	8.00
1957	12,770,190	—	—	—	5.00	7.00
1958	9,336,910	—	—	—	—	6.00
1959	13,503,461	—	—	—	—	6.00
1960	22,835,327	—	—	—	—	5.00
1961	18,164,368	—	—	—	—	5.00
1962	29,559,266	—	—	—	—	5.00
1963	21,180,652	—	—	—	—	5.00
1964	36,479,343	—	—	—	—	5.00

CROWNED PORTRAIT; CARIBOU REVERSE 1965-1966

A new obverse with the Queen showing more mature facial features and wearing a tiara was introduced on all denominations in 1965.

Designer & Modeller:
  Portrait - Arnold Machin

The physical and chemical specifications are as the 1954-1964 issues.

Date	Quantity Minted	MS-60
1965	44,708,869	5.00
1966	25,626,315	5.00

COMMEMORATIVE FOR CENTENNIAL OF CONFEDERATION 1967

A reverse design featuring a walking wildcat (bobcat) was selected as part of the commemorative set of coins for this year. During the year, the rising price of silver entailed reducing the silver content from .800 to .500. The two varieties are not distinguishable by eye.

Designer: Reverse - Alex Colville
Modeller: Reverse - Myron Cook
Composition: .800 silver, .200 copper, or
.500 silver, .500 copper

The other physical specifications are as for the 1965-1966 issues.

Date	Quantity Minted	EF-40	AU-50	MS-60
1967 Commemorative, .800 silver	49,136,303	3.00	4.00	6.00
1967 Commemorative, .500 silver	Incl. above	3.00	4.00	6.00

CARIBOU REVERSE RESUMED 1968-1972

During the 1968 coining it was necessary to discontinue the use of silver and substitute nickel for it. Nickel coins are darker in colour and are attracted to a magnet.

Composition: .500 silver, .500 copper
(1968);
1.00 nickel (1968-72)

The physical specifications are as for the 1965-1967 issues.

Date	Quantity Minted	MS-60
1968 .500 Silver	71,464,000	4.00
1968 Nickel	88,686,931	1.00
1969	133,037,929	1.00
1970	10,302,010	4.00
1971	48,170,428	.75
1972	43,743,387	.75

COMMEMORATIVE FOR CENTENNIAL OF FOUNDING OF R.C.M.P. 1973

The special reverse on the 1973 twenty-five cent piece commemorates the centennial of the founding of the North West Mounted Police, which later became the Royal Canadian Mounted Police. A new obverse with a smaller, more detailed portrait and fewer rim denticles placed farther from the rim was prepared for use with the commemorative reverse, However, a small quantity of coins was struck with the 1972 obverse, creating two varieties for the year. The quantity of the Small Bust variety struck for circulation is believed not to exceed 10,000.

Designer: Reverse - Paul Cedarberg (PC behind horse)

Modeller: Small Bust Obverse - Patrick Brindley, modifying the existing Machin portrait; Reverse - Walter Ott

Small Bust

Large Bust

The physical and chemical specifications are as for the 1969-1972 issues.

Date	Quantity Minted	F-12	VF-20	EF-40	AU-50	MS-60
1973 R.C.M.P., Small Bust	134,958,589	—	—	—	—	.75
1973 R.C.M.P., Large Bust	Incl. above	125.00	150.00	175.00	225.00	300.00

CARIBOU REVERSE RESUMED; LARGE PORTRAIT 1974-1978

With the return to the caribou reverse for the twenty-five cent piece in 1974, the use of the Large Portrait obverse was resumed.

The physical and chemical specifications are as for the 1969-1973 issues.

Date	Quantity Minted	MS-60
1974	192,360,598	.75
1975	141,148,000	.75
1976	86,898,261	.75
1977	99,634,555	.75
1978	176,475,408	.75

MODIFIED OBVERSE 1979-1980

Beginning with the 1979 issue and as part of a general standardization of the coinage, the portrait of the Queen was reduced. The intention was to make the size of the portrait proportional to the diameter of the coin, regardless of the denomination. This obverse is not the same as that employed in connection with the 1973 R.C.M.P. commemorative.

The physical and chemical specifications are as for the 1969-1978 issues.

Date	Quantity Minted	MS-60
1979	131,042,905	.60
1980		.60

FIFTY CENTS

VICTORIA

Since the Province of Canada did not issue this denomination, new coinage tools had to be produced when the Dominion placed its first order for coins. For the obverse L.C. Wyon used the same portrait model as he did for the twenty-five cents: a crowned effigy of Victoria based on a model by William Theed. The reverse featured the St. Edward's crown atop crossed boughs of sweet maple, tied at the bottom by a ribbon. By the end of the reign four major obverses and two reverses had been utilized. With the exception of the first two obverses (see below), a detailed description and listing of these varieties by year will be included in a separate catalogue (see INTRODUCTION).

Designer, Modeller & Engraver:
Leonard C. Wyon
Composition: .925 silver, .075 copper
Weight: 11.62 grams
Diameter: 29.72 mm
Edge: Reeded
Die Axes: ↑↓

Heaton Mint issues of 1871-1881 and the Mint, Birmingham issue of 1890 have an "H" on the reverse under the wreath. London Mint strikings have no letter.

VARIETIES 1870

The initial obverse for this denomination lacked the initials of the designer on the truncation of the Queen's neck. The second obverse, also employed for the 1870 coinage, has the L.C.W., as well as a shamrock just behind the front cross in the Queen's tiara.

1870 Without L.C.W.
no shamrock behind front cross

1870 L.C.W. on Truncation
shamrock behind front cross

Date and Mint Mark	Quantity Minted	G-4	VG-8	F-12	VF-20	EF-40	AU-50	MS-60
1870 No L.C.W.	450,000	150.00	300.00	750.00	2,000.00	4,000.00	6,000.00	12,000.00
1870 L.C.W.	Incl. above	25.00	50.00	125.00	250.00	500.00	2,000.00	3,500.00
1871	200,000	30.00	55.00	125.00	300.00	1,000.00	3,000.00	5,500.00
1871H	45,000	50.00	100.00	175.00	600.00	1,200.00	3,500.00	6,000.00

VARIETIES 1872H

Numerous repunching varieties exist on the 1872H coinage, but the only one interesting enough to include in this catalogue involves a blundered obverse die. While repunching defective letters in the obverse legend the engraver inadvertantly used an "A" punch to repair a defective "V" in VICTORIA, converting the Queen's name into "VICTORIA".

1872 Inverted A over V in VICTORIA

Date and Mint Mark	Quantity Minted	G-4	VG-8	F-12	VF-20	EF-40	AU-50	MS-60
1872H Normal	80,000	25.00	50.00	125.00	300.00	800.00	2,500.00	5,000.00
1872H A/V	Incl. above	40.00	80.00	175.00	400.00	1,000.00	3,000.00	6,000.00
1881H	150,000	25.00	50.00	100.00	300.00	600.00	2,000.00	4,000.00
1888	60,000	60.00	125.00	250.00	600.00	1,200.00	2,500.00	5,000.00
1890H	20,000	400.00	800.00	1,500.00	3,000.00	6,000.00	12,000.00	20,000.00
1892	151,000	30.00	60.00	120.00	300.00	600.00	2,000.00	5,000.00
1894	29,036	100.00	200.00	400.00	1,000.00	2,500.00	8,000.00	15,000.00
1898	100,000	25.00	50.00	100.00	300.00	600.00	1,800.00	4,000.00
1899	50,000	45.00	75.00	175.00	500.00	1,000.00	3,500.00	7,500.00
1900	118,000	22.50	45.00	100.00	250.00	600.00	1,800.00	3,500.00
1901	80,000	25.00	50.00	110.00	300.00	700.00	2,000.00	4,000.00

FIFTY CENTS

EDWARD VII   **1902 - 1910**

The reverse of the Edward VII fifty cents followed the same design as the lower silver denominations: the word "CANADA" was made part of the legend, moved from its former position at the bottom of the obverse, and the Imperial State crown replaced St. Edward's crown. The first reverse used the Victorian maple wreath almost untouched.

Designer & Modeller:
    Obverse - G.W. DeSaulles
    (DES. under the bust)
Engraver: Victorian Leaves Reverse -
    G.W. DeSaulles;
    Edwardian Leaves Reverse -
    W.H.J. Blakemore
Composition: 11.62 grams (1902-10);
    11.66 grams (1910)
Diameter: 29.72 mm
Edge: Reeded
Die Axes: ↑↓ (1902-07);
    ↑↑ (1908-10)

The Mint, Birmingham issue of 1903 has an "H" mint mark on the reverse under the wreath. London Mint issues (1902-1907) and Ottawa Mint issues (1908-1910) have no letter.

Date and Mint Mark	Quantity Minted	G-4	VG-8	F-12	VF-20	EF-40	AU-50	MS-60
1902	120,000	15.00	25.00	60.00	250.00	500.00	1,000.00	2,000.00
1903H	140,000	18.00	30.00	75.00	300.00	800.00	1,600.00	3,200.00
1904	60,000	45.00	90.00	200.00	600.00	1,500.00	4,000.00	8,000.00
1905	40,000	45.00	90.00	225.00	700.00	1,700.00	4,500.00	9,000.00
1906	350,000	12.00	18.00	50.00	135.00	400.00	1,250.00	2,500.00
1907	300,000	12.00	17.00	50.00	135.00	350.00	1,200.00	2,200.00
1908	128,119	15.00	25.00	65.00	175.00	450.00	1,250.00	2,500.00
1909	203,118	12.00	18.00	60.00	150.00	450.00	1,250.00	2,500.00

Because the Victorian Leaves variety fifty-cent pieces being coined at the Ottawa Mint had almost no rim, it was requested that the parent Royal Mint in London make new reverse tools. In addition to a wider rim the new variety (Edwardian Leaves reverse) had several altered leaves and a different cross atop the crown. The most noticeable difference is the two outside leaves at the right side of the date. On the Victorian Leaves reverse these leaves have long points which nearly touch the denticles, but on the Edwardian Leaves reverse these leaves have shorter, more curved points farther from the denticles.

1910 Victorian Leaves Reverse   1910 Edwardian Leaves Reverse

Date	Quantity Minted	G-4	VG-8	F-12	VF-20	EF-40	AU-50	MS-60
1910 Victorian Leaves	649,521	12.00	18.00	60.00	150.00	450.00	1,250.00	2,500.00
1910 Edwardian Leaves	Incl. above	12.00	18.00	60.00	150.00	450.00	1,250.00	2,500.00

FIFTY CENTS

GEORGE V   **1911 - 1936**

"GODLESS" OBVERSE 1911

Public outcry greeted the new George V coins issued in 1911 because the obverse legend lacked reference to the King's ruling "by the grace of God." The coinage tools were modified during the year and a new legend containing the Lating abbreviation "DEI GRA:" appeared on the 1912 and subsequent issues. The reverse was a continuation of the Edwardian Leaves variety of the previous reign.

Designer & Modeller:
Sir E.B. MacKennal
(B.M. on truncation)
Composition: .925 silver, .075 copper
Weight: 11.66 grams
Diameter: 29.72 mm
Edge: Reeded
Die Axes: ↑↑

Date	Quantity Minted	G-4	VG-8	F-12	VF-20	EF-40	AU-50	MS-60
1911	209,972	15.00	25.00	135.00	750.00	1,500.00	2,000.00	4,000.00

MODIFIED OBVERSE LEGEND 1912-1936

Composition: .925 silver, .075 copper
(1912-1919);
.800 silver, .200 copper
(1920-1936)

The physical specifications are as for the 1911 issue.

Date	Quantity Minted	G-4	VG-8	F-12	VF-20	EF-40	AU-50	MS-60
1912	285,867	—	12.00	25.00	100.00	350.00	1,500.00	3,500.00
1913	265,889	—	14.00	25.00	100.00	350.00	1,500.00	3,500.00
1914	160,128	20.00	40.00	100.00	300.00	750.00	2,000.00	5,000.00
1916	459,070	—	15.00	25.00	75.00	300.00	900.00	1,800.00
1917	752,213	—	12.00	20.00	55.00	200.00	550.00	1,250.00
1918	854,989	—	11.00	18.00	50.00	200.00	400.00	800.00
1919	1,113,429*	—	10.00	18.00	50.00	175.00	350.00	700.00
1920	584,691**	—	11.00	20.00	65.00	200.00	450.00	1,000.00

* 144,200 fifty-cent pieces of .925 silver were melted in 1920; it is believed they were all dated 1919.

FIFTY CENTS 1921

This popular and very scarce coin was originally minted in considerable quantity. During the early and mid-1920's the demand for fifty-cent pieces was very light; only 28,000 pieces were issued between 1921 and early 1929. These are assumed to have been almost entirely 1920's. When a greater demand for this denomination arose later in 1929, the Master of the Ottawa Mint decided to melt the stock of 1920 and 1921 coins (amounting to some 480,392 pieces) and recoin the silver into 1929 coins. He took this decision because he feared that the public would suspect they were receiving counterfeits if a large quantity of coins with "old" dates were issued. It is believed that the 75 or so 1921's that have survived came from specimen sets sold to collectors or from circulation strikes sold to Mint visitors.

Date	Quantity Minted	G-4	VG-8	F-12	VF-20	EF-40	AU-50	MS-60
1921	206,398**	4,500.00	7,000.00	10,000.00	15,000.00	22,000.00	30,000.00	40,000.00
1929	228,328	—	12.00	20.00	50.00	150.00	400.00	800.00
1931	57,581	—	14.00	25.00	80.00	350.00	1,200.00	2,000.00
1932	19,213	40.00	60.00	125.00	400.00	800.00	2,000.00	4,000.00
1934	39,539	10.00	18.00	40.00	120.00	450.00	1,250.00	2,500.00
1936	38,550	10.00	18.00	40.00	100.00	400.00	1,000.00	2,000.00

** In 1929 480,392 pieces of this denomination, consisting of 1920 and 1921 dates, were melted.

FIFTY CENTS

GEORGE VI

"ET IND: IMP:" OBVERSE 1937-1947

A stylized Canadian coat-of-arms designed by George Edward Kruger-Gray was selected for the George VI fifty-cent piece, first issued in 1937. The initial obverse bore a legend containing an abbreviation for the Latin phrase, ET INDAE IMPERATOR, meaning "and Emperor of India", denoting the King was Emperor of that vast country.

Designer & Modeller:
Portrait - T.H. Paget
(H.P. below bust);
Reverse - G.E. Kruger-Gray
(K.G flanking lower part of crown on shield)
Composition: .800 silver, .200 copper
Weight: 11.66 grams
Diameter: 29.72 mm
Edge: Reeded
Die Axes: ↑↑

Date	Quantity Minted	F-12	VF-20	EF-40	AU-50	MS-60
1937	192,016	12.00	18.60	25.00	60.00	125.00
1938	192,018	14.00	25.00	90.00	200.00	350.00
1939	287,976	12.00	22.00	40.00	125.00	275.00
1940	1,996,566	10.00	15.00	20.00	30.00	65.00
1941	1,714,874	10.00	15.00	20.00	30.00	60.00
1942	1,974,165	10.00	15.00	20.00	30.00	60.00
1943	3,109,583	10.00	15.00	20.00	30.00	50.00
1944	2,460,205	10.00	15.00	20.00	30.00	60.00
1945	1,959,528	10.00	15.00	20.00	30.00	50.00
1946	950,235	10.00	15.00	30.00	80.00	150.00

VARIETIES 1947

There are two styles of 7 for the 1947 issue; the first is a tall figure with a tail curving to the left at the bottom (Straight 7), similar to that on the 1937 issue. The second (Curved 7) has a bottom that curves to the right.

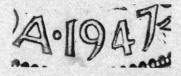 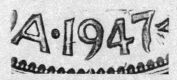

1947 Straight 7   1947 Curved 7

Date	Quantity Minted	VG-8	F-12	VF-20	EF-40	AU-50	MS-60
1947 Straight 7	424,885	—	10.00	15.00	30.00	100.00	200.00
1947 Curved 7	Incl. above	—	10.00	15.00	30.00	100.00	200.00

MAPLE LEAF ISSUE 1947

With the granting of independence to India, the Royal Canadian Mint was faced with a dilemma in early 1948. The new obverse coinage tools with the Latin abbreviation "ET IND: IMP:" omitted would not arrive for several months, yet there was a great need for all denominations of coins. The Mint satisfied the demand by striking coins dated 1947 and bearing an obverse with outmoded titles. To differentiate this issue from the regular strikings of 1947, a tiny maple leaf was placed after the date. Both styles of 7 (see above) were employed for the Maple Leaf coinage, creating four varieties of the 1947 date in all.

1947 Maple Leaf, Straight 7   1947 Maple Leaf, Curved 7

Date	Quantity Minted	VG-8	F-12	VF-20	EF-40	AU-50	MS-60
1947 ML, Straight 7	38,433	40.00	55.00	75.00	125.00	200.00	400.00
1947 ML, Curved 7	Incl. above	1,500.00	2,000.00	2,500.00	3,000.00	3,500.00	5,000.00

MODIFIED OBVERSE LEGEND 1948-1952

In 1948, following the arrival of the master tools with the new obverse legend, production of the 1947 Maple Leaf coinage was suspended. For the remainder of the year coins were produced with the new obverse and the true date, 1948.

The physical and chemical specifications are as for the 1937-1947 issues.

Date	Quantity Minted	VG-8	F-12	VF-20	EF-40	AU-50	MS-60
1948	37,784	60.00	80.00	110.00	160.00	225.00	400.00
1949	858,991	—	10.00	15.00	20.00	50.00	100.00
1950	2,384,179	8.00	10.00	12.00	14.00	18.00	27.00
1951	2,421,730	8.00	10.00	12.00	14.00	16.00	25.00
1952	2,596,465	8.00	10.00	12.00	14.00	16.00	25.00

FIFTY CENTS

ELIZABETH II

1953 to date

LAUREATED PORTRAIT; LARGE COAT-OF-ARMS REVERSE 1953-1954

During 1953 two obverse varieties were employed. Known as the No Shoulder Fold and Shoulder Fold varieties (see page 83 for full description) they were combined with two major reverse varieties. The No Shoulder Fold obverse was used with both the Small and Large Date reverses, though only a modest quantity of the latter were struck. The Small Date reverse was carried over from George VI issues. The Shoulder Fold obverse appeared only with the Large Date reverse.

Designer & Modeller: Portrait - Mrs. Mary Gillick, (M.G. on truncation);
Large Date Reverse - Thomas Shingles, copying existing model
Engraver: No Shoulder Fold Obverse - Thomas Shingles, using the Gillick portrait model;
Shoulder Fold Obverse - Thomas Shingles, modifying existing NSF coinage tools
Composition: .800 silver, .200 copper
Weight: 11.66 grams
Diameter: 29.72 mm
Edge: Reeded
Die Axes: ↑↑

No Shoulder Fold Obverse 1953
letters have pronounced flaring

Shoulder Fold Obverse 1953-1964
letters have subdued flaring

Small Date Reverse 1953

Large Date Reverse 1953-1964

Date	Quantity Minted	VG-8	F-12	VF-20	EF-40	AU-50	MS-60
1953 Small Date, NSF	1,630,429	—	—	10.00	12.00	15.00	20.00
1953 Large Date, NSF	Incl. above	18.00	35.00	45.00	60.00	175.00	350.00
1953 Large Date, SF	Incl. above	—	10.00	14.00	25.00	40.00	70.00
1954	506,305	—	11.00	12.00	25.00	40.00	75.00

MODIFIED REVERSE 1955-1958

Continuing difficulties with the Coat-of-Arms reverse design resulted in the introduction of a major modification in 1955. The problem was the obverse portrait tended to draw away too much metal at the moment the coin was struck, leaving insufficient metal to completely fill the design on the reverse die. Thus, the coins sometimes showed a weakness in the design at and around the crown and top of the shield. This problem was largely solved by the new reverse with a smaller version of the coat-of-arms.

Designer & Modeller:
Thomas Shingles, copying existing models

The physical and chemical specifications are as for the 1953-1954 issues.

Date	Quantity Minted	VG-8	F-12	VF-20	EF-40	AU-50	MS-60
1955	763,511	—	11.00	12.00	20.00	30.00	50.00
1956	1,379,499	—	—	—	10.00	12.00	15.00
1957	2,171,689	—	—	—	10.00	12.00	15.00
1958	2,957,266	—	—	—	10.00	12.00	15.00

NEW COAT-OF-ARMS REVERSE; LAUREATED OBVERSE 1959-1964

In 1959 the new Canadian coat-of-arms which had been approved for government use in 1957 was adapted for the fifty-cent piece. One of the major changes compared to the previous design was the addition of a ribbon at the bottom bearing "A MARI USQUE AD MARE," meaning "from sea to sea" and making reference to the territorial extent of the country. The 1959 issue had horizontal lines in the bottom panel, indicating the colour incorrectly as blue. To indicate the correct colour, white, these lines were removed from the 1960 and subsequent issues. The obverse continued unchanged.

Designer & Modeller:
Reverse - Thomas Shingles
(T S flanking shield at bottom)

The physical and chemical specifications are as the 1953-1958 issues.

Date	Quantity Minted	MS-60
1959	3,095,535	12.00
1960	3,488,897	12.00
1961	3,584,417	12.00
1962	5,208,030	12.00
1963	8,348,871	10.00
1964	9,177,676	10.00

CROWNED PORTRAIT; NEW COAT-OF-ARMS REVERSE 1965-1966

A new obverse with the Queen showing more mature facial features and wearing a tiara was introduced in 1965.

Designer & Modeller:
    Portrait - Arnold Machin

The physical and chemical specifications are as the 1953-1964 issues.

Date	Quantity Minted	MS-60
1965	12,629,974	10.00
1966	7,683,228	10.00

COMMEMORATIVE FOR CENTENNIAL OF CONFEDERATION 1967

A design for the reverse showing a howling wolf was chosen as part of the set of commemorative coins for this year. The obverse continued unchanged.

Designer: Reverse - Alex Colville
Modeller: Reverse - Myron Cook

The physical and chemical specifications are as for the 1953-1966 issues.

Date	Quantity Minted	MS-60
1967 Confederation Commemorative	4,211,395	10.00

NEW COAT-OF-ARMS REVERSE RESUMED;
REDUCED SIZE NICKEL COINAGE 1968-1976

When the coat-of-arms reverse design was resumed in 1968, the strikes were in nickel. In order to make the coins easier to strike in the harder metal the diameter was considerably reduced.

Composition: 1.00 Nickel
Weight: 8.10 grams
Diameter: 27.13 mm
Edge: Reeded
Die Axes: ↑↑

Date	Quantity Minted	MS-60
1968	3,966,932	1.00
1969	7,113,929	1.00
1970	2,429,516	1.50
1971	2,166,444	1.00
1972	2,515,632	1.00
1973	2,546,096	1.00
1974	3,436,650	1.00
1975	3,710,000	1.00
1976	2,940,719	1.00

MODIFIED DESIGNS 1977

The 1977 coinage featured pronounced changes on both sides. The obverse bears a smaller bust with increased hair detail, smaller lettering, and larger beads placed farther from the rim. The reverse shows a smaller coat-of-arms and for the first time beads instead of denticles at the rim.

Modeller: Obverse - Patrick Brindley, modifying the Machin portrait

The physical and chemical specifications are as for the 1968-1976 issues.

Date	Quantity Minted	MS-60
1977	709,939	5.00

MODIFIED DESIGNS 1978-1980

In 1978 the Mint's attempts to settle upon standard designs continued. The beaded motif for the reverse was dropped and a design essentially the same as that for 1968-1976 was restored. Two minor varieties of the 1978 reverse are known, but their detailed description and listing is left to a separate catalogue (see INTRODUCTION). The 1978 obverse was a combination of the 1968-1976 and 1977 designs. The unmodified Machin portrait was restored, but the smaller lettering of 1977 was retained.

Modeller: Portrait - Arnold Machin

The physical and chemical specifications are as for the 1968-1977 issues.

Date	Quantity Minted	MS-60
1978	3,341,892	1.00
1979	3,425,000	.75
1980		.75

ONE DOLLAR — SILVER

GEORGE V   1935 - 1936

SILVER JUBILEE COMMEMORATIVE 1935

Canada's first silver dollar for circulation, also the first commemorative coin, marked the 25th anniversary of the accession of King George V. The Bank of Canada $25 bill also commemorated the special event. The reverse of the silver dollar was a modern design by sculptor Emmanuel Hahn, showing an Indian and a voyageur, a travelling agent for a fur company, paddling a canoe by an islet on which there are two wind-swept trees. In the canoe are bundles of goods; the bundle at the right has HB, representing the Hudson's Bay Company. The vertical lines in the background represent the northern lights. This modern design began a trend which produced the beautiful reverses for 1937.

The obverse was the commemorative side of the coin with the Latin legend indicating the King was in the 25th year of his reign. The portrait was by Percy Metcalfe and was never used for any other Canadian coinage, but had been used previously for the obverses of some New Zealand and Australian coinages.

Generally, the coins were issued in cardboard tubes of 20.

Designer & Modeller:
    Portrait - Percy Metcalfe;
    Reverse - Emmanuel Hahn
    (EH in water left end of canoe)
Composition: .800 silver, .200 copper
Weight: 23.33 grams
Diameter: 36.00 mm
Edge: Reeded
Die Axes: ↑↑

Date	Quantity Minted	F-12	VF-20	EF-40	AU-50	MS-60
1935 Jubilee Commemorative	428,707	25.00	35.00	45.00	50.00	80.00

STANDARD OBVERSE 1936

In 1936 the issue of silver dollars continued, with the reverse remaining unchanged. The obverse was the regular MacKennal design used for 1 to 50¢ pieces of 1912-1936. The tools for this obverse had already been prepared in 1911 for use on the 1911 dollar (cf. DC-6 on page 230).

Designer & Modeller:
  Portrait - Sir E.B. MacKennal
  (B.M. on truncation)

The physical and chemical specifications are as for the 1935 issue.

Date	Quantity Minted	F-12	VF-20	EF-40	AU-50	MS-60
1936	339,600	25.00	30.00	40.00	45.00	80.00

ONE DOLLAR — SILVER

GEORGE VI   1937 - 1952

VOYAGEUR REVERSE 1937-1938

New reverse designs were under consideration for the 1937 issues; however, it was decided to retain the voyageur design, since it was already modern.

Designer & Modeller:
Portrait - T.H. Paget
(H.P. below bust)
Composition: .800 silver, .200 copper
Weight: 23.33 grams
Diameter: 36.00 mm
Edge: Reeded
Die Axes: ↑↑

Date	Quantity Minted	F-12	VF-20	EF-40	AU-50	MS-60
1937	207,406	25.00	30.00	40.00	45.00	80.00
1938	90,304	45.00	60.00	75.00	100.00	200.00

COMMEMORATIVE FOR ROYAL VISIT 1939

Canada's second commemorative coin was created when the reverse of the 1939 silver dollar was used to mark the visit of George VI and Queen Elizabeth to Canada. The design consists of the centre block of the Parliament buildings in Ottawa and the Latin phrase, "FIDE SVORVM REGNAT," meaning "He rules by the faith of his people."

The usual means of issuing coins was through the Bank of Canada, but for this special coinage it was decided to make them available through the Post Office as well. Consequently, 369,500 of the original mintage of nearly 1.4 million were issued direct to the Post Office. This mintage proved to be larger than public demand and between 1939 and 1945 nearly 160,000 pieces were returned to the Mint and melted.

Designer & Modeller:
Reverse - Emmanuel Hahn
(E H flanked the building in the original model, but were removed by order of Canadian government officials)

The physical and chemical specifications are as for the 1937-1938 issues.

Date	Quantity Minted	F-12	VF-20	EF-40	AU-50	MS-60
1939	1,363,816*	15.00	20.00	25.00	30.00	35.00

* 158,084 pieces were returned to the Mint and melted between 1939 and 1945.

VOYAGEUR REVERSE RESUMED; "ET IND: IMP:" OBVERSE 1945-1947

Beginning with the 1945 silver dollars a more brilliant appearance was achieved. This was due to the use of chromium-plated coinage dies. For previous issues unplated dies with a rougher surface had been used.

The chemical and physical specifications are as the 1937-1939 issues.

Date	Quantity Minted	F-12	VF-20	EF-40	AU-50	MS-60
1945	38,391	125.00	150.00	250.00	375.00	700.00
1946	93,055	35.00	50.00	70.00	150.00	300.00

VARIETIES 1947

Two styles of 7 were used to date the 1947 dies: a tall figure with the lower tail pointing back to the right (Pointed 7) and a shorter 7 with the lower tail pointing almost straight down (Blunt 7).

1947 Pointed 7   1947 Blunt 7

Date	Quantity Minted	F-12	VF-20	EF-40	AU-50	MS-60
1947 Pointed 7	65,595	150.00	175.00	225.00	450.00	1,500.00
1947 Blunt 7	Incl. above	65.00	90.00	115.00	150.00	300.00

MAPLE LEAF ISSUE 1947

    In early 1948 the Royal Canadian Mint was faced with a problem. New obverse coinage tools with the Latin abbreviation "ET IND: IMP:" omitted to indicate that the King's titles had changed to concur with India's recently granted independence would not arrive for several months. Yet, there was a great need for all denominations of coins. The Mint satisfied the demand by striking coins dated 1947 and bearing an obverse with outmoded titles. To differentiate this issue from the regular strikings of 1947, a tiny maple leaf was placed after the date. Only the Blunt 7 was employed for dating this issue.

1947 Maple Leaf Issue,
struck in 1948

Date	Quantity Minted	F-12	VF-20	EF-40	AU-50	MS-60
1947 Maple Leaf	21,135	165.00	200.00	250.00	350.00	800.00

MODIFIED OBVERSE LEGEND; VOYAGEUR REVERSE 1948

Following the arrival in 1948 of the master tools with the new obverse legend production of the 1947 Maple Leaf coinage was suspended. For the remainder of the year coins were produced with the new obverse and the true date, 1948.

The physical and chemical specifications are as for the 1937-1947 issues.

Date	Quantity Minted	F-12	VF-20	EF-40	AU-50	MS-60
1948	18,780	900.00	1,200.00	1,400.00	1,800.00	2,500.00

COMMEMORATIVE FOR ENTRY OF NEWFOUNDLAND
INTO CONFEDERATION 1949

On December 31, 1949 Newfoundland became the tenth province of the Dominion of Canada. This historic event was recognized on the Canadian coinage with a special reverse for the 1949 silver dollar. The design shows the ship "Matthew" in which it is thought John Cabot discovered Newfoundland in 1497. Below it is the Latin phrase, "FLOREAT TERRA NOVA", meaning "May the new found land flourish." The design was inspired by Newfoundland's commemorative postage stamp of 1947, based on a model of the ship by Ernest Maunder. The obverse continued unchanged from that of 1948.

The 1949 dollars were struck more carefully than those of previous years and were issued in plastic or cardboard tubes of 20 to protect them. Many of these coins remain in "proof-like" condition today. Thomas Shingles was the engraver, doing his work entirely by hand, without the aid of a "reducing" machine.

It was decided to strike these coins, dated 1949, as long as there was a demand for them. In 1950 some 40,718 pieces were coined. The 1949 and 1950 strikings have been combined to give the total production for the type.

Designer: Reverse - Thomas Shingles,
based upon Ernest Maunder's
model of the "Matthew"
(T.S. above horizon at right)
Engraver: Reverse - Thomas Shingles

The physical and chemical specifications
are as for the 1937-1948 issues.

Date	Quantity Minted	F-12	VF-20	EF-40	AU-50	MS-60
1949	672,218	25.00	30.00	40.00	45.00	55.00

VOYAGEUR REVERSE RESUMED 1950-1952

ARNPRIOR DOLLARS 1950 & 1951

During the year 1950 a technical problem arose that was to plague the Mint throughout the 1950's. At each end of the canoe are four (not three as is so often claimed) shallow water lines. In the process of polishing or repolishing the dies parts of these lines tended to disappear, creating differences within a given year's coinage. Collectors have decided arbitrarily that a certain pattern of partial water lines at the right-hand end of the canoe should be collected separately and command a premium over dollars with perfect water lines or other partial lines configurations.

The so-called Arnprior configuration (see page 166 for more details) consists of 2½ (often incorrectly called 1½) water lines at the right. Any trace of the bottom water line disqualifies a coin from being an Arnprior. One should also beware of coins that have had part of the water lines fraudulently removed.

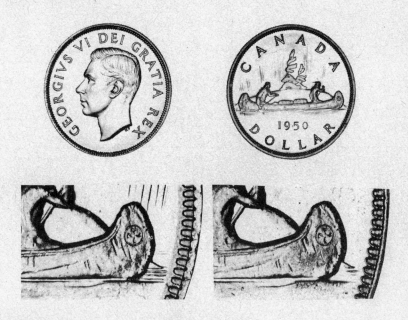

Normal (4) Water Lines at Right   Arnprior (2½) Water Lines at Right

Date	Quantity Minted	F-12	VF-20	EF-40	AU-50	MS-60
1950 Normal Water Lines	261,002	18.00	25.00	30.00	35.00	50.00
1950 Arnprior	Incl. above	30.00	40.00	50.00	75.00	125.00
1951 Normal Water Lines	416,395	15.00	20.00	25.00	30.00	40.00
1951 Arnprior	Incl. above	35.00	50.00	75.00	125.00	225.00

VARIETIES 1952

In 1952 a modified reverse with no water lines at all, was put into use. In addition to removing the water lines, this reverse differs from the Water Lines variety in having a remodeled (larger) islet tip at the right end of the canoe. This variety is fundamentally different from the Arnpriors in that it was deliberately not accidentally created. The Water Lines variety was also used in 1952.

1952 Water Lines Variety

1952 No Water Lines Variety

Date	Quantity Minted	VF-20	EF-40	AU-50	MS-60
1952 Water Lines	406,148	20.00	25.00	30.00	40.00
1952 No Water Lines	Incl. above	25.00	30.00	35.00	50.00

ONE DOLLAR — SILVER

ELIZABETH II

LAUREATED PORTRAIT; VOYAGEUR REVERSE 1953-1957

As was true of all the lower denominations, the 1953 silver dollars came with two obverses, called the No Shoulder Fold and Shoulder Fold varieties (see page 83 for full explanation). On this denomination these obverses are combined with different reverses. The No Shoulder Fold variety appears with the Wire Edge reverse, the Water Lines reverse of 1950-1952, and the Shoulder Fold obverse with the Wide Border reverse.

Designer & Modeller: Portrait - Mrs. Mary Gillick (M.G. on truncation)
Engraver: No Shoulder Fold Obverse - Thomas Shingles, using the Gillick portrait;
    Shoulder Fold Obverse - Thomas Shingles, modifying existing NSF coinage tools
Composition: .800 Silver, .200 Copper
Weight: 23.33 grams
Diameter: 36.00 mm
Edge: Reeded
Die Axes: ↑↑

No Shoulder Fold Obverse 1953
letters have pronounced flaring

Shoulder Fold Obverse 1953-1964
letters have subdued flaring

Date	Quantity Minted	VF-20	EF-40	AU-50	MS-60
1953 NSF, Narrow Rim	1,073,218	—	20.00	25.00	30.00
1953 SF, Wide Border	Incl. above	—	20.00	25.00	35.00
1954	241,306	20.00	25.00	30.00	40.00

ARNPRIOR DOLLAR 1955

In December, 1955 the Mint made up an order of 2,000 silver dollars for a firm in Arnprior, Ontario. These coins had 2½ water lines at the right of the canoe, similar to the configuration which occurred on some of the 1950-1951 dollars. It was the 1955 dollars that first attracted the attention of collectors, but the term Arnrpior has been applied to any dollar with a similar configuration of defective water lines. See the 1950-1951 silver dollars issues for additional comments.

1955 Normal (4) Water Lines at Right   1955 Arnprior (2½) Water Lines at Right

Date	Quantity Minted	VF-20	EF-40	AU-50	MS-60
1955 Normal Water Lines	260,155	20.00	25.00	30.00	40.00
1955 Arnprior	Incl. above	125.00	160.00	200.00	275.00
1956	198,880	25.00	30.00	35.00	45.00

ONE WATER LINE DOLLAR 1957

Part of the 1957 issue was struck from dies which retained only one of the long water lines at the right end of the canoe. This difference arose in the same way as the Arnprior dollars (cf. 1950-1951 issues for commentary) and is of questionable importance.

1957 Normal (4) Water Lines at Right   1957 One Water Line at Right

Date	Quantity Minted	VF-20	EF-40	AU-50	MS-60
1957 Normal Water Lines	480,899	—	20.00	25.00	35.00
1957 One Water Line	Incl. above	20.00	25.00	30.00	45.00

BRITISH COLUMBIA COMMEMORATIVE 1958

The reverse of the 1958 dollar commemorates the centenary of the Caribou gold rush and the establishment of British Columbia as a Crown Colony. The design shows a totem pole section with mountains in the background. The top element in the totem is a raven, used by some Indians to symbolize death. As a result, it was rumoured that those Indians disliked the dollars, causing them to be called "death dollars." The obverse was the same as that on the 1954-1957 issues.

Designer & Modeller:
Reverse - Stephan Trenka
(ST on right-hand of lower base
of totem pole)

The physical and chemical specifications are as for the 1953-1957 issues.

Date	Quantity Minted	AU-50	MS-60
1958 Totem Pole	3,039,630	20.00	25.00

VOYAGEUR REVERSE RESUMED 1959-1963

During this period minor changes were made in the reverse details, the description of which is left to a separate work (see INTRODUCTION). The obverse was continued from the previous year.

Date	Quantity Minted	MS-60
1959	1,398,342	25.00
1960	1,337,758	22.50
1961	1,141,303	22.50
1962	1,636,248	20.00
1963	3,126,446	20.00

CONFEDERATION MEETINGS COMMEMORATIVE 1964

The reverse of the 1964 silver dollar carried a special design marking the centennial of the 1864 meetings in Charlottetown, P.E.I. and Quebec City, Quebec which prepared the way for Confederation in 1867. The design depicts, conjoined within a circle, the French fleur-de-lis, the Irish shamrock, the Scottish thistle and the English rose. The obverse coupled with the commemorative reverse was a reworking of the Shoulder Fold variety.

Designer: Reverse - Dinko Vodanovic
(D.V. near the Q of Quebec)
Modeller: Reverse - Thomas Shingles
(T.S. near the C of Quebec);
Obverse - Myron Cook,
modifying existing model

The physical and chemical specifications are as for the 1953-1963 issues.

Date	Quantity Minted	MS-60
1964 Meetings Commemorative	4,434,391	20.00

CROWNED PORTRAIT; VOYAGEUR REVERSE 1965-1966

A new obverse with the Queen showing more mature facial features and wearing a tiara was introduced on all denominations in 1965. The first obverse for the dollar had to be replaced because it gave such poor die life. The difficulty was a flat field (Small Beads variety). A single trial die (Medium Beads variety) established that an obverse with the field sloping up at the edge was preferable, so new master tools were prepared (Large Beads variety) and those dies became the standard variety. In addition two reverses, bearing slightly different 5's, were employed, creating five varieties in all for 1965. Through an error a small quantity of 1966 dollars was struck with the outmoded Small Beads obverse.

Designer: Portrait - Arnold Machin

The physical and chemical specifications are as for the 1953-1964 issues.

Small Beads Obverse 1965-1966
rear jewel in tiara is well attached

Medium Beads Obverse 1965
rear jewel in tiara is nearly detached

Large Beads Obverse
rear jewel in tiara is well attached

1965 Pointed 5 (at bottom)   1965 Blunt 5 (at bottom)

Date	Quantity Minted	AU-50	MS-60
1965 Small Beads, Pointed 5 (variety 1)	7,863,885	—	20.00
1965 Small Beads, Blunt 5 (variety 2)	Incl. above	—	20.00
1965 Medium Beads, Pointed 5 (variety 5)	Incl. above	25.00	30.00
1965 Large Beads, Pointed 5 (variety 3)	Incl. above	—	20.00
1965 Large Beads, Blunt 5 (variety 4)	Incl. above	—	20.00
1966 Small Beads	9,239,315	1,250.00	1,500.00
1966 Large Beads	Incl. above	—	20.00

COMMEMORATIVE FOR CENTENNIAL OF CONFEDERATION 1967

A design for the reverse showing a Canada goose in flight was chosen as part of the set of commemorative coins for this year. The obverse was the Large Beads variety of 1965-1966.

Designer: Reverse - Alex Colville
Modeller: Reverse - Myron Cook

The physical and chemical specifications are as for the 1953-1966 issues.

Date	Quantity Minted	MS-60
1967 Confederation Commemorative	5,816,176*	20.00

* 141,741 pieces were melted in 1967.

ONE DOLLAR — NICKEL

ELIZABETH II   **1968 to date**

VOYAGEUR REVERSE RESUMED; REDUCED SIZE COINAGE 1968-1969

When the voyageur reverse design was resumed in 1968, the strikes were in nickel. In order to make coining easier for the harder metal the diameter was reduced considerably.

Engraver: Myron Cook, using existing
models
Composition: 1.00 Nickel
Weight: 15.62 grams
Diameter: 32.13 mm
Edge: Reeded
Die Axes: ↑↑

Date	Quantity Minted	AU-50	MS-60
1968	4,755,080	1.25	1.75
1969	4,215,055	1.25	1.75

MANITOBA CENTENNIAL COMMEMORATIVE 1970

The year 1970 saw Canada's first commemorative nickel dollar, with a special reverse featuring a prairie crocus in recognition of the centenary of Manitoba's entry into Confederation. The obverse continued unchanged from the 1968-1969 issues.

Designer: Reverse - Raymond Taylor
(RT to right of crocus plant)
Modeller: Reverse - Walter Ott

The physical and chemical specifications are as for the 1968-1969 issues.

Date	Quantity Minted	AU-50	MS-60
1970 Manitoba Commemorative	3,493,189	1.50	3.00

BRITISH COLUMBIA CENTENNIAL COMMEMORATIVE 1971

The nickel dollar for 1971 commemorates the entry in 1871 of British Columbia into Confederation. Its design is based on the arms of the province, with a shield at the bottom and dogwood blossoms at the top. The obverse was the same as on previous nickel dollar issues.

Designer & Modeller:
Reverse - Thomas Shingles
(TS at bottom of shield)

The physical and chemical specifications are as for the 1968-1970 issues.

Date	Quantity Minted	AU-50	MS-60
1971 British Columbia Commemorative	3,659,045	1.50	3.00

VOYAGEUR REVERSE RESUMED 1972

In 1972 the standard voyageur reverse was resumed; it and the obverse were the same as on the 1968-1969 issues.

The physical and chemical specifications are as for the 1968-1971 issues.

Date	Quantity Minted	AU-50	MS-60
1972	2,193,000	1.40	2.50

P.E.I. CENTENNIAL COMMEMORATIVE 1973

The special reverse on the nickel dollar of 1973 marks the 100th anniversary of the entry of Prince Edward Island into Confederation. The design depicts the provincial legislature building. A new obverse with a smaller, more detailed portrait, and fewer rim denticles placed farther from the rim is brought into use with this reverse.

Designer: Reverse - Terry Manning
            (TM at left of building)
Modeller: Obverse - Patrick Brindley;
            Reverse - Walter Ott
            (WO at right of building)

The physical and chemical specifications are as for the 1968-1972 issues.

Date	Quantity Minted	AU-50	MS-60
1973 P.E.I. Commemorative	2,683,000*	1.50	3.00

* 25,000 of the mintage was struck in 1974.

WINNIPEG COMMEMORATIVE 1974

The 1974 issue of nickel dollars commemorates the centenary of the city of Winnipeg, Manitoba. The design consists of a large 100; in the first 0 is a view of Main Street in 1874 and in the second 0 is a view of the same location 100 years later. For the first time the special collectors' issue of silver dollars for that year had the same design.

Designer: Reverse - Paul Pederson
(PP above the date)
Modeller: Reverse - Walter Ott and
Patrick Brindley
(B below Winnipeg)

The physical and chemical specifications are as for the 1968-1973 issues.

Date	Quantity Minted	AU-50	MS-60
1974 Winnipeg Commemorative, nickel	2,268,027	3.00	5.00

VOYAGEUR REVERSE RESUMED 1975-1976

The designs employed for the voyageur dollars of 1975-1976 were essentially continuations of previous designs, except for some minor variations on the obverse. Their detailed description and listing is left to a separate catalogue (see INTRODUCTION).

The physical and chemical specifications are as for the 1968-1974 issues.

Date	Quantity Minted	AU-50	MS-60
1975	3,256,000	1.25	2.00
1976	1,717,010	2.25	4.00

MODIFIED REVERSE 1977

A major alteration was made in the reverse of the 1977 dollar. A new model was prepared in which the size of the device was reduced and the legend was in smaller lettering, much farther from the rim. The rim denticles were replaced with beads. Two minor varieties exist on the obverse, but these will not be listed separately here (see INTRODUCTION).

Modeller: Reverse - Terry Smith, copying existing models

The physical and chemical specifications are as for the 1968-1976 issues.

Date	Quantity Minted	AU-50	MS-60
1977	1,393,745	2.00	3.50

MODIFIED DESIGNS 1978-1980

Continued major changes occurred in the nickel dollar coinage in 1978. In a reversal of design policy, the Mint returned to designs more like those used prior to 1977. On the obverse the unmodified Machin portrait was restored, but the beads were farther from the rim than on the 1968-1972 issues. The reverse had a design similar to that of 1975-1976, complete with rim denticles instead of beads, but the northern lights were rendered as raised lines, as they were for the 1977 issue.

The physical and chemical specifications are as for the 1968-1977 issues.

Date	Quantity Minted	AU-50	MS-60
1978	2,948,488	1.25	2.00
1979	2,544,000	1.25	2.00
1980		1.25	2.00

FIVE DOLLARS — GOLD

GEORGE V   1912 - 1914

From the first year of operation for the Ottawa Mint it was planned that gold should be coined in dollar denominations as well as British sovereigns. However, the preparations proceeded slowly and it was not until 1911 that final designs were decided upon (cf. DC-7 & DC-8 on page 231) for the $5 and $10 coins. Originally it had been planned to strike denominations of $2.50, $5, $10 and $20, but by sometime in 1911 these expectations were trimmed to only the two middle denominations.

Coins for circulation were first issued in 1912. Their production was halted in 1914, when Canada adopted new wartime legislation to restrict the flow of gold. At that time notes issued by the Dominion government ceased to be redeemable in gold. This redeemability was not restored until 1926.

The design for the reverse features the old Canadian coat-of-arms superimposed upon two boughs of maple.

Designer: Portrait - Sir E.B. MacKennal
              (B.M. on truncation);
              Reverse - W.H.J. Blakemore
Composition: .900 gold, .100 copper
Weight: 8.36 grams
Diameter: 21.59 mm
Edge: Reeded
Die Axes: ↑↑

Date	Quantity Minted	VF-20	EF-40	AU-50	MS-60
1912	165,680	300.00	375.00	425.00	600.00
1913	98,832	300.00	375.00	425.00	650.00
1914	31,122	900.00	1,100.00	1,200.00	1,300.00

TEN DOLLARS — GOLD

GEORGE V

The designs of this denomination are the same as those of the $5 except for the change in value.

Designer: Portrait - Sir E.B. MacKennal
(B.M. on truncation);
Reverse - W.H.J. Blakemore
Composition: .900 gold, .100 copper
Weight: 16.72 grams
Diameter: 26.92 mm
Edge: Reeded
Die Axes: ↑↑

Date	Quantity Minted	VF-20	EF-40	AU-50	MS-60
1912	74,759	925.00	975.00	1,050.00	1,300.00
1913	149,232	950.00	1,025.00	1,100.00	1,300.00
1914	140,068	1,050.00	1,150.00	1,200.00	1,400.00

OTTAWA MINT SOVEREIGNS

The British £1 pieces (sovereigns) coined at the Ottawa Mint between 1908 and 1919 occupy a controversial position in Canadian numismatics. Some argue that these pieces are Canadian and must be collected as part of the Canadian series, while others claim that they are British and are separate from the decimal series of the Dominion of Canada.

From the time of the opening of the Ottawa Mint it was the intention of the Dominion government to mint decimal gold coins; however, the fact that the Ottawa Mint was a branch of the Royal Mint in London meant it was obligated to mint sovereigns on request. And while sovereigns were legal tender in Canada, so were gold coins of the United States. Neither type of gold circulated to any significant degree in Canada in the 20th century. Most companies who requested the Ottawa Mint to strike sovereigns did so because they wanted the coins for export purposes. Finally, the fact that some sovereigns were coined at the Ottawa Mint does not automatically make them Canadian, any more than other coinages (eg. Newfoundland or Jamaica) produced there.

ONE POUND (SOVEREIGNS)

EDWARD VII   **1908 - 1910**

As with all other branch mint sovereigns of the period, the Edward VII Canadian sovereigns are identical to the corresponding London Mint issues except for the branch mint mark. The 1908 strikes were specimen coins only and the tiny mintage was merely to establish the series.

Designer & Modeller:
Portrait - G.W. DeSaulles
(DES below bust)
Reverse - Beneditto Pistrucci
(B.P. below ground line at right
Composition: .917 gold, .083 copper
Weight: 7.99 grams
Diameter: 22.05 mm
Edge: Reeded
Die Axes: ↑↓

The "C" mint mark (for Canada) is on the ground line above the centre of the date.

Date and Mint Mark	Quantity Minted	VF-20	EF-40	AU-50	MS-60
1908C	636	2,000.00	2,500.00	3,000.00	4,000.00
1909C	16,273	450.00	550.00	650.00	1,000.00
1910C	28,012	425.00	525.00	600.00	900.00

ONE POUND (SOVEREIGNS)

GEORGE V   **1911 - 1919**

     The mintages for the Ottawa Mint sovereigns of George V continued the modest trend set in the previous reign. The total of all sovereigns from Ottawa barely equalled the yearly mintage at London or one of the Australian branch mints.

     The 1916C issue is rare, with about 10 or so pieces known. The rarity of this issue is probably due to most of the mintage being melted, although this is by no means an established fact. Until the last few years the 1916 London issue was also rare, but thousands of them were released from a British bank.

     The reverse of the George V sovereigns is the same as that for Edward VII.

Designer & Modeller:
           Portrait - E.B. MacKennal
           (B.M. on truncation)
Composition: .917 gold, .083 copper
Weight: 7.99 grams
Diameter: 22.05 mm
Edge: Reeded
Die Axes: ↑↓

Date and Mint Mark	Quantity Minted	VF-20	EF-40	AU-50	MS-60
1911C	256,946	300.00	310.00	325.00	350.00
1913C	3,715	800.00	1,200.00	1,500.00	2,000.00
1914C	14,891	500.00	700.00	900.00	1,100.00
1916C	6,111	15,000.00	20,000.00	25,000.00	30,000.00
1917C	58,845	300.00	310.00	325.00	350.00
1918C	106,516	300.00	310.00	325.00	350.00
1919C	135,889	300.00	310.00	325.00	350.00

COLLECTORS' COINS

From the 19th century onward, mints have often struck small quantities of special coins for collectors in addition to those produced for general circulation. In the Canadian context these collectors' coins have been of several different qualities and finishes, depending upon the particular period and the mint which produced them. Three terms can be correctly applied to Canadian collectors' coins, and it is important for the reader to understand them.

PROOF-LIKE: A term originated in 1953 by J.E. Charlton to describe special silver dollars and sets which were obviously superior to circulation strikes, but whose surfaces were not as bright as those of other collectors' coins (Specimens) being struck at that time. It was commonly asumed that Proof-like coins were simply circulation strikes which had been carefully handled to avoid abrasions. This is not the case; these coins are struck using selected dies and blanks and on slower moving presses than for circulation coins. Because of their superior finish, the Proof-like coins are sometimes mistakenly classed as Specimens or Proofs. It should be noted that Proof-like coins are not as sharply struck, and the higher denominations often have a slight roughness at the Queen's shoulder as a result. Proofs and Specimens are usually double struck under much greater pressure which results in a flawless surface, sharp wire edge and better detail.

SPECIMEN: A general term applying to any specially produced collectors' coin. Most often it is used in connection with the best quality Canadian collectors' coins struck between 1858 and 1972. Specimen coins are usually double struck, with very sharp details and square edges, but are not of the same superlative quality as Proofs. Before 1973, the Royal Canadian Mint did not have the equipment sufficient to strike Proof coins.

PROOF: The highest quality of collectors' coin, generally with frosted relief and highly polished mirror fields. The Olympic Proof coins were the first Canadian Proofs produced in this century. To date, the only other 20th century Canadian Proofs have been the $100 gold pieces.

In the listings that follow, single dollars and gold coins are listed first, followed by cases for Specimen sets, and finally ending with sets. Mintage figures and original issue prices are given where possible.

PROOF-LIKE AND SPECIMEN SILVER DOLLARS 1935 - 1967

Collectors' one dollar coins are listed separately even though some were originally available only in sets. This is because of the long-standing popularity of this denomination with collectors.

Between 1935 and 1947 the only quality of collectors' dollar that was made was Specimen. The situation becomes more confusing after that date, however, because both Specimen and Proof-like dollars and sets were produced in most years. It is sometimes difficult to distinguish the two qualities and, considering the substantial price difference between them, it is advisable to have the quality confirmed by an expert.

Date and Description	Proof-like Silver Dollars		Specimen Silver Dollars	
	Mintage	Value	Mintage	Value
1935 (two coins in red leather case)	—	—	Unknown (2)	$8,000.00
1935 (one coin, not in case)	—	—	Unknown	$4,000.00
1936	—	—	Unknown	$5,000.00
1937 (satin finish)	—	—	1,295	$ 350.00
1937 (mirror fields)	—	—	Unknown	$ 750.00
1938	—	—	Unknown	$7,500.00
1939 (satin fields)	— (1)	—	Unknown	$2,500.00
1939 (mirror fields)	—	—	Unknown	$2,500.00
1945	—	—	Unknown	$2,500.00
1946	—	—	Unknown	$2,500.00
1947 Pointed 7	—	—	Unknown	$7,500.00
1947 Blunt 7	—	—	Unknown	$5,000.00
1947 Maple Leaf	—	—	Unknown	$5,000.00
1948	—	—	Unknown	$5,000.00
1949	Unknown (3)	$ 75.00	Unknown	$2,500.00
1950 Normal Water Lines	Unknown	$ 250.00	Unknown	$2,000.00
1951 Normal Water Lines	Unknown	$ 250.00	Unknown	$2,000.00
1952 Water Lines	—	—	Unknown	$2,000.00
1952 No Water Lines	Unknown	$ 250.00	Unknown	$2,000.00
1953 No Shoulder Fold	—	—	160	$1,250.00
1953 Shoulder Fold	1,200	$ 500.00	Incl. above	$1,250.00
1954	5,300	$ 200.00	—	—
1955 Normal Water Lines	7,950	$ 175.00	—	—
1955 Arnprior	Incl. above	$ 300.00	—	—
1956	10,212	$ 100.00	—	—
1957	16,241	$ 50.00	—	—
1958	33,237	$ 50.00	—	— (4)
1959	45,160	$ 25.00	—	—
1960	82,728	$ 20.00	—	—
1961	120,928	$ 20.00	—	—
1962	248,901 (2)	$ 20.00	—	—
1963	963,525	$ 20.00	—	—
1964	2,862,441	$ 20.00	Unknown	$ 400.00
1965 Variety 1	2,904,352	$ 20.00	Unknown	$ 400.00
1965 Variety 2	Incl. above	$ 20.00	—	—
1965 Variety 3	Incl. above	$ 150.00	—	—
1965 Variety 4	Incl. above	$ 75.00	—	— (4)
1966 Small Beads Obverse	672,514	$2,000.00	—	—
1966 Large Beads Obverse	Incl. above	$ 20.00	—	—
1967	1,036,176	$ 20.00	337,688 (5)	$ 25.00

(1) No Proof-like coins were issued 1935-1948.
(2) Mintage figures are for coins issued separately and in sets.
(3) The mintage of 1949 Proof-like dollars was very high. The vast majority of the pieces issued for circulation were Proof-like and were released in plastic tubes of 20 pieces.
(4) No Specimen coins were issued.
(5) Only available in Centennial commemorative set.

PROOF-LIKE AND SPECIMEN NICKEL DOLLARS 1968 - 1980

Collectors' dollars continued to be made after the changeover to nickel for the circulating dollar. In the first two years Proof-like was probably the only quality produced, but beginning in 1970 and continuing through 1976, both Proof-like and Specimen dollars were struck. The Specimen coins were included in the special 1970 presentation set and the prestige sets of 1971-1976. From 1970 to 1976 separate Proof-like nickel dollars were issued in cases. The original issue prices were $1.25 (1968-1969), $2.00 (1970-1973), $2.50 (1974-1976). In 1977 the issue of a separate nickel dollar was discontinued and all collectors' coins were of Specimen quality, i.e. Proof-like coins were no longer produced. Mintage figures are for coins issued separately and in sets together.

Date	Proof-like Nickel Dollars			Specimen Nickel Dollars		
	Mintage		Value	Mintage	Value	
1968	1,408,143	(1)	$2.75	—	—	(2)
1969	594,258		$2.75	—	—	
1970	ca. 645,869		$3.50	ca. 1,000	$300.00	
1971	468,729		$3.50	66,860	$ 5.00	
1972	405,865		$3.50	36,349	$ 5.00	
1973	466,881	(3)	$3.50	119,891	$ 5.00	
1974	363,786		$7.50	85,230	$ 7.50	
1975	322,325		$4.00	97,263	$ 5.00	
1976	274,106		$6.00	87,744	$ 6.00	
1977	—		$6.00	410,082	$ 5.00	
1978	—		$6.00	448,000	$ 5.00	
1979	—	(4)	$6.00	410,842	$ 5.00	
1980	—		$6.00	N/A	$ 5.00	

(1) Issued individually in pliofilm pouches or in Proof-like sets.
(2) None issued.
(3) Cased individually and in Proof-like sets.
(4) Only available in Proof-like sets.

CASED .500 FINE SILVER DOLLARS 1971 - 1980

Beginning in 1971 the Mint returned to the production of one dollar coins in silver. However, unlike previous issues they were collectors' coins only and were .500 silver instead of .800 silver. Most issues have been commemoratives, and all are of Specimen quality.

All of these coins have been issued in cases. The normal case is covered with black leather. On some occasions limited numbers of special cases were employed for more restricted distribution. They will be noted in the listings below. From 1974 onward the dollars have been housed in clear plastic capsules before being put in the cases.

BRITISH COLUMBIA CENTENNIAL COMMEMORATIVE 1971

The first non-circulating silver dollar issued to the public was a commemorative for the entry of British Columbia into Confederation in 1871. Its design is based upon the provincial arms. The obverse features a modification of the Machin portrait in which the Queen's hair is extensively redone to give more detail.

Designer: Reverse - Patrick Brindley
Modeller: Obverse - Patrick Brindley, modifying the Machin portrait model; Reverse - Patrick Brindley

Composition: .500 silver, .500 copper
Weight: 23.33 grams
Diameter: 36.01 mm
Edge: Reeded
Die Axes: ↑↑
Original Issue Price: $3.00

Date	Quantity Minted	Specimen
1971 British Columbia Commemorative	585,674	20.00

VOYAGEUR REVERSE 1972

The reverse of the 1972 silver dollar is the voyageur design somewhat modified from its last use on the 1966 silver dollar. One of the most noticeable differences is the substitution of beads for denticles at the rim. The obverse is the same as that established for the 1971 dollar.

Modeller: Reverse - Patrick Brindley, modifying the Hahn model

The physical and chemical specifications are as for the 1971 issue.

Original Issue Price: $3.00

Date	Quantity Minted	Specimen
1972 Voyageur Reverse	341,598	20.00

COMMEMORATIVE FOR CENTENNIAL OF FOUNDING OF R.C.M.P. 1973

In 1973 the reverse of the silver dollar recognized the founding of the North West Mounted Police, which later became the Royal Canadian Mounted Police. The obverse design of the previous two years was retained. The special blue case is the same size and shape as the regular case, except it is blue and has a gold-coloured R.C.M.P. crest on the top.

Designer: Reverse - Paul Cedarberg (PC at left of date)
Modeller: Reverse - Patrick Brindley (B at right of date)

The physical and chemical specifications are as for the 1971-1972 issues.

Original Issue Price: $3.00

Date	Quantity Minted	Specimen
1973 R.C.M.P. Commemorative, regular black case	1,031,271	18.00
1973 R.C.M.P. Commemorative, special blue case*	Incl. above	30.00

* This case is the same size and shape as the regular case, except it is blue and has a gold-coloured R.C.M.P. crest on the top.

WINNIPEG COMMEMORATIVE 1974

The 100th anniversary of the establishment of Winnipeg, Manitoba as a city was marked by the reverse of the 1974 silver dollar. The design is identical to that for the nickel dollar (cf. page 175). The obverse remained unchanged from previous issues.

Designer & Modeller:
    Reverse - Paul Pederson

The physical and chemical specifications are as for the 1971-1973 issues.

Original Issue Price: $3.50

Date	Quantity Minted	Specimen
1974 Winnipeg Commemorative, silver	728,947	18.00

CALGARY COMMEMORATIVE 1975

For the centenary of the founding of Calgary, Alberta, the silver dollar of 1975 bore a special reverse showing a cowboy atop a bucking bronco. Oil wells and the modern city skyline appear in the background. The obverse continued unchanged from previous issues.

Designer: Reverse - D.D. Paterson
Modeller: Reverse - Patrick Brindley

The physical and chemical specifications are as for the 1971-1974 issues.

Original Issue Price: $3.50

Date	Quantity Minted	Specimen
1975 Calgary Commemorative	930,956	18.00

LIBRARY OF PARLIAMENT COMMEMORATIVE 1976

The reverse of the 1976 silver dollar was employed to commemorate the 100th anniversary of the completion of the Library of Parliament. This attractive building was the only part of the original centre block of the Parliament buildings that was saved during the disastrous fire of 1916. It is still in use and is a popular tourist attraction in Ottawa.

The obverse was continued unchanged from the previous year.

Designer: Walter Ott and
Patrick Brindley
(B at left of building and
WO monogram at right)

Modeller: Reverse - Walter Ott

The physical and chemical specifications are as for the 1971-1975 issues.

Original Issue Price: $4.00

Date	Quantity Minted	Specimen
1976 Library Commemorative, regular black case	578,708	25.00
1976 Library Commemorative, special blue case*	Incl. above	50.00

* This case is covered with blue leather with an oxidized silver Canadian coat-of-arms on the top. It measures 9.5 x 8.5 cm.

QUEEN ELIZABETH II SILVER JUBILEE COMMEMORATIVE 1977

During 1977 the Queen celebrated the 25th anniversary of her accession to the throne. Many countries, including Canada, recognized the event with a special commemorative coinage. The design on the reverse depicts the Throne of the Senate of Canada, which is used by the Queen or the governor-general for ceremonial occasions.

The obverse was specifically designed for this coin and bears a special legend and the dates 1952-1977.

Designer: Obverse - Royal Canadian
Mint staff, using the Machin
portrait
Reverse - Raymond Lee

Modeller: Reverse - Ago Aarand

The physical and chemical specifications are as for the 1971-1976 issues.

Original Issue Price: $4.25

187

Date	Quantity Minted		Specimen
1977 Silver Jubilee Commemorative, regular black case	744,848		20.00
1977 Silver Jubilee Commemorative, special maroon case*	Incl. above		50.00

* This case is covered with maroon velvet with an oxidized silver Canadian coat-of-arms on the top. It measures 10.0 x 9.0 cm.

11th COMMONWEALTH GAMES COMMEMORATIVE 1978

The 1978 silver dollar commemorated the 11th Commonwealth Games, held in Edmonton, Alberta, August 3-12 of that year. The reverse design features the symbol of the Games in the centre and the official symbols of the ten sports which comprise the Games along its perimeter.

The obverse was made specifically for this issue.

Designer: Obverse - Royal Canadian
Mint staff
Reverse - Raymond Taylor

The physical and chemical specifications are as for the 1971-1977 issues.

Original Issue Price: $4.50

Date	Quantity Minted		Specimen
1978 Commonwealth Games Commemorative	709,602		.18.00

GRIFFIN COMMEMORATIVE 1979

The first voyage by a commercial ship on the Great Lakes was recognized on the reverse of the 1979 silver dollar.

Designer: Walter Schlemp
Modeller: Terry Smith

The physical and chemical specifications are as for the 1971-1978 issues.

Original Issue Price: $5.50

Date	Quantity Minted	Specimen
1979 Griffin Commemorative	ca. 826,695	20.00

ARCTIC TERRITORIES COMMEMORATIVE 1980

The year 1980 marks the centenary of the transfer of the Arctic Islands from the British government to the government of the Dominion of Canada. This added significantly to the land area of the Dominion. The obverse continued unchanged from the 1970-1979 issues.

Designer: Reverse - Donald D. Paterson
Modeller: Reverse - Walter Ott

The physical and chemical specifications are as for the 1971-1979 issues.

Original Issue Price: $22.00

Date	Quantity Minted	Specimen
1980 Arctic Territories Commemorative		27.50

OLYMPIC $5 AND $10 COINS 1973 - 1976

In 1976 Montreal, Canada hosted the XXI Olympiad. To commemorate and help finance Canada's first Olympics, the federal government agreed to produce a series of 28 silver and 2 gold coins (see page 199 for the $100 gold coins). There are seven series of silver coins. Each series has two $5 and two $10 coins, making 14 of each denomination in all. Each series depicts different Olympic themes on the reverses and has a common design (except for the date) on the obverse. The date on the coins is usually the year of minting. Orders for the Olympic coins were accepted up to the end of December 1976, so a small unit continued to function into 1977 on the Olympic Coin Program.

In order to give some credibility to the Olympic silver coins being current, about 1,000,000 Series I coins were distributed at face value through banks. However, the rest of the Series I coins and all Series II to VII issues were sold at a premium over the face value. Most of these coins were sealed in clear styrene capsules.

$5 COIN	$10 COIN
Composition: .925 silver, .075 copper	**Composition:** .925 silver, .075 copper
Weight: 24.30 grams	**Weight:** 48.60 grams
Diameter: 38.00 mm	**Diameter:** 45.00 mm
Edge: Reeded	**Edge:** Reeded
Die Axes: ↑↑	**Die Axes:** ↑↑

Coin No. 1
World Map

Coin No. 2
World Map

Coin No. 3
Montreal Skyline

Coin No. 4
Kingston and Sailboats

Theme: Geographic
Official Release Date: December 13, 1973
Designer of Reverses: Georges Huel, worked by invitation
Modellers: Coin No. 1 ($10 Map of the World): none (design was photochemically etched)
  Coin No. 2 ($5 Map of the World): none (design was photochemically etched)
  Coin No. 3 ($10 Montreal Skyline): Ago Aarand
  Coin No. 4 ($5 Kingston and Sailboats): Terrance Smith

	Single Coins (Unc. or Proof)		Cased Custom Set	Cased Prestige Set	Cased Proof Set
	$5 Coin	**$10 Coin**	**(2 x $5, 2 x $10)**	**(2 x $5, 2 x $10)**	**(2 x $5, 2 x $10)**
Series					
I	$18.00	$35.00*	$105.00	$105.00	$105.00

*Except for the mule with the Map of the World on the reverse. $500.00

Coin No. 5
Head of Zeus

Coin No. 6
Athlete with Torch

Coin No. 7
Temple of Zeus

Coin No. 8
Olympic Rings and Wreath

Theme: Olympic Motifs
Official Release Date: September 16, 1974
Designer of Reverses: Anthony Mann, winner of an invitational competition
Modellers: Coin No. 5 ($10 Head of Zeus): Patrick Brindley
Coin No. 6 ($5 Athlete with Torch): Patrick Brindley
Coin No. 7 ($10 Temple of Zeus): Walter Ott
Coin No. 8 ($5 Olympic Rings and Wreath): Walter Ott

	Single Coins (Unc. or Proof)		Cased Custom Set	Cased Prestige Set	Cased Proof Set
Series	$5 Coin	$10 Coin	(2 x $5, 2 x $10)	(2 x $5, 2 x $10)	(2 x $5, 2 x $10)
II	$18.00	$35.00*	$105.00	$105.00	$105.00

*Except for the mule with the obverse dated 1974. $500.00

Coin No. 9
Lacrosse

Coin No. 10
Canoeing

Coin No. 11
Cycling

Coin No. 12
Rowing

Theme: Early Canadian Sports
Official Release Date: April 16, 1975
Designer of Reverses: Ken Danby, winner of an invitational competition
Modellers: Coin No. 9 ($10 Lacrosse): Walter Ott
Coin No. 10 ($5 Canoeing): Patrick Brindley
Coin No. 11 ($10 Cycling): Ago Aarand
Coin No. 12 ($5 Rowing): Terrance Smith

	Single Coins (Unc. or Proof)		Cased Custom Set	Cased Prestige Set	Cased Proof Set
Series	$5 Coin	$10 Coin	(2 x $5, 2 x $10)	(2 x $5, 2 x $10)	(2 x $5, 2 x $10)
III	$18.00	$35.00	$105.00	$105.00	$105.00

Coin No. 13
Men's Hurdles

Coin No. 14
Marathon

Coin No. 15
Women's Shot Put

Coin No. 16
Women's Javelin

Theme: Olympic Track & Field Sports
Official Release Date: August 12, 1975
Designer of Reverses: Leo Yerxa, winner of an invitational competition
Modellers: Coin No. 13 ($10 Men's Hurdles): Patrick Brindley
Coin No. 14 ($5 Marathon): Walter Ott
Coin No. 15 ($10 Women's Shot Put): Patrick Brindley
Coin No. 16 ($5 Women's Javelin): Walter Ott

Series	Single Coins (Unc. or Proof)		Cased Custom Set	Cased Prestige Set	Cased Proof Set
	$5 Coin	$10 Coin	(2 x $5, 2 x $10)	(2 x $5, 2 x $10)	(2 x $5, 2 x $10)
IV	$18.00	$35.00	$105.00	$105.00	$105.00

Coin No. 17
Paddling

Coin No. 18
Diving

Coin No. 19
Sailing

Coin No. 20
Swimming

Theme: Olympic Summer Sports
Official Release Date: December 1, 1975
Designer of Reverses: Linda Cooper, winner of an open national competition
Modellers: Coin No. 17 ($10 Paddling): none (design was photochemically etched)
            Coin No. 18 ($5 Diving): none (design was photochemically etched)
            Coin No. 19 ($10 Sailing): none (design was photochemically etched)
            Coin No. 20 ($5 Swimming): none (design was photochemically etched)

Series	Single Coins (Unc. or Proof)		Cased Custom Set	Cased Prestige Set	Cased Proof Set
	$5 Coin	$10 Coin	(2 x $5, 2 x $10)	(2 x $5, 2 x $10)	(2 x $5, 2 x $10)
V	$18.00	$35.00	$105.00	$105.00	$105.00

Coin No. 21
Field Hockey

Coin No. 22
Fencing

Coin No. 23
Soccer

Coin No. 24
Boxing

Theme: Olympic Team & Body Contact Sports
Official Release Date: March 1, 1976
Designer of Reverses: Shigeo Fududa, winner of an open international competition
Modellers: Coin No. 21 ($10 Field Hockey): none (design was photochemically etched)
　　　　　 Coin No. 22 ($5 Fencing): none (design was photochemically etched)
　　　　　 Coin No. 23 ($10 Soccer): none (design was photochemically etched)
　　　　　 Coin No. 24 ($5 Boxing): none (design was photochemically etched)

Series	Single Coins (Unc. or Proof)		Cased Custom Set (2 x $5, 2 x $10)	Cased Prestige Set (2 x $5, 2 x $10)	Cased Proof Set (2 x $5, 2 x $10)
	$5 Coin	$10 Coin			
VI	$18.00	$35.00	$105.00	$105.00	$105.00

Coin No. 25
Olympic Stadium

Coin No. 26
Olympic Village

Coin No. 27
Olympic Velodrome

Coin No. 28
Olympic Flame

Theme: Olympic Souvenirs
Official Release Date: June 1, 1976
Designer of Reverses: Elliott Morrison, winner of an invitational competition
Modellers: Coin No. 25 ($10 Olympic Stadium): Ago Aarand
Coin No. 26 ($5 Olympic Village): Sheldon Beverage
Coin No. 27 ($10 Olympic Velodrome): Terrance Smith
Coin No. 28 ($5 Olympic Flame): Walter Ott

Series	Single Coins (Unc. or Proof)		Cased Custom Set (2 x $5, 2 x $10)	Cased Prestige Set (2 x $5, 2 x $10)	Cased Proof Set (2 x $5, 2 x $10)
	$5 Coin	$10 Coin			
VII	$18.00	$35.00	$105.00	$105.00	$105.00

GOLD 20 DOLLARS

CENTENNIAL OF CONFEDERATION COMMEMORATIVE 1967

The highlight of the coins issued in 1967 to mark the centenary of Canadian Confederation was a $20 gold coin. It was issued only as part of a $40.00 specimen set in a black leather-covered case (see page 213), but many were later removed from the sets for separate trading. The reverse design is an adaption of the Canadian coat-of-arms, as on the 50¢ piece of 1960-1966. It is the only coin in the Centennial set that bears the single date 1967 instead of 1867-1967.

Designer: Portrait - Arnold Machin;
Reverse - Royal Canadian Mint staff

Modeller: Obverse - Myron Cook, using the Machin portrait model;
Reverse - Myron Cook, using the Thomas Shingles model of the Canadian coat-of-arms

Composition: .900 gold, .100 copper
Weight: 18.27 grams
Diameter: 27.05 mm
Edge: Reeded
Die Axes: ↑↑

Date	Quantity Minted	Specimen
1967 Confederation Commemorative	337,688	425.00

GOLD 100 DOLLARS

OLYMPIC COMMEMORATIVES 1976

As part of the series of collectors' coins to commemorate and help finance the XXI Olympiad, two separate $100 gold coins were issued in 1976. The reverse design for each shows an ancient Grecian athlete being crowned with laurel by the goddess Pallas Athena. The Uncirculated edition (uniformly shiny surface) is 14k gold and has rim denticles. The Proof edition (mirror fields and matte devices and legends) is 22k gold, slightly smaller, and lacks rim denticles.

Designer: Portrait - Arnold Machin;
Reverse - Dora de Pedery-Hunt
Modeller: Obverse - Walter Ott, using the Machin portrait model;
Reverse - Dora de Pedery-Hunt and Walter Ott
Composition: .583 gold, .417 copper alloy
Weight: 13.338 grams
Diameter: 27.00 mm
Edge: Reeded
Die Axes: ↑↑
Original Issue Price: $105.00

Date	Quantity Minted	Specimen
1976 14k Uncirculated Olympic Commemorative	572,387	200.00

Designer & Modeller: as above
Composition: .917 gold, .083 copper alloy
Weight: 16.966 grams
Diameter: 25.00 mm
Edge: Reeded
Die Axes: ↑↑
Original Issue Price: $150.00

Date	Quantity Minted	Proof
1976 22k Proof Olympic Commemorative	335,779	400.00

ELIZABETH II SILVER JUBILEE COMMEMORATIVE 1977

Following the sales success of the Olympic $100 coins, the government decided to embark upon a program to issue a $100 coin every year. The 1977 coin formed part of a two-coin set, the other coin was the silver dollar, issued in recognition of the Queen's Silver Jubilee. The special reverse shows a bouquet of flowers made up of the official flowers of the provinces and territories. All of the issue was of Proof quality, with mirror fields and matte devices and legends.

Designer: Portrait - Arnold Machin;
Reverse - Raymond Lee
Modeller: Reverse - Walter Ott
Composition: .917 gold, .083 silver
Weight: 16.589 grams
Diameter: 27.00 mm
Edge: Reeded
Die Axes: ↑↑
Original Issue Price: $140.00

Date	Quantity Minted	Proof
1977 Silver Jubilee Commemorative	180,396	500.00

CANADIAN UNITY COIN 1978

The reverse of the Proof $100 gold coin for 1978 depicts twelve Canada geese flying in formation. The image represents the ten provinces and two territories, and so promotes Canadian unity.

Designer: Portrait - Arnold Machin;
Reverse - Roger Savage
Modeller: Obverse - Royal Canadian Mint
staff, using the Machin model;
Reverse - Ago Aarand
Composition: .917 gold, .083 silver
Weight: 16.965 grams
Diameter: 27.00 mm
Edge: Reeded
Die Axes: ↑↑
Original Issue Price: $150.00

Date	Quantity Minted	Proof
1978 Unity Coin	200,000	425.00

INTERNATIONAL YEAR OF THE CHILD COMMEMORATIVE 1979

Children playing hand in hand beside a globe adorns the reverse of the 1979 $100 gold piece struck in honour of the International Year of the Child. The issue is in Proof only.

Designer: Portrait - Arnold Machin;
Reverse - Carala Tietz
Modeller: Obverse - Royal Canadian Mint
staff, using the Machin portrait
model
Reverse - Victor Cote

The physical and chemical specifications are as for the 1978 issue.

Original Issue Price: $185.00

Date	Quantity Minted	Proof
1979 International Year of the Child Commemorative	250,000	425.00

ARCTIC TERRITORIES COMMEMORATIVE 1980

The gold $100 coin for 1980 is a commemorative marking the 100th anniversary of the transfer of the Arctic Islands from the British government to the government of the Dominion of Canada. Its reverse shows an Inuk paddling a kayak near a small iceberg and has no lettering or date. The obverse features the Machin bust of Queen Elizabeth, with the legend and date.

Designer: Portrait - Arnold Machin;
Reverse - Arnoldo Marchetti
Modeller: Reverse - Sheldon Beverage

The physical and chemical specifications are as for the 1978-1979 issues.

Original Issue Price: $430.00

Date	Quantity Minted	Proof
1980 Arctic Islands $100 Commemorative		475.00

$50 MAPLE LEAF BULLION COINS 1979 - 1980

   Beginning in 1979 the Canadian government decided to produce a gold bullion issue to compete with similar pieces (such as the Krugerrand of South Africa) issued by other countries. Although the Canadian issue has a face value of $50, the value of the gold it contains is much greater than $50. Each coin contains one troy ounce (31.1 grams) of .999 fine gold, and its selling price is based on the current spot market price of gold bullion. The government has committed to strike 1,000,000 Maple Leaf coins for 1979 and 2,000,000 coins for each subsequent year.

Date and Denomination	Quantity Minted	Value
1979 Gold Maple Leaf $50	1,000,000	Price based on spot gold at
1980 Gold Maple Leaf $50	2,000,000 (proposed)	the day of sale or purchase

SPECIMEN CASES AND SETS 1858 - 1952

The sets of Specimen coins produced between 1858 and 1952 are among the most spectacular items in Canadian numismatics and are keenly sought after. These coins were usually beautifully struck and represent Canadian coinage at its best.

The finish imparted to Specimen coins has varied over the years. During the Victorian period, it was frosted raised elements with bright, mirror fields. In the reigns of Edward VII and George V an overall satin (sometimes called matte) finish was in vogue. The 1937 coins of George VI came with both finishes. Between 1938 and the mid-1940's the finish was frosted raised elements with bright fields. However, by the late 1940's the Specimen coins tend to have an overall polished appearance.

Specimen sets were often issued in official cases. These cases are sometimes encountered without any coins in them, and so are numbered, described and priced as separate entities, beginning on page 207, after the listings that follow.

CASED AND UNCASED SPECIMEN SETS 1858 - 1952

Date and Description	Price

NEW BRUNSWICK 1862

1862 Double Set: 2 x 1¢, 2 x 5¢, 2 x 10¢ (Normal Date), 2 x 20¢. Plain Edge,
in Case #2. .... $15,000.00
1862 Single Set: 1¢, 5¢, 10¢ (Normal Date), 20¢. Plain Edge, in Case #3. ...... $7,000.00

NOVA SCOTIA 1861

1861: ½¢, 1¢ (Large Rosebud). Not in case. $1,000.00

NEWFOUNDLAND 1864-1940

1864-65 Double Set: 1864 - 2 x 1¢ (NF-18); 1865 - 2 x 5¢, 2 x 10¢, 2 x 20¢,
2 x $2. Plain Edge, in Case #4. .... $10,000.00
1870 Double Set: 2 x 5¢, 2 x 10¢, 2 x 20¢, 2 x 50¢, 2 x $2. Plain Edge,
possibly in case. $25,000.00
1880: 1¢ (Narrow 0, but not the same as the currency issue), 5¢, 10¢,
20¢, 50¢, $2. Plain Edge, not in case. $20,000.00
1882H: 5¢, 10¢, 20¢, 50¢, $2. Reeded Edge, not in case. $15,000.00
1904H: 1¢, 5¢, 10¢, 20¢, 50¢. Silver with Reeded Edges, not in case. $5,000.00
1912: 5¢, 10¢, 20¢. Reeded Edge, not in case. $3,000.00
1917C: 1¢, 5¢, 10¢, 25¢, 50¢. Silver has Reeded Edges and officially
filed rims, not in case. $3,000.00
1919C: 1¢, 5¢, 10¢, 25¢, 50¢. Silver has Reeded Edges, not in case. $3,000.00
1938: 1¢, 5¢, 10¢. Silver has Reeded Edges, not in case. $2,500.00
1940C: 1¢ (no mint mark), 5¢, 10¢ (no mint mark). Silver has Reeded
Edges, not in case. $2,500.00

PROVINCE OF CANADA 1858

1858 Double Set: 2 x 1¢, 2 x 5¢ (Small Date), 2 x 10¢, 2 x 20¢. Plain Edge,
in Case #1. .... $15,000.00
As above, except one 5¢ is the Large Date over Small Date variety. $16,000.00

Dominion of Canada 1911-1912
Double Set

Date and Description	Price

DOMINION OF CANADA 1870-1952

1870 Double Set: 2 x 5¢ (one Wide Rims, the other Narrow Rims),
2 x 10¢ (Narrow 0), 2 x 25¢, 2 x 50¢ (L.C.W.).
Plain Edges, in Case #5. .... $25,000.00
1870 Single Set: 5¢ (Wide or Narrow Rims), 10¢ (Narrow 0), 25¢,
50¢ (L.C.W.). Reeded Edge, not in case. $12,500.00
1872H: 5¢, 10¢, 25¢, 50¢. Reeded Edges, not in case. $15,000.00
1875H: 5¢ (Large Date), 10¢, 25¢. Reeded Edge, not in case. $25,000.00
1880H: 5¢, 10¢, 25¢ (Narrow 0). Reeded Edges, not in case. $7,500.00
1881H: 1¢, 5¢, 10¢, 25¢, 50¢. Reeded Edges, not in case. $15,000.00
1902H: 5¢ (Large H), 10¢, 25¢. Not in case. $7,500.00
1903H: 5¢, 10¢, 50¢. Not in case. $10,000.00
1908: 1¢, 5¢, 10¢, 25¢, 50¢. In Cases #6, #7, #7a or #7b.
(Original Issue Price: $2.00) $2,000.00
1911: 1¢, 5¢, 10¢, 25¢, 50¢. In Case #9a. (Original Issue Price: $2.00) $10,000.00
1911-12: 1¢, 5¢, 10¢, 25¢, 50¢, £1, $5, $10. In Case #10.
(Original Issue Price: $24.00) $25,000.00
1921: 1¢, 5¢, 10¢, 25¢, 50¢. Not in case. $100,000.00
1922: 1¢, 5¢. Not in case. $1,000.00
1923: 1¢, 5¢. Not in case. $1,000.00
1924: 1¢, 5¢. Not in case. $1,000.00
1925: 1¢, 5¢. Not in case. $2,000.00
1926: 1¢, 5¢ (Near 6). Not in case. $2,500.00
1927: 1¢, 5¢, 25¢. Not in case. $4,000.00
1928: 1¢, 5¢, 10¢, 25¢. Not in case. $3,000.00
1929: 1¢, 5¢, 10¢, 25¢, 50¢. Not in case. $9,000.00

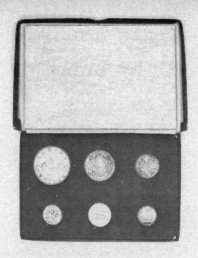

Dominion of Canada 1937
6 Coins in Cardboard Case #11

Dominion of Canada 1937
4 Coins in Case #9c

Date and Description	Price
1930: 1¢, 5¢, 10¢, 25¢. Not in case.	$4,000.00
1931: 1¢, 5¢, 10¢, 25¢, 50¢. In Case #9b.	$9,000.00
1932: 1¢, 5¢, 10¢, 25¢, 50¢. Not in case.	$12,500.00
1934: 1¢, 5¢, 10¢, 25¢, 50¢. Not in case.	$10,000.00
1936: 1¢, 5¢, 10¢, 25¢, 50¢. Not in case.	$9,000.00
1936: 1¢ (Dot), 5¢, 10¢ (Dot), 25¢ (Dot), 50¢, $1. Not in case.	RARE
1937: 1¢, 5¢, 10¢, 25¢, 50¢, $1. Satin Finish, in cardboard Case #11. (Original Issue Price: $3.25, including 25¢ for postage), 1,295 sets issued.	$1,000.00
1937: 1¢, 5¢, 10¢, 25¢. Mirror Fields, in Case #9c.	$750.00

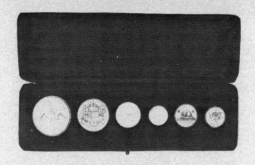

Dominion of Canada 1937
6 Coins in Case #9d

Date and Description	Price
1937: 1¢, 5¢, 10¢, 25¢, 50¢, $1. Mirror Fields, in Case #9d.	$2,500.00
1938: 1¢, 5¢, 10¢, 25¢, 50¢, $1. In Case #9e.	$15,000.00
1944: 1¢, 5¢, 10¢, 25¢, 50¢. Not in case.	RARE
1945: 1¢, 5¢, 10¢, 25¢, 50¢, $1. In Case #9e.	$5,000.00
1946: 1¢, 5¢, 10¢, 25¢, 50¢, $1. In Case #9e.	$5,000.00
1947: 1¢, 5¢, 10¢, 25¢, 50¢ (Curved 7), $1 (Pointed 7). In Case #9e.	$5,000.00
As above, except the $1 is the Blunt 7 variety.	$5,000.00
1947ML: 1¢, 5¢, 10¢, 25¢, 50¢ (Curved 7), $1. In Case #9e.	$12,500.00
1948: 1¢, 5¢, 10¢, 25¢, 50¢, $1. In Case #9e.	$7,500.00
1949: 1¢, 5¢, 10¢, 25¢, 50¢, $1. In Case #9e.	$5,000.00
1950: 1¢, 5¢, 10¢, 25¢, 50¢, $1 (Normal Water Lines). In Case #9e.	$2,500.00
As above, except the $1 is the Arnprior variety.	$2,500.00
1951: 1¢, 5¢ (Both Types), 10¢, 25¢, 50¢, $1 (Normal Water Lines). Not in case.	$2,500.00
1952: 1¢, 5¢, 10¢, 25¢, 50¢, $1 (Water Lines). In Case #9e.	$2,500.00

OFFICIAL (EMPTY) CASES FOR SPECIMEN SETS 1858 - 1952

Except for the cardboard box for the 1937 satin-finish sets issued through the Bank of Canada, all cases are leather covered. The cases used for sets between 1913 and 1952 were 1911 cases with the outer inscription covered and the inside modified to hold the appropriate denominations. Prices are given for cases in average condition.

In the listings below u = upper and l = lower.

Case #1 1858

CHARLTON NUMBER	INTENDED CONTENTS	EXTERIOR COLOUR & DIMENSIONS	INTERIOR COLOURS	PRICE FOR EMPTY CASE
1	1858 1¢, 5¢, 10¢, 20¢ 1¢, 5¢, 10¢, 20¢	Black, 7.5 x 11.5 cm	u: white l: dark blue	$500.00
2	New Brunswick 1862 1¢, 5¢, 10¢, 20¢ 1¢, 5¢, 10¢, 20¢	Details unknown. May be same as case #1.		$500.00
3	New Brunswick 1862 1¢, 5¢, 10¢, 20¢	Details unknown.		$300.00
4	Newfoundland 1864 (1¢); 1865 (others) 1¢, 5¢, 10¢, 20¢, $2 1¢, 5¢, 10¢, 20¢, $2	Details unknown. May be the same as case #1.		$500.00

Case #8 1911

CHARLTON NUMBER	INTENDED CONTENTS	EXTERIOR COLOUR & DIMENSIONS	INTERIOR COLOURS	PRICE FOR EMPTY CASE
5	1870 5¢, 10¢, 25¢, 50¢	Dark brown, 6.5 x 10.5 cm.	u: white l: dark blue	$300.00
6	1908 1¢, 5¢, 10¢, 25¢, 50¢	Maroon, 5.3 x 15.5 cm	u: purple, impressed in gold lettering: "First Coinage in Canada/ 1908/Ottawa" l: purple	$100.00
7	1908 1¢, 5¢, 10¢, 25¢, 50¢	Red, 5.3 x 15.5 cm	u & l: purple	$100.00
7a	1908 1¢, 5¢, 10¢, 25¢, 50¢	Red, 5.3 x 15.5 cm top impressed in gold lettering: "First Coinage in Canada/ 1908./Royal Mint Ottawa"	u & l: purple	$200.00
7b	1908 1¢, 5¢, 10¢, 25¢, 50¢	Red, 5.3 x 15.5 cm	u: purple with affixed red leather strip impressed in gold lettering: "First Coinage of Canadian Mint/Ottawa/1908" l: purple	$100.00
8	1911 1¢, 5¢, 10¢, 25¢, 50¢, $1 £1, $5, $10	Red, 8.9 x 19.7 cm top impressed in gold lettering: "Specimen Coins/Silver and Bronze/Ottawa Mint/ 1911"	u & l: purple	$500.00
9	1911 1¢, 5¢, 10¢, 25¢, 50¢, $1	Red, 5.3 x 19.7 cm top impressed in gold lettering:"Specimen Coins/Silver and Bronze/Ottawa Mint/ 1911"	u & l: purple	$200.00

Case #10 1911

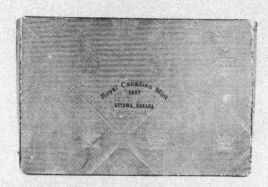

Case #11 1937

CHARLTON NUMBER	INTENDED CONTENTS	EXTERIOR COLOUR & DIMENSIONS	INTERIOR COLOURS	PRICE FOR EMPTY CASE
9a	1911 1¢, 5¢, 10¢, 25¢, 50¢	As case #9	As case #9	$200.00
10	1911 1¢, 5¢, 10¢, 25¢, 50¢ 1912 $5, $10 1911 £1	Red, 8.9 x 19.7 cm top impressed in gold lettering: "Specimen Coins/Ottawa Mint/ 1911-12"	u & l: purple	$500.00
9b	1931 1¢ (small), 5¢ (nickel), 10¢, 25¢, 50¢	As case #9	As case #9	$300.00
11	1937 1¢, 5¢, 10¢, 25¢, 50¢, $1	Red cardboard, 10.2 x 15.3 cm, with horizontal ridges, crowns and sceptres and in black lettering: "Royal Canadian Mint/1937/Ottawa, Canada"	u: coarse white cloth l: royal blue cardboard	$50.00

Case #9c 1937

Case #9e 1938-1952

CHARLTON NUMBER	INTENDED CONTENTS	EXTERIOR COLOUR & DIMENSIONS	INTERIOR COLOURS	PRICE FOR EMPTY CASE
9c	1937 1¢, 5¢, 10¢, 25¢	As case #9, except date covered by paper Union Jack	As case #9	$150.00
9d	1937 1¢, 5¢, 10¢, 25¢, 50¢, $1	As case #9, except the inscription is covered by a blue leather strip upon which is impressed in gold a view of the centre section of the Royal Canadian Mint surrounded on the sides and bottom by a ribbon. "1937" is below. On the ribbon is "Royal Canadian Mint"	As case #9	$200.00
9e	1938-1952 1¢, 5¢, 10¢, 25¢, 50¢, $1	As case #9d, except for the absence of "1937"		$200.00

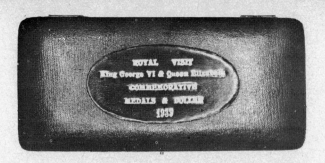

Case #8a 1939

Case #12 1953

CHARLTON NUMBER	INTENDED CONTENTS	EXTERIOR COLOUR & DIMENSIONS	INTERIOR COLOURS	PRICE FOR EMPTY CASE
8a	1939 54 mm medal, $1, 54 mm medal	As case #8, except the inscription is covered by an oval blue patch impressed in gold lettering: Royal Visit/ King George VI & Queen Elizabeth/ Commemorative/ Medals & Dollar/1939"		$100.00
12	1953 1¢, 5¢, 10¢, 25¢, 50¢, $1	Red, top impressed in gold with a view of the centre section of the Royal Canadian Mint surrounded on the sides and bottom by a ribbon bearing "Royal Canadian Mint "	u & l: purple	$200.00

PROOF-LIKE AND SPECIMEN SETS 1953 - 1970

Although some silver dollars of Proof-like quality were issued prior to 1953, it has not been confirmed that any entire sets were issued. Certainly some minor coins in the sets of 1950-1952 are Proof-like, but either the few Proof-likes made were mixed up with circulation strikes in making up the sets or certain denominations were not made as Proof-likes to begin with. In any case the majority of the coins in the sets sold to the public by the mint in 1950-1953 were nothing more than circulation strikes that had not gone through mint bags. Beginning in 1954 and continuing through 1969, all mint sets which the Royal Canadian Mint sold to the public were Proof-like. The quality was somewhat inferior in 1965 due to greatly increased production and in 1968-1969 due to the inexperience of the mint in producing larger Proof-like coins in nickel. The original issue prices of Proof-like sets were: $2.20 (1953), $2.50 (1954-1959), $3.00 (1960-1964), $4.00 (1965-1970).

During the period 1953 to 1970, Specimen sets were also produced in some years. This generally does not pose a difficulty because the Specimen coins were either issued in special packaging or are of markedly better quality than the corresponding Proof-like coins.

Proof-like sets issued from 1953 to 1960 came in flat white cardboard holders housed in cellophane envelopes. On some 1960 holders appeared the black stamp, "ROYAL CANADIAN MINT / OTTAWA, CANADA." From 1961 to 1970 the Proof-like sets were issued in a sealed pliofilm pack embossed with "ROYAL CANADIAN MINT" in the gutters between the coins.

Proof-like Set Issued 1953-1960

Proof-like Set Issued 1961 to Date

Date and Description	Proof-like Sets		Specimen Sets	
	Mintage	Value	Mintage	Value
1953 No Shoulder Fold (in case #12)	1,200	$1,000.00	Unknown	$2,500.00
1953 Shoulder Fold	Included	$1,000.00	Unknown	$2,500.00
1954 Shoulder Fold	3,000	$500.00	—	—
1954 No Shoulder Fold	Included	$650.00	—	—
1955 Normal Water Lines Dollar	6,300	$375.00	—	—
1955 Arnprior Dollar	Included	$500.00	—	—
1956	6,500	$250.00	—	—
1957	11,862	$125.00	—	—
1958	18,259	$125.00	—	—
1959	31,577	$50.00	—	—
1960	64,097	$35.00	—	—
1961	98,373	$25.00	—	—
1962	200,950	$25.00	—	—
1963	673,006	$25.00	—	—
1964	1,653,162	$25.00	Unknown	$750.00
1965 Variety 1 Dollar	2,904,352	$25.00	Unknown*	$750.00
1965 Variety 2 Dollar	Included	$25.00	—	—
1966 Small Beads Dollar	672,514	$25.00	—	—
1966 Large Beads Dollar	Incl.	$25.00	—	—
1967	963,714	$25.00	See below	
1968	521,641	$4.00	—	—
1969	326,203	$4.00	—	—
1970	349,120	$10.00	See below	

* Superb strikes, with no roughness on the Queen's shoulder.

CASED CONFEDERATION COMMEMORATIVE SET 1967

SILVER MEDALLION PRESENTATION SET

In 1967 the Royal Canadian Mint produced two special cased coin sets to mark the 100th anniversary of Confederation. The set in the red leather-covered case contained one each of the 1¢ to $1 (Proof-like quality) and a sterling silver medallion designed and modelled by Thomas Shingles. The original issue price was $12.00.

1967 Centennial 1¢, 5¢, 10¢, 25¢, 50¢, $1, plus silver medallion $50.00

GOLD PRESENTATION SET

The premier 1967 coin set contained a $20 gold coin (see page 198) and one each of the 1¢ to $1, all of Specimen quality. The coins were housed in a black leather-covered case. The original issue price was $40.00, and 337,688 were issued.

1967 Centennial 1¢, 5¢, 10¢, 25¢, 50¢, $1, plus $20 gold piece $475.00

Cased Specimen Set 1970

CASED SPECIMEN SET 1970

In 1970 the Royal Canadian Mint considered the possibility of resuming the sale of cased Specimen sets to the public on a regular basis. In connection with this and also to provide Prime Minister Pierre Trudeau with special sets for presentation purposes during his trip to China that year, a quantity of Specimen sets in narrow cases was made up. After Trudeau's trip, some of these sets were sold to the public for $13.00 each. The total quantity of 1970 Specimen sets issued in Canada is believed to be less than 1,000 and the only way 1970 Specimen coins were available was in these sets. When the mint made Specimen sets generally available starting in 1971, they were housed in a larger, different style case.

1970 Specimen set in black case $750.00

COLLECTORS' COIN SETS 1971 - 1980

In 1971 the Royal Canadian Mint expanded its product line so that a total of three different coin sets was available to the public.

REGULAR SET (6 COINS)

This was a continuation of the set offered previously. It contains one of each denomination (for a total of six coins) packaged in a flat pliofilm pouch. From 1971 to 1976 the quality of the coins was Proof-like; since that time it has been Specimen. The original issue prices have been: $4.00 (1971-1973), $5.00 (1974-1975), $5.15 (1976-1977), $5.25 (1978), $6.25 (1979) and $8.00 (1980).

CUSTOM SET (TWO 1¢ PIECES)

The Custom Set contains one of each denomination, with an extra cent to show the obverse. It is housed in a square vinyl-covered case. From 1971 to 1976 the quality of the coins was Proof-like; since that time it has been Specimen. The original selling prices have been: $6.50 (1971-1973), $8.00 (1974-1975), $8.15 (1976-1977), $8.75 (1978), $10.75 (1979) and $12.50 (1980). The packaging details are as follows:

1971: coins in black vinyl-covered case with Canada's coat-of-arms and the word "CANADA" stamped in gold on the top.

1972 - 1973: as 1971, except the vinyl is red.

1974 - 1978: as 1971, except the vinyl is maroon.

1979 to Date: as 1974-1978, except a gold maple leaf replaces the coat-of-arms and "CANADA".

PRESTIGE SET (TWO $1 PIECES)

When it was first introduced in 1971, the Prestige Set had two nickel dollars (and no silver dollar), with the second nickel dollar used to show the obverse. This was also true for 1972, but from 1973 on the second nickel dollar was replaced with a silver dollar. The quality of the coins in the Prestige Set has always been Specimen. The original issue prices have been: $12.00 (1971-1973), $15.00 (1974-1975), $16.00 (1976-1977), $16.50 (1978), $18.50 (1979) and $36.00 (1980). The sets have been housed in rectangular black leather-covered cases, the details of which are as follows:

1971 - 1973: coins mounted in case covered with black leather with an oxidized silver Canadian coat-of-arms on the front.

1974 to Date: coins held in page-like plastic frame so both sides of the coins can be viewed in satin-lined case covered with black leather with an oxidized silver Canadian coat-of-arms on the front.

Date	Regular Set (Six Coins)		Custom Set (7 Coins) With Two 1¢ Pieces		Prestige Set (7 Coins) With Two $1 Pieces	
	Mintage	Value	Mintage	Value	Mintage	Value
1971	253,311	$7.50	33,517	$10.00	66,860	$25.00
1972	224,275	$6.50	38,198	$10.00	36,349	$75.00
1973 Large Bust 25¢	243,695	$750.00	49,376	$650.00	119,891	$650.00
1973 Small Bust 25¢	Included	$7.50	Included	$10.00	Included	$20.00
1974	312,589	$8.50	44,296	$10.00	85,230	$20.00
1975	197,372	$7.50	36,851	$10.00	97,263	$20.00
1976	171,737	$15.00	28,162	$13.00	87,744	$35.00
1977	225,307	$14.00	42,198	$13.00	142,577	$40.00
1978	260,000	$10.00	41,000	$12.50	147,000	$20.00
1979	187,624	$10.00	31,174	$12.50	155,698	$35.00
1980	Unknown	$10.00	Unknown	$12.50	Unknown	$45.00

PATTERNS, TRIAL PIECES & OFFICIAL FABRICATIONS

A PATTERN is a piece submitted as a design sample by engravers when a new coinage is contemplated. If the design is adopted for regular coinage with the same date, the piece ceases to be a pattern. If the design is adopted with a later date, the piece remains a pattern. Patterns are usually struck as proofs.

A TRAIL PIECE or ESSAI is from dies already accepted for regular coinage. It may bear a date or mint mark other than on the coins issued for circulation or it may be in a different metal.

AN OFFICIAL FABRICATION is a piece that was created for some special purpose unconnected with design proposals or experiments on coinage design or metals. For example, the New Brunswick pieces bearing the dates 1870, 1871 and 1875 were obviously not connected with an attempt to revive a separate coinage for that province after Confederation.

The best listing of patterns, trial pieces and official fabrications has been by Fred Bowman in his book "Canadian Patterns." The present listing is greatly revised compared to Bowman's and new numbers are used. However, Bowman's original numbers are also included for those pieces which were listed in his book.

PROVINCE OF CANADA

CHARLTON NUMBER	BOWMAN NUMBER	PATTERNS

PC-1   B-4   One Cent 1858, bronze. Uniface - obverse blank. Not a proof. Reverse - wreath of maple leaves and seed pods with beaded circle containing ONE/CENT/1858. (National Currency Collection)

PC-2   B-4   One Cent 1858, bronze. Uniface - obverse blank. Proof. Reverse - similar to PC-1 except the date is more closely spaced and the device is farther from the inner beaded circle. (National Currency Collection)

PC-3   B-3   One Cent 1858, bronze. Proof. Obverse - adopted legend with diademed bust of Victoria. Reverse - pattern design as on PC-2. (Wayte Raymond Sale 1928)

PC-4   B-6   Twenty Cents 1858, silver. Plain edge proof, dies ↑↑ . Obverse - adopted design. Reverse - adopted design for New Brunswick. (National Currency Collection)

PC-5   B-5   One Cent 1859 (in Roman numerals), bronze. Proof. Obverse - adopted design. Reverse - Britannia reverse for a pattern British halfpenny. (Parsons Collection 1936)

TRIAL PIECES

PC-6   One Cent 1858, cupro-nickel. Dies ↑↑ . Adopted design; struck from proof dies on an unpolished blank of double thickness. (National Currency Collection)

PC-7   One Cent 1858, cupro-nickel. Proof; dies ↑↑ . Adopted design; normal thickness. (National Currency Collection)

NOVA SCOTIA

PATTERNS

NS-1

Half Cent 1860. Reverse - crown surrounded by wreath of roses; date below wreath. (The illustration is from a matrix. It is uncertain whether patterns bearing this date were actually produced.)

NS-2

One Cent 1860. Reverse - crown surrounded by wreath of roses; date below wreath. (The illustration is from a matrix. It is uncertain whether patterns bearing this date were actually produced.)

NS-3   B-11

Half Cent 1861, bronze. Proof; dies ↑ ↑ . Obverse - large bust of Victoria by James Wyon. Reverse - pattern design as on NS-1. (National Currency Collection)

NS-4   B-7

One Cent 1861, bronze. Proof; dies ↑ ↑ . Obverse - large bust of Victoria by James Wyon. Reverse - pattern design as on NS-2. (National Currency Collection)

NS-5   B-13   Half Cent 1861, bronze. Proof; dies ↑↓ . Obverse - adopted (small bust) design by L.C. Wyon. Reverse - pattern design as NS-3. (National Currency Collection)

NS-6   B-8   One Cent 1861, bronze. Not a proof; dies ↑↑ . Obverse - adopted (small bust) design by L.C. Wyon. Reverse - pattern design as NS-4. (National Currency Collection)

NS-7   B-12   Half Cent 1861, bronze. Proof; dies ↑↑ . Obverse - pattern design as on NS-3. Reverse - adopted design (crown and date surrounded by a wreath of mayflowers and roses). (New Netherlands Coin Sale 1960)

NS-8   B-10   One Cent 1861, bronze. Proof; dies ↑↑ and ↑↓ . Obverse - pattern design as on NS-4. Reverse - adopted design (1861), large rose bud variety. (National Currency Collection)

NS-8a B-10 One Cent 1861, bronze. Proof; dies ↑ ↑ . As NS-8, except the reverse is the small rose bud variety (adopted design for 1861-1864).

NS-9 B-14 Half Cent 186–, bronze. Proof. As NS-5, except for the incomplete date.

NS-10 B-9 One Cent 186–, bronze. As NS-6, except for the incomplete date.

NEW BRUNSWICK

CHARLTON NUMBER	BOWMAN NUMBER	PATTERNS

NB-1 B-15 One Cent 1861, bronze. Proof; dies ↑ ↑ . Obverse - large bust design by James Wyon as on NS-6, etc. Reverse - adopted design. (National Currency Collection)

NB-2 B-20 Ten Cents 1862, silver. Reeded edge proof; dies ↑ ↑ . Obverse - adopted design. Reverse - legend and date surrounded by arabesque design somewhat similar to that used for Newfoundland. The arabesque reverse on this piece was also used for a pattern ten-cent piece for Hong Kong. (National Currency Collection)

TRIAL PIECES

NB-3 One Cent 1862, bronze. Proof. As adopted design, except for the date. Struck to make the date uniform for the 1862 proof sets.

OFFICIAL FABRICATIONS

NB-4 B-23 Twenty Cents 1862, silver. Plain edge proof; dies ↑ ↑ . Obverse - plain, except for the legend G.W. WYON/OBIT/MARCH 27TH 1862/AETAT/26 YEARS. Reverse - adopted design. This is an obituary medalet for George W. Wyon, who was resident engraver at the Royal Mint. The fact that this reverse was chosen for the piece suggests that it was engraved by George Wyon. (National Currency Collection)

221

The following six pieces (NB-5 to NB-10) obviously have nothing to do with contemplated designs for New Brunswick, since they bear dates after Confederation. It is believed they were struck for exhibition purposes where only the type was considered important.

NB-5   B-18   Five Cents 1870, silver. Reeded edge proof; dies ↑ ↑ . Obverse - adopted design. Reverse - adopted design for the Dominion of Canada (wire rim variety). (National Currency Collection)

NB-6   B-21   Ten Cents 1870, silver. Reeded edge proof; dies ↑ ↑ . Obverse - adopted design. Reverse - adopted design for the Dominion of Canada and New Brunswick. (National Currency Collection)

NB-7   B-22   Ten Cents 1871, silver. Reeded edge proof; dies ↑ ↑ . As NB-6, except for the date. (Caldecott Sale 1912)

NB-8   B-24   Twenty Cents 1871, silver. Plain and reeded edge proofs; dies ↑ ↑ . As the adopted design, except for the date. (National Currency Collection)

NB-9   B-19   Five Cents 1875, silver. Reeded edge proof; dies ↑ ↑ . Obverse - adopted design. Reverse - adopted design for the Dominion of Canada. (National Currency Collection)

NB-10   Five Cents 1875H, silver. reeded edge proof. As NB-9, except for the H mint mark. (Douglas Robins 1974)

CHARLTON NUMBER	BOWMAN NUMBER	PATTERNS

BC-1   B-37   Ten Dollars 1862, silver. Dies ↑↓ . Obverse - crown and legend. Reverse - wreath, denomination and date. (National Currency Collection)

BC-2   B-36   Twenty Dollars 1862, silver. Dies ↑↑ . Design similar to BC-1. (National Currency Collection)

BC-3   B-37   Ten Dollars 1862, gold. Design as BC-1. (B.C. Provincial Archives)

BC-4   B-36   Twenty Dollars 1862, gold. Design as BC-2. (B.C. Provincial Archives)

NEWFOUNDLAND

PATTERNS

The following five patterns (NF-1 to NF-5) are the result of a directive given by Master of the Royal Mint Thomas Graham in which he stated that the designs for the reverses of the Newfoundland coins should be those of New Brunswick. This was later altered.

CHARLTON NUMBER	BOWMAN NUMBER	
NF-1		One Cent 1864. Reverse - similar to the design adopted for the New Brunswick cent. Presently unknown as a struck piece, but may exist.
NF-2	B-28	Five Cents 1864, bronze. Plain edge. Obverse - adopted design. Reverse - crown and wreath design adopted for New Brunswick, etc. (W.W.C. Wilson Sale 1925)
NF-3	B-29	Ten Cents 1864, bronze. Plain edge. Obverse - adopted design. Reverse - crown and wreath design adopted for New Brunswick, etc. (British Museum)

NF-4	B-32	Twenty Cents 1864, bronze. Indented corded edge; dies ↑ ↓ . Obverse - adopted design. Reverse - crown and wreath design adopted for New Brunswick. (National Currency Collection)

NF-5	B-31	Two Dollars 1864, bronze. Plain edge; dies ↑ ↓ . Obverse - adopted design. Reverse - crown and wreath from the New Brunswick, etc. ten cents with the legend TWO/DOLLARS/1864 in the centre. (National Currency Collection)

NF-6   B-25   One Cent, bronze. Dies ↑ ↑ ; not a proof. Obverse - similar to adopted design, except the legend reads VICTORIA QUEEN. Reverse - similar to adopted design, except one leaf is missing from the top of each side of the wreath. (National Currency Collection)

NF-7   B-27   One Cent 1865, bronze. Proof; dies ↑ ↑ . Obverse - adopted design for Nova Scotia and New Brunswick. Reverse - pattern designs as for NF-6, except for the date.

NF-8   Five Cents 1865, silver. Plain edge proof; dies ↑ ↓ . Obverse - adopted design. Reverse - similar to the adopted design, except the arches are much thinner. (National Currency Collection)

NF-9   Ten Cents 1865, silver. Plain edge proof; dies ↑ ↓ . Obverse - adopted design. Reverse - similar to the adopted design, except the arches are much thinner. (National Currency Collection)

NF-10   Twenty Cents 1865, silver. Plain edge proof; dies ↑ ↓ . Obverse - adopted design. Reverse - similar to the adopted design, except the arches are much thinner. (National Currency Collection)

NF-11   Five Cents 1865, silver. Plain edge proof; dies ↑ ↓ . Obverse - adopted design. Reverse - as the adopted design, except the arches and dots have raised edges. (National Currency Collection)

NF-12   Ten Cents 1865, silver. Plain edge proof; dies ↑ ↓ . Obverse - adopted design. Reverse - as the adopted design, except the arches and dots have raised edges. (National Currency Collection)

NF-13   Twenty Cents 1865, silver. Plain edge proof; dies ↑ ↓ . Obverse - adopted design. Reverse - similar to the adopted design, except for some details of the arches and the presence of a raised line just inside the rim denticles. (National Currency Collection)

NF-14   B-33   Two Dollars 1865, gold. Plain edge proof; dies ↑ ↑ . Obverse - adopted design. Reverse - similar to the adopted design, except the legend and date are in block type. (National Currency Collection)

NF-15   B-34   Two Dollars 1865, gold. Plain edge proof. Obverse - small bust of Victoria (from the five cents) in beaded circle with the legend VICTORIA D:G REG:/ NEWFOUNDLAND. Reverse - pattern design as on NF-14.

NF-16   B-35   Fifty Cents 1870, bronze. Plain edge proof; dies ↑ ↑ . Obverse - adopted design. Reverse - as the adopted design, except the denticles are longer and touch the device. (National Currency Collection)

NF-17   Two Dollars 1870, gold. Plain edge proof. Obverse - pattern designs as on NF-15. Reverse - adopted design.

NF-18   B-26   One Cent 1864, bronze. Proof; dies ↑ ↑ . As the adopted design, except for the date. This is the piece that is believed to have been included in the specimen sets of 1864-1865. Proofs of the adopted design of the cent dated 1865 seem not to have been produced. (National Currency Collection)

NF-19   Fifty Cents 1882, silver. Reeded edge proof. As the adopted design, except for the absence of the H mint mark. (British Museum)

NF-20   Ten Cents 1945C, nickel. Struck on a thin blank; not a proof. This piece is rather weakly struck because of the thinness of the blank, suggesting that it is nothing more than a mint error. (National Currency Collection)

DOMINION OF CANADA

DC-1   B-38   One Cent 1876H, bronze. Proof; dies ↑ ↑. Obverse - adopted laureated head design for the Province of Canada. Reverse - adopted design. The existence of this pattern suggests that the government of the Dominion of Canada initially considered using the Province of Canada laureated obverse for its new cent. (National Currency Collection)

DC-2   Ten Cents (no date), bronze. Reeded edge proof. Obverse - adopted design (Haxby Obv. 6). Reverse - plain, except for a "B" engraved on the piece after it was struck. Probably unique. (National Currency Collection)

DC-3   Fifty Cents 1870, bronze. Plain edge proof; dies ↑ ↑. Obverse - no L.C.W. on the truncation, but otherwise very similar to Haxby Obv. 2. Reverse - slight differences in some leaves compared to the adopted design. (National Currency Collection)

DC-5   One Cent 1911, bronze. Specimen. As the adopted design for 1912-1920, except for the date; i.e. the obverse legend has DEI GRA:. (Royal Mint Collection)

DC-6   B-40   One Dollar 1911, silver. Reeded edge specimen; dies ↑ ↑ . Obverse - the standard MacKennal design later adopted for the 1936 dollar. Reverse - crown, wreath, legend and date. (Tony Carrato 1979)

In the Dominion of Canada Currency Act of 1910, which received Royal Assent on the 4th of May, 1910, provision was made for the striking of a Canadian silver dollar. The schedule appended to the Act specified a coin of 360 grains weight and a standard fineness of .925 silver. The Dominion Government, having decided to add a silver dollar to the coinage, purchased a new coining-press from Taylor and Challen of Birmingham, England, for the express purpose of striking coins of this size. A pair of dies for the new coin were prepared by the Die and Medal Department of the Royal Mint, London, and at least two specimens were struck. When cases were prepared for the specimen sets of the first Canadian coinage of George V, a space was left for the dollar. Later, however, the Dominion authorities decided against the issue of a silver dollar at that time, although no reason was given for this decision.

Only two specimens of the 1911 silver dollar are known to exist; one is in the Royal Mint Museum and the other was sold at the 1979 ANA sale for $160,000. U.S.

DC-6a   One Dollar 1911, lead. As DC-6, except for the metal. Probably unique. This piece was only recently discovered by the numismatic world, having been in storage in Ottawa since 1911. It is believed to be a sample piece struck at the Ottawa Mint to be used for gaining approval to proceed with the production of coins for circulation. (National Currency Collection)

DC-7   B-41   Five Dollars 1911, gold. Reeded edge specimen; dies ↑↑ . As the adopted design for 1912-1914, except for the date. (Royal Mint Collection)

DC-8   B-42   Ten Dollars 1911, gold. Reeded edge specimen; dies ↑↑ . As the adopted design for 1912-1914, except for the date. (Royal Mint Museum)

In 1926 Dominion notes (the treasury notes issued by the government of the Dominion of Canada) were made redeemable in gold for the first time since 1914. Since the time of the production of the gold $5 and $10 of 1912-1914, it had been concluded that the coat-of-arms borne on their reverses was incorrect. Therefore, new reverses were engraved in the event that a gold coinage would again have to be struck. Bronze patterns were produced to have samples of the designs. A few of these, probably made for the designer, G.E. Kruger-Gray, have the obverse design machined off, "SPECIMEN" punched in instead, and the entire piece acid-etched.

DC-9

Five Dollars 1928, bronze. Reeded edge; dies ↑ ↑. Obverse - as the adopted design for the 1912-1914 issues. Reverse - modified Canadian arms by G.E. Kruger-Gray. (National Currency Collection)

DC-10

Ten Dollars 1928, bronze. Reeded edge, dies ↑ ↑. Obverse - as the adopted design for the 1912-1914 issues. Reverse - modified Canadian arms by G.E. Kruger-Gray. (National Currency Collection)

DC-11

Five Dollars 1928, bronze. Reeded edge. Obverse - planed off flat just inside the denticles after striking; SPECIMEN has been punched in by hand. Reverse - pattern design as on DC-9. The entire piece has been acid-etched (officially) giving it a light brown colour. (National Currency Collection)

DC-12

Ten Dollars 1928, bronze. Reeded edge. Obverse - planed off flat just inside the denticles after striking; SPECIMEN has been punched in by hand. Reverse - pattern design as on DC-10. The entire piece has been etched as for DC-11.

DC-13   One Dollar 1964, tin. Plain edge; not a proof. Obverse - blank, except for small symbol ·F· . Reverse - similar to the adopted design, except for being higher in relief and having thin rounded rim denticles instead of wide square ones. Piefort, Unique. This unusual price is a matrix trial. (National Currency Collection.

DC-14   One Dollar 1967, silver. Reeded edge; not a specimen. Similar to the adopted design, except the fields on both sides are flat instead of concave and the rim beads differ slightly in size and position.

TRIAL PIECES

DC-15   Fifty Cents (no date), white metal. Trial impression of portrait of Victoria only; as on Haxby Obv. 2, 1870-1872. (National Currency Collection)

DC-16   Five Cents 1875, silver. Reeded edge proof; dies ↑ ↓ . As the adopted design, except for the absence of the H mint mark. (National Currency Collection)

DC-17   One Cent (1876H), cupro-nickel. Proof. As the adopted design. These pieces are believed to have been struck for exhibition purposes, without regard to the fact that there was no currency issue corresponding exactly to them. (American Numismatic Society)

DC-18   One Cent 1876, bronze. Proof; dies ↑ ↑. As the adopted design, except for the absence of the H mint mark. (National Currency Collection)

The five brass pieces listed below (DC-19 to DC-23) were produced at the Paris Mint. It is there that the original matrices for these denominations were engraved as the Royal Mint was too busy producing coins for Great Britain.

DC-19   One Cent 1937, brass. Specimen; dies ↑ ↓. As the adopted design. Slightly thicker than normal. (National Currency Collection)

DC-20   Five Cents 1937, brass. Specimen; dies ↑ ↓ . As the adopted design. Slightly thicker than normal. (National Currency Collection)

DC-21   Ten Cents 1937, brass. Reeded edge specimen; dies ↑ ↓ . As the adopted design. Slightly thicker than normal. (National Currency Collection)

DC-22   Twenty-Five Cents 1937, brass. Reeded edge specimen; dies ↑ ↓ . As the adopted design. Slightly thicker than normal. (National Currency Collection)

DC-23   Fifty Cents 1937, brass. Reeded edge specimen; dies ↑ ↓ . As the adopted design. Thicker than normal. (National Currency Collection)

DC-24   Twenty-Five Cents 1937, bronze. Reeded edge; dies ↑ ↑ . As the adopted design. Normal thickness. (National Currency Collection)

DC-25   Five Cents 1942, nickel. Dies ↑ ↑ ; not a specimen. As the 12-sided design adopted for the tombac pieces. (National Currency Collection)

DC-26   One Cent 1943, copper-plated steel. Dies ↑ ↑ ; not a specimen. As the adopted design. (National Currency Collection)

DC-27   Five Cents 1943, steel. Specimen. As the design adopted for the tombac pieces. (Piece seen, but composition not confirmed).

DC-28   Five Cents 1944, tombac. As the design adopted for the chrome-plated steel pieces. (Piece seen, but composition not confirmed).

DC-29   Five Cents 1951, chrome-plated steel. Specimen; dies ↑ ↑ . As the commemorative design struck in nickel. (National Currency Collection)

DC-30   Five Cents 1952. Specimen; dies ↑ ↑ . As the adopted design, except differs in composition, which has not yet been determined. White coloured, instead of the normal bluish. (National Currency Collection)

DC-31   Fifty Cents 1959, tin. Uniface on thick, oversize blank. Obverse - blank except for the engraved inscription (added after the piece was struck) FIRST TRIAL/ Oct 27th/1958. Reverse - as the adopted design, except lacks rim denticles. Unique. (National Currency Collection)

DC-32   Twenty Cents 1871, silver. Reeded and plain edge specimen; dies ↑ ↓ . As the adopted design for the Province of Canada, except for the date. This piece does not represent a proposed twenty cents for the Dominion of Canada. It is believed to have been struck for exhibition to show the Province of Canada twenty cents. Only the type was important; no concern was given to using a date corresponding to the coins actually issued for circulation. (National Currency Collection)

TEST TOKENS

On occasion the Mint has produced special tokens for machine-testing or other purposes. These tokens are the diameter of standard Canadian coins, but they may or may not be in the same metal as the coins to which they correspond.

**CHARLTON
NUMBER**

TT-1   Fifty Cents Size, bronze. Dies ↑ ↑ , reeded edge. Obverse: OTTAWA MINT / TRIAL RUN. Reverse: NOVEMBER/1907.
Struck to adjust the coining presses prior to the first production of Canadian coins at the new Ottawa Branch of the Royal Mint.

TT-2   Ten Cent Size, nickel. Dies ↑ ↑ , reeded edge. Obverse & Reverse: bouquet of flowers and fleur-de-lis with legend R.C.M. TEN TOKENS 1965.
Struck to provide an example of the quality of coins produced by the Royal Canadian Mint and to provide a piece for adjusting vending machines for nickel coins.

TT-3   As TT-2, except the R.C.M. has been removed from the design.

Photo Not
To Scale

TT-4   Twenty-Five Cent Size, nickel. Dies ↑ ↑ , reeded edge. Obverse & Reverse: three Canada geese flying to left with legend TWENTY FIVE TOKENS / 1965 / R.C.M. (for Royal Canadian Mint).
Struck to provide an example of the quality of coins produced by the Royal Canadian Mint and to provide a piece for adjusting vending machines for nickel coins.

TT-5   As TT-4, except the R.C.M. has been removed from the design.

Photo Not
To Scale

TT-6   Fifty Cent Size, nickel. Dies ↑ ↑ , reeded edge. Obverse & Reverse: standing ram facing
right with mountains in background and legend 50 TOKENS / R.C. MINT / 1965.
Struck to provide an example of the quality of coins produced by the Royal Canadian Mint.

TT-7   As TT-6, except struck in brass.

TT-8   Twenty-Five Cent Size, cupro-nickel. Dies ↑ ↑ , reeded edge. Obverse: conjoined busts of
King George VI and Queen Elizabeth as used on the school children's Royal Visit medal of
1939. Reverse: three Canada geese flying to left with legend TWENTY FIVE TOKENS /
1965 / CANADA.

APPENDIX I

GOLD CONTENT OF CANADIAN GOLD COINS

Denom.	Date and Mint Mark	Gross Weight (Grams)	Fineness	Pure Gold Content (Grams)	(Troy Oz.)
NEWFOUNDLAND:					
$2	1865-1888	3.33	.917	3.05	.100
CANADA					
£1	1908C-1910C	7.99	.917	7.32	.236
£1	1911C-1919C	7.99	.917	7.32	.236
$5	1912-1914	8.36	.900	7.52	.242
$10	1912-1914	16.72	.900	15.05	.484
$20	1967	18.27	.900	16.45	.529
$50	1979-1980	31.10	.999	31.10	1.000
$100	1976 (Unc.)	13.33	.583	7.78	.250
$100	1976 (Proof)	16.96	.917	15.55	.499
$100	1977	16.96	.917	15.55	.499
$100	1979	16.96	.917	15.55	.499
$100	1980	16.96	.917	15.55	.499

APPENDIX Ia

BULLION VALUES OF CANADIAN GOLD COINS

(Computed from $400/troy ounce to $1,000/troy ounce in increments of $50 Canadian)

Denom.	Date & Mint Mark	$400	$450	$500	$550	$600	$650	$700	$750	$800	$850	$900	$950	$1000
NEWFOUNDLAND														
$2	1865-1888	40.00	45.00	50.00	55.00	60.00	65.00	70.00	75.00	80.00	85.00	90.00	95.00	100.00
CANADA														
£1	1908C-1910C	94.40	106.20	118.00	129.80	141.60	153.40	165.20	177.00	188.80	200.60	212.40	224.20	236.00
£1	1911C-1919C	94.40	106.20	118.00	129.80	141.60	153.40	165.20	177.00	188.80	200.60	212.40	224.20	236.00
$5	1912-1914	96.80	108.90	121.00	133.10	145.20	157.30	169.40	181.50	193.60	205.70	217.80	229.90	242.00
$10	1912-1914	193.60	217.80	242.00	266.20	290.40	314.60	338.80	363.00	387.20	411.40	435.60	459.80	484.00
$20	1967	211.60	238.05	264.50	290.95	317.40	343.85	370.30	396.75	423.20	449.65	476.10	502.55	529.00
$50	1979-1980	400.00	450.00	500.00	550.00	600.00	650.00	700.00	750.00	800.00	850.00	900.00	950.00	1000.00
$100	1976 (Unc.)	100.00	112.50	125.00	137.50	150.00	162.50	175.00	187.50	200.00	212.50	225.00	237.50	250.00
$100	1976 (Proof)	199.60	224.55	249.50	274.45	299.40	324.35	349.30	374.25	399.20	424.15	449.10	474.05	499.00
$100	1977	199.60	224.55	249.50	274.45	299.40	324.35	349.30	374.25	399.20	424.15	449.10	474.05	499.00
$100	1979	199.60	224.55	249.50	274.45	299.40	324.35	349.30	374.25	399.20	424.15	449.10	474.05	499.00
$100	1980	199.60	224.55	249.50	274.45	299.40	324.35	349.30	374.25	399.20	424.15	449.10	474.05	499.00

APPENDIX II

SILVER CONTENT OF CANADIAN SILVER COINS

Denom.	Fineness	Silver Content (Grams)	Silver Content (Troy Oz.)
$1	.925	—	—
$1	.800	18.661	.600
$1	.500	11.662	.375
50¢	.925	10.792	.347
50¢	.800	9.330	.300
50¢	.500	—	—
25¢	.925	5.370	.173
25¢	.800	4.665	.150
25¢	.500	2.923	.094
10¢	.925	2.146	.069
10¢	.800	1.866	.060
10¢	.500	1.170	.038
5¢	.925	1.080	.034
5¢	.800	.933	.030
5¢	.500	—	—

APPENDIX IIa

BULLION VALUES OF CANADIAN SILVER COINS
(Computed from $10/ounce to $70/ounce in increments of $5 Canadian)

Denom.	Fineness	$10	$15	$20	$25	$30	$35	$40	$45	$50	$55	$60	$65	$70
$1	.800	6.00	9.00	12.00	15.00	18.00	21.00	24.00	27.00	30.00	33.00	36.00	39.00	42.00
$1	.500	3.75	5.63	7.50	9.37	11.25	13.12	15.00	16.87	18.75	20.62	22.50	24.37	26.25
50¢	.925	3.47	5.20	6.94	8.67	10.41	12.14	13.88	15.61	17.35	19.08	20.82	22.55	24.29
50¢	.800	3.00	4.50	6.00	7.50	9.00	10.50	12.00	13.50	15.00	16.50	18.00	19.50	21.00
25¢	.925	1.73	2.60	3.46	4.32	5.19	6.05	6.92	7.78	8.65	9.51	10.38	11.24	12.11
25¢	.800	1.50	2.25	3.00	3.75	4.50	5.25	6.00	6.75	7.50	8.25	9.00	9.75	10.50
25¢	.500	.94	1.40	1.88	2.35	2.82	3.29	3.76	4.23	4.70	5.17	5.64	6.11	6.58
10¢	.925	.69	1.04	1.38	1.72	2.07	2.41	2.76	3.10	3.45	3.79	4.14	4.48	4.83
10¢	.800	.60	.90	1.20	1.50	1.80	2.10	2.40	2.70	3.00	3.30	3.60	3.90	4.20
10¢	.500	.38	.56	.76	.95	1.14	1.33	1.52	1.71	1.90	2.09	2.28	2.47	2.66
5¢	.925	.34	.51	.68	.85	1.02	1.19	1.36	1.53	1.70	1.87	2.04	2.21	2.38
5¢	.800	.30	.45	.60	.75	.90	1.05	1.20	1.35	1.50	1.65	1.80	1.95	2.10